"Some Christians feel that the subject of 'Israel' is political at best and carnal at worst. This passionately written book dispels such unbiblical thinking, opening up the deeply spiritual treasures that remain part of Israel's God-given heritage. If you love Jesus and His Kingdom, you will be blessed and enriched by this book, and you will find yourself loving God's purposes for Israel as well."

—**Dr. Michael L. Brown**, president, FIRE School of Ministry, Concord, NC

"A quick scan of the daily newspaper or evening news lets us know that God's timetable for the age has taken a quantum leap forward. At the center of that plan stand His covenant people and His covenant land. It is essential that we as believers understand and embrace the critically decisive role Israel plays in God's end-time purposes, and that we participate in the prophetic shift toward the emerging destiny of the Church and Israel. Sandra Teplinsky's new book will give you insight into God's heart and purpose for Israel in this hour, and how that applies to you personally as part of the body of Messiah."

—**Jane Hansen Hoyt**, president/CEO, Aglow International

"*Israel's Anointing* is a catalyst for revival! In the spirit of Elijah, it turns the hearts of the children (the Church) to their spiritual fathers (Israel), and the hearts of the fathers to their children. Sandy Teplinsky combines biblical and prophetic revelation with fiery passion for God to disclose mysteries and engage us with our ancient spiritual heritage. An important book for this hour of history!"

—**Lou Engle**, founder, the Call, International House of Prayer, Kansas City, MO

"There are few who can communicate the blueprint of heaven to the earth realm. After reviewing Sandy Teplinsky's *Israel's Anointing*, however, I can honestly say this is a prototype book. With the Church age diminishing and the Kingdom age increasing, *Israel's Anointing* fully communicates God's heart of 'one new man' on the earth. Sandy gracefully blends the old and the new to form a great treasure. If you will embrace what has been written, you will find many yokes in your life broken. This is one of the defining books of this time in history."

—**Dr. Chuck D. Pierce**, president, Glory of Zion International Ministries; harvest watchman, Global Harvest Ministries

"*Israel's Anointing* is a cutting-edge book for the whole body of Messiah. Sandy's compelling writing style combines with prophetic insight and biblical truth to draw you into God's presence as you read. Her book sheds much-needed light on critical issues important to both Gentile and Jewish believers, guiding us toward matu⸺ ⸻man in Messiah. Be forewarned,

however: Sandy's passion for Yeshua (Jesus), His people, the Scriptures and end-times revival is contagious!"

—**Jonathan Bernis**, Messianic rabbi; president,
Jewish Voice Ministries International

"Occasionally a book comes along that grabs my heart and brings me into the midst of God's eternal purposes. *Israel's Anointing* is just such a book. With great balance and biblical understanding, this book lays before us the path that must be taken for the Church to walk in power and in accordance with God's plan for the end of the age."

—**Dave Butts**, chairman, America's National Prayer
Committee; president, Harvest Prayer Ministries

"Sandra Teplinsky's *Israel's Anointing* intertwines two destinies: the calling of the Church to connect to her Jewish origins, and the challenge to Jewish believers to be a light to the nations and to unite with their brothers and sisters from the nations, so that we can all press into the future with strength. As a Jewish believer, Sandra is herself a prophetic statement to her people and the Church. She unequivocally proclaims Israel's need for her Messiah while reminding the Church that Jesus was a Jew, still is a Jew and will return as a Jew to reign as King over a world at peace."

—**Don Finto**, director, the Caleb Company; pastor emeritus, Belmont
Church, Nashville; author, *Your People Shall Be My People*

"Sandra Teplinsky's book *Israel's Anointing* releases revelation for the whole Bride of Christ. This is a powerful book, drawing us to love-based clarity of thought. It will be used by God to help unfold some of the mysteries of God."

—**Heidi Gayle Baker**, Ph.D., founding director, Iris Ministries

"Sandra Teplinsky has offered a book of balanced scholarship and sensitive treatment of God's redemptive love for all peoples—Jew and Gentile—while retrieving to a high degree the depths of divine revelatory mysteries embedded in four thousand years of God's unique involvement with Israel and the Jewish people, and offering them up afresh for the Church at large. Herein are uncovered gems of insight, facets of which you will find nowhere else, that deepen our understanding of God's purposes, the wonder of His story and clear signs as to current movements toward the consummation of His story.

"Fittingly, in this year of the sixtieth birthday of the modern state of Israel, this book is nothing less than an epic philosophy of history comprising in its scope major themes of God's work of restoration in process throughout the universe. The book gives due place to Israel's significance, and does so in a holistic, Hebraic and heartfelt medium, without which the message of these truths is not complete."

—**William D. Bjoraker**, Ph.D., Operation Ezekiel and
William Carey International University

"As a wife and mother serving the Lord in Israel, I find Sandy's book extremely encouraging and relevant. All of creation is groaning in labor before the Messiah's Second Coming. We who follow Him are being groomed to take our place as His Bride. We must avail ourselves of every resource He provides to help us stay focused in these coming days, and this book is a treasure-packed cache! Here we find practical and timely tools to breathe through the birthing pains of today and tomorrow, strength to keep our eyes on our Jewish Bridegroom-King and a vision of the glorious coming Kingdom we will share with Him."

—**Rachel Boskey**, Final Frontier Ministries, www.davidstent.org

"Once again Sandy Teplinsky has written a book that is not a rehash of what others are writing but an expression of fresh, deep insight into hearing 'what the Spirit is saying to the churches' today. *Israel's Anointing* is a heart-grabbing, thought-provoking challenge to the Body of Christ (Messiah) worldwide to come to grips with what it means in practical terms to embrace our Jewish roots. Sandy's fresh revelations carried us much deeper into the heart of God for His chosen people. We found ourselves drawn away from the cares of this world into an even greater longing to know our Jewish Bridegroom-King in all His fullness."

—**Rick and Patti Ridings**, international worship leaders; founders and directors, *Succat Hallel* ("House of Praise"), www.jerusalempraise.com

"Revival and war are running mates. *Israel's Anointing* is not a book for everyone. Sandy's book is dangerous, controversial, captivating and challenging—certainly not a book for the fainthearted! It takes us from a romanticized theology of Israel into governmental revelation, giving us powerful keys for the hour and times we live in. Her book moves powerfully to impact cultures and nations with the sword of the Lord to awaken mercy and truth, justice and judgment, and radical love. It will awaken intercessors and strategists to bring revival and revolution in all spheres of life.

"As a Messianic Jew herself, Sandy Teplinsky lays a well-researched foundation in the Word that works in tandem with the Spirit in a way few books on Israel do. As a lawyer she puts forth her case in stellar fashion. As I read *Israel's Anointing*, my heart burned with a passion to see God's chosen people come to Yeshua. This book is a call to war and a call to love, as the warrior bride is awakened for the coming of the Bridegroom!"

—**Jill Austin**, international speaker; president and founder, Master Potter Ministries, www.masterpotter.com

"It is time to partake of Israel's anointing. When the Jewish spiritual DNA merges with the Christian spiritual DNA, it makes room for the full glory of God. Sandra Teplinsky's book prepares the way."

—**Sid Roth**, host, *It's Supernatural!* TV

"In *Israel's Anointing* Sandy Teplinsky manages to do what is almost impossible. Since Israel reemerged on the scene in a big way sixty years ago, the Church has struggled with how to celebrate the Holy Land where Jesus walked, how to honor the Jewish heritage and people our faith comes from, and how to understand the Hebrew roots of Christianity—all the while celebrating the Gospel given freely to the Gentiles. Sandy is one of the few who have so woven all these things skillfully together while avoiding the legalism trap many fear. As one who has celebrated some of the Jewish feasts, I have greatly benefited from the edification that takes place when I trace my physical and spiritual heritage back to Abraham, Isaac and Israel. Sandy continues the journey of discovery."

—**Steve Shultz**, publisher, the Elijah List; author, *Can't You Talk Louder, God?*

Israel's
Anointing

Your Inheritance *and*
End-Time Destiny *through* Israel

Sandra Teplinsky

Chosen
a division of Baker Publishing Group
Grand Rapids, Michigan

© 2008 by Sandra Teplinsky

Published by Chosen Books
A division of Baker Publishing Group
P.O. Box 6287, Grand Rapids, MI 49516-6287
www.chosenbooks.com

Second printing, August 2008

Printed in the United States of America

All rights reserved. No part of this publication may be reproduced, stored in a retrieval system, or transmitted in any form or by any means—for example, electronic, photocopy, recording—without the prior written permission of the publisher. The only exception is brief quotations in printed reviews.

Library of Congress Cataloging-in-Publication Data
Teplinsky, Sandra.
    Israel's anointing : your inheritance and end time destiny through Israel / Sandra Teplinsky.
        p. cm.
    Includes bibliographical references (p.   ) and index.
    ISBN 978-0-8007-9437-8 (pbk.)
    1. Israel (Christian theology) 2. End of the world. I. Title.
BT93.T433 2008
231.7′6—dc22   2008011586

Unless otherwise indicated, Scripture is taken from the HOLY BIBLE, NEW INTERNATIONAL VERSION®. NIV®. Copyright © 1973, 1978, 1984 by International Bible Society. Used by permission of Zondervan. All rights reserved.

Scripture marked AMPLIFIED is taken from the Amplified® Bible. Copyright © 1954, 1958, 1962, 1964, 1965, 1987 by The Lockman Foundation. Used by permission.

Scripture marked CJB is taken from the *Complete Jewish Bible*, copyright © 1998 by David H. Stern. Published by Jewish New Testament Publications, Inc. www.messianicjewish.net/jntp. Distributed by Messianic Jewish Resources. www.messianicjewish.net. All rights reserved. Used by permission.

Scripture marked NKJV is taken from the New King James Version. Copyright © 1982 by Thomas Nelson, Inc. Used by permission. All rights reserved.

In keeping with biblical principles of creation stewardship, Baker Publishing Group advocates the responsible use of our natural resources. As a member of the Green Press Initiative, our company uses recycled paper when possible. The text paper of this book is comprised of 30% post-consumer waste.

To Tasha and her peers everywhere
who are young radicals for Messiah

Contents

Acknowledgments   11
Foreword   13

1. Ancient Paths Revived   15
2. Kingdom Convergence   21
3. The Mystery of Jew and Gentile in Messiah   40
4. Coming for a Bride   56
5. Sabbath Rest   75
6. Highway of Holiness   92
7. Messianic Justice   111
8. From Zion's Battlegrounds   130
9. Messianic Millennium Coming   150
10. Standing Firm to the End   169

Bibliography   191
Notes   197
Index   211

Acknowledgments

This book would never exist without the undeserved help of family and friends, my personal heroes and heroines of persevering faith and support. Foremost is my husband, Kerry, God's greatest gift to me in this life. His Messiah-like wisdom and patience, unswerving love and loyalty—as well as research and editorial skills—never cease to amaze me. Next comes my sweet-spirited daughter, Tasha, for sacrificing another year of her mom's time and attention, as well as for contributing to the book cover design.

Eternal gratitude goes to my treasured team of dedicated intercessors. Though too many to name individually, their labors in the Spirit are reflected on every page. My deep appreciation to proofreaders Dr. Bill Bjoraker, Sue Haffely, Janna Christenson, and Cindi and Myles Fink; and to Joshua Chang and my extraordinary Eastside Life Group for encouraging me every step of the way. Thank you to my discerning and gracious editor, Trish Konieczny, and especially to Chosen Books' editorial director, Jane Campbell, for believing in this project and nurturing it to fruition. (Jane, you are a gift to this generation of readers.)

All glory and everlasting gratitude to Yeshua (Jesus) my Messiah for the grace to write *Israel's Anointing*, and for whose incomparable honor it exists.

Foreword

Interest concerning God's heart for Israel is on the rise. New organizations are being formed; new houses of prayer are springing up across the nations, carrying portions of God's heart for Israel and the Jewish people worldwide. Teaching is being released from voices both old and new in the body of Messiah. This is good news!

But the waters seem a bit murky as some step out into what has been, for them, unknown territory. Sincere efforts are taking place, for sure. But there is some confusion in the camp as well. Wrong teachings on things like "two-house" theories are permeating different sectors.

Some of the theories even suggest that there is more than one way of salvation: one for the Jew and another for the Gentile. Yet I think I remember Jesus being the One who said, "I am the way and the truth and the life. *No one* comes to the Father except through me." Did we forget? And in our romantic melancholy, are we forgetting the main and plain teachings of the Gospel of the Kingdom?

Some today are emphasizing that you must identify which of the twelve tribes of Israel you are from, genealogically speaking. Interesting enough—but I thought salvation was a matter of faith in the Son of God and the power of the blood of Jesus, not of your own bloodline.

Please don't get me wrong: I celebrate the feasts of Israel. I pray for the peace of Jerusalem. I call out to the Lord in identificational repentance that the blinders on the eyes of the Church concerning replacement theology will fall away. I have been deeply involved for years in the issues of *aliyah* and the return of the Jewish people to their homeland.

Yet I am left with a big "Huh?" over some of what is occurring in some popular circles. While I rejoice in the Lord greatly that the subject of Israel and God's end time purposes are getting onto the screens of believers today, as a watchman I am concerned lest we become deceived into making trivial issues the main issues. There are lots of side issues today and lots of potholes to avoid!

So if you are searching for clarity and a resource that will drive you to the Word of God and propel you into proper biblical interpretation—all the while steering you into God's prophetic purposes for our generation and beyond—then I have good news. Your search is over!

You are holding in your hands one of the most concise yet thorough volumes written to date concerning the proper placement of Israel. Sandra Teplinsky has done a marvelous job stating truth, creating hunger and motivating her readers to study to show themselves approved as workmen for God.

Now, don't just read this book. Get out your Bible and search things out for yourself. But do more than that: Pray as you read. The Spirit of truth will lead you into His truth as you ask Him to be your divine Guide. You can trust the Holy Spirit!

Sandy, you have done the Body of Christ a great service through your sacrificial efforts in this inspiring book. May more voices of clarity arise in this hour for such a time as this!

—Dr. James W. Goll, cofounder, Encounters Network
author, *The Prophetic Intercessor, Praying for Israel's Destiny,*
The Lost Art of Intercession and many more

1

Ancient Paths Revived

Stand at the crossroads and look; ask for the ancient paths, ask where the good way is, and walk in it.

Jeremiah 6:16

Long ago, God's people in the Promised Land stood at a crossroads. The world around them was shaking, and they would never be the same again. Radical change and reformation lay ahead. In such a season, how would they reach their destiny? "Ask for the ancient paths," the prophet Jeremiah discerned. It was time, the Spirit was saying, to walk in them.

Today, God is opening the heavens, reviving Israel's anointing for Christians to walk in. Once again, the prophetic season is shifting. The destiny of His Church is intersecting anew with Israel's destiny. As a result, the last days body of believers will increasingly resemble the early New Covenant Church, restored in power, love and purity. For this restoration, Israel is integral. A catalyst for revival, she endues us with fresh Kingdom reality from her spiritual progenitors and heritage. Therefore, a company is emerging whose time has come: the Church with Israel, converging in Christ, mediating His Kingdom and preparing the way of His return. You are invited to participate; in fact, it will not be the same without you.

As a Jewish believer in Jesus, I want to see blessings from Israel imparted to the international Body of Christ. Why? Some of God's ways of old have long been set aside. Yet through them, He reveals Himself uniquely and intimately in passionate holiness. He wants you and me to walk in—then mediate to others—renewed realms of His supernatural salvation. At the same time, He is stirring fresh zeal in us to prepare for the days ahead, stay the course and stand firm to the end—even to the consummate coming of our Bridegroom-King. For all this, we will access a long-dormant inheritance in Israel.

Accordingly, after decades of Messianic ministry, I have witnessed a significant shift in the Church. Steadily growing numbers of believers across the globe are identifying with the Jewish people. They understand that Messiah was, is, and will return as a Jew. More and more, God's New Covenant people are hearing and embracing His heart for His Old Covenant ones. Not coincidentally, Jews are coming to faith in *Yeshua* (Jesus' Hebrew name) in numbers not seen since the book of Acts.

As Gentile and Jewish believers join together, a sublime mystery is materializing in our day. At new levels, God is creating "one new man out of the two" (Ephesians 2:15). This one new man is characterized as a *bride* purified for her Betrothed. At the same time she is a *warrior* (see Revelation 19:7; 12:11). For both a wedding and a war are at hand; the One who is just and true said it must be so. His coveted coming will not take place without opposition. Those who comprise this "Messianic Warrior Bride" company are being outfitted for battle. Refined by fire, they will emerge unstoppably ablaze for the King. They will minister His Kingdom and mediate revival in all manner of ways, and in wide-scale Holy Spirit power, fulfill the Great Commission to which they have been called.

This book is about preparing God's people for revival *now*, and for the closing, crescendo events of this age—and beyond.

Each chapter addresses a major shift that will reshape the Body in coming years. These shifts will come from tapping into our revived spiritual heritage in Israel. Some chapters and shifts revolve around a single book of the Bible; most are based on themes that develop throughout the Scriptures. The chapters build on each other, taking us from ancient paths into the prophetic future. We will stand at the crossroads and look, seek the good ways, and together walk anew in them.

What is at stake, and how is it relevant to you? One of my favorite verses answers these questions: "Rejoice greatly, O daughter of Zion! . . . Behold, your King is coming to you." (Zechariah 9:9, NKJV; see also Matthew 21:5). *Our Messiah is coming!* Indeed, He has already come—and *heaven is even now bursting into the earth realm.* The miraculous is overtaking the mundane. Yet there is more. He is coming again to set in place a totally tangible Kingdom according to the law of love—justice with joy, resplendent righteousness, peace and prosperity—encompassing the earth. As never before, all humanity will be subject to the dominion of Deity. The increase of His Kingdom will *never* end (see Isaiah 9:7). Care to prepare? Again, Israel is integral.

Prophetic Parameters

Israel's Anointing has been written both to Gentile and Jewish believers. My heart is to share with Gentile believers certain select and timeless, Messiah-centered treasures from our Old Covenant heritage (see Matthew 13:52). These truths are God's gifts, that you might be equipped and empowered to know, love and serve Him intimately, creatively and with explosive joy in these last days. For my fellow Messianic Jews, my prayer is that you would gain ever-expanding revelation of the breadth and depth of our calling—and of our Yeshua—in the ardor of His affections and anointing (see Ephesians 3:16–19). Because, really, are we not all about *Him*?

Israel's Anointing is not only prophetic, but also practical in nature. I want your heart stirring and your spirit soaring as you learn of God's ways from His Word. I want you to know your Savior from a Hebraic perspective that remains extremely relevant to the challenge of present-day, 21st-century living. But be forewarned. You may find yourself provoked to jealousy for more and more of your Jewish Bridegroom-King—and you may never be the same. Once you connect to the ever-mounting glory of His Kingdom—heaven on earth in which you personally participate—you may find that changes everything.

This book is not about politics in the Middle East. It does reflect, and aims to inspire, love for the Jewish nation. However, you will find only love for the Arabs here. Like all other nations, Israel and the Arabic peoples await a salvation only their Messiah can achieve. The pages that follow will help you understand this prophetic unfolding.

As a former attorney and now as a teacher of the Word of God, I admit to passionate love for truth. I desire to encourage others in their own lifelong journey through the Scriptures. I also believe that in this season the Spirit is equipping believers with a new mental acuity. Love-based sharpness of thought is a dimension of the mind of Christ that is being restored so the Church can move forward in His full counsel. This anointing is not at all contrary, but rather complementary, to heart-level passion for Jesus, supernatural revelation and surrender to the Spirit (see Luke 10:27). For this reason, ample references are noted for those desiring to pursue further study. At the same time, the text is written to serve as a launch point for personal devotion and intercession. May worship and prayer flow from you as you read the pages that follow!

New Words of Old

In a book of this nature, some clarification of terms is important. Occasionally I use Hebrew words with translation provided. I substitute Jesus' name in English many times with His Hebrew name, *Yeshua*, since often that is what I love to call Him. In some instances, I refer to God as *Yahweh*, the English pronunciation of His personal name derived from the Hebrew tetragrammaton, *YHVH*. The Hebrew Scriptures (Tanakh) are identified as the *Old Covenant*. Following biblical usage, I employ the word *Israel* interchangeably with *Jewish nation*, meaning either the ethnic descendants of Abraham, Isaac and Jacob or the geographic land, or both. The particular meaning should be clear from the context.

When the term *Messianic Jew* appears, it means, for the purposes of this book, any believer in Jesus who is biologically or ethnically Jewish and intentionally identifies as such. It does not necessarily carry any connotations regarding adherence to the wide panoply of practices associated with contemporary Messianic Judaism. It never implies superiority—or inferiority—to non-Jewish believers. *Christendom* refers here to historically and politically institutionalized Christianity. In contrast, *Church* is synonymous with the collective Body of Christ—sometimes called Body of Messiah—or with the word *Christian(s)*. It includes both Jewish and Gentile believers, with rare exception for the sake of a specific point. Where the occasional phrase *Messianic Warrior Bride* or *warrior bride* appears, it does not suggest that followers of Jesus are or should be predominantly, stereotypically feminine. It does reflect that He is coming back for a corporate Bride crazy in love with Him (see Revelation 19:7)! Finally, the remainder of this book usually refers to the present time as the end times or last days (see 1 Peter 1:20; Hebrews 1:2). Apocalyptic events associated with the final closing of the age are sometimes identified as the last of the last days, or end of the end times.

Occasionally, select Jewish traditions and rabbinic interpretations are shared that lend themselves, in context, to the exaltation of Yeshua. These are offered as helpful illustrations of biblical thought from a Hebraic perspective to enrich relationship with the Savior. Never do I intend for them to detract from a focus on God, the supremacy of His written Word or the Gospel of Jesus Christ.

In the course of writing the book you hold in your hands, I found myself surprisingly immersed in various realms of God. At times, holy awe captivated me. At other times, exhilaration at the expectation of things to come overtook me. Occasionally, intercessory sorrow welled up in my spirit. My prayer is that through these pages you, too, will be drawn deeper and deeper into the heart of Messiah. So I invite you to sit at His feet with me, anticipating new insights. I think you will emerge transformed.

2

Kingdom Convergence

All these are the beginning of birth pains . . . but he who stands firm to the end will be saved.

Matthew 24:8, 13

Jesus aptly described our day: "These are the beginning of birth pains." The Savior was referring to shaking events that would shift realities to signal and make way for His return.

I will never forget the first time I witnessed the birth of a baby. The labor was hard and long. Finally, the infant's head emerged. Holy anticipation filled the room. Then—suddenly—it was over. Within seconds the newborn had journeyed her way into the world. And just as suddenly, everything changed for everyone present. Joy exploded. Like nothing I had ever experienced, a spark of eternity intersected dramatically with the natural, blood-and-guts process of life in the earth realm.

So it is with the Kingdom of God. Infinity is infiltrating earth today in answer to the prayers of past millennia: "Your kingdom come, your will be done on earth as it is in heaven" (Matthew 6:10). The King is coming—in glorious Person—as this present age transitions to the next. But as in the natural, so it is in the supernatural; there is no birth without blood, guts and, yes, even pain. In this chapter we see why.

Birth Pains

One day Yeshua took His disciples to the Mount of Olives overlooking Jerusalem for a Bible study. "What will be the sign of your coming and of the end of the age?" they asked (Matthew 24:3).

The Master did not deny the premise of the question. Indeed He would come at the end of the age. It would be wise to know the signs heralding the event. He answered the disciples promptly and to the point. First, He said, would come wide-scale deception, then wars, famines and earthquakes. These would be only the beginning of "birth pains."[1]

The Greek word translated "birth pains" in many modern Bible versions is *odin. Odin* refers to odious distress. It is translated "sorrows" by the King James Version and "horrors" by others.[2] All versions can be considered correct, but the usage of "birth pains" captures a vital point. The odious distress or suffering is related to the inception of something new—a birth. The word *odin* directs our vision beyond the travail or temporary affliction to something ahead much greater and grander.

Yeshua says that a steadfast heart, fixated not on the *odin* but on its goal, will stay the course. Because of the increase of evil alongside good during this time, "the love of *most*"—even believers—"will grow cold." (That is a bit sobering!) "But," He adds, "he who stands firm to the end will be saved" (Matthew 24:12–13, emphasis added).

I trust you want to understand, and participate in, what God is doing in these last days. Some who have never searched out the Scriptures pertaining to this hour may find their faith wavering. Like many of the spiritual leaders of Jesus' time, they may take conscious or unconscious offense at His sovereign, unexpectedly different ways. Their love may grow cold. Jesus cautions this will happen to *most*.

But if you love the Lord and pray with even a modicum of militance, "Your kingdom come, Your will be done," you do not want to risk cooling off to Him. Nor do you desire to merely wince and grit your teeth during this pivotal period. Like me, you want to stand firm in Kingdom fervor, substance and dimension in your life. You want revival! Your heart cries out for the manifest presence of God, the salvation of souls and the righteous deeds of the saints. You already taste the joy set before you and your Beloved, and you will do what it takes for more. You want to be part of the emerging Messianic Warrior Bride, engaged to the end in Kingdom expansion—because you want your life spent on Him.

In the 21st century, birth pains of Jesus' resplendent return are coming fast and hard. Times are proving uniquely replete with rapid, radical change—like wide-scale natural disasters, political and economic upheavals, Islamic terror—and, despite sweeping moral depravity, *revival of previously unimaginable magnitude*. The Holy Spirit is awakening lost humanity as false gods topple, from Marxism to Islam, materialism and more. God's glory is penetrating the planet. Kingdom expansion will continue on through these birth pains, and we will increasingly access heaven right here on earth. In the process, the Body of Christ is being groomed for a wondrous destiny conceived in the eternal recesses of the Godhead.

Satan is striking back, terrorized that his time is short. But the Omnipotent One is very much in control. Hell's gory incursion will not outmatch heaven's glorious intrusion into the affairs of nations and neighborhoods. Through increasing darkness on earth, this present generation of believers will be refined so we shine in purity and power. We will be used to prepare the way of the Lord's return.

The Messianic Warrior Bride

As birth pains intensify, Israel and the Church will converge toward a common destiny. To "converge" means to move from different directions toward one point and unite in a common interest or focus, developing similar characteristics.[3] The two are converging because, as we will later see, neither can attain to their ultimate destiny apart from the other. God's Old and New Covenant peoples are inextricably bound together. In Christ, the two are now becoming one, maturing into His bride. But this last days betrothed one is also a warrior. Loving the Lord with all our heart, soul and mind—as a Bride awaits a Bridegroom—is fierce in its force, shattering evil and overcoming the world (see 1 John 3:8b; 5:3–4). Such love is warlike.

The Messianic Warrior Bride is an unfolding mystery of God, a people being formed in this generation. Fueled by unquenchable desire for Yeshua, this army of lovers is marked by relentless drive for the things of His Kingdom. They traverse the earth realm in holy authority obtained from heaven. This battalion comprises believers, including Jewish believers, from every nation—including Israel. For on Israel rests an ancient anointing that God is reviving to propel His people into new realities "on earth as it is in heaven" (Matthew 6:10).

The Messianic Warrior Bride is not about an attitude of crusading triumphalism or carnal emotionalism. It is not about who is better or more blessed: Jewish or Gentile believers. In Jesus, ethnicity is neither a barrier nor a boon for blessing. Rather, this fellowship of friends is about a King who is coming, a love He is unleashing with power for prevailing, and a Kingdom restoration of all things—in the context of Jews and Gentiles joined together for Jesus.

The Kingdom of God

God's Kingdom is often described as His rule and reign in any given dimension. The word *king* together with the word

domain communicates the general concept of kingdom. Therefore, when the Son of God came two thousand years ago, He
brought spectacularly good news: "The kingdom of heaven is
near," or, according to early translations, "at hand" (Matthew
4:17). Heaven and earth were converging in new dimensions
through the Person of Yeshua.

Much of Messiah's teaching centered on the theme of the
Kingdom of heaven on earth. He instructed His followers to
minister the same message in word and deed (see Matthew
10:7–8). He had in mind, as did those to whom He spoke, par-
don from sin—and much more. The Gospel of the Kingdom is
about forgiveness, which then sets us on course into tremendous,
wholly new, eternal realities.

To an extent far greater than you may perceive, the Kingdom
of God is already within you if you have surrendered your life
to Jesus. As you read these words, you really *are* seated with
Him in heavenly places. In spirit, you and I have free access
to God's celestial throne of grace (see Luke 17:21; Ephesians
2:6; Hebrews 4:16). As we extend the authority His Holiness
delegates to us, we mediate His dominion government around
us. This intersection of the natural and supernatural causes the
miraculous to become commonplace. All manner of sacred signs
and wonders follow those who believe (see Mark 16:16–18). Yet
the Kingdom is about still more. It is about what happens when
the King personally comes back.

The Old Covenant speaks at length about Messiah's Kingdom
rule and reign of righteousness on earth when He returns. The
concept unfolds when God promises to David a descendant
who will inherit his throne forever (see 2 Samuel 7:12–13; Isaiah
9:6–7). The New Covenant identifies Yeshua, Son of Man/Son
of God, as this descendant (see Luke 1:32–33; Acts 2:29–30).
Deity embodied in dust, Yeshua inherits not only the Kingdom
of heaven but this Davidic kingdom as well—encompassing
earthly Israel and the nations (see Revelation 11:15; 19:16; Isaiah 9:7; Zechariah 14:9, 16). So it is no coincidence that after
two thousand years, Israel finds herself once more at a global

spiritual epicenter. It is to the Jewish nation, the apple of His eye (see Zechariah 2:8), that Messiah is coming to establish holy headquarters in Jerusalem. From there His manifest Kingdom, in tangible splendor, will transform the earth in glory (see Isaiah 11:6–10).

A series of convulsions will transition us from this age to the next. The Jewish people often refer to this period of tribulation as the Day of Jacob's Trouble (see Jeremiah 30:7). Yet it is not the grisly gloom, but the glorious goal, that Israel's prophets keep in sight. To them, the pain is about paradise coming to the planet. Their vision is set on Messiah and His Kingdom-come-to-earth. The New Covenant authors understood this background well and further developed its magnificent theme. Among other things, they tell us the Messianic age lasts a thousand years (see Revelation 20:2–7). For this reason it is often called the millennial Kingdom, or simply the Millennium.

Some believers have been taught that life here on earth will only get better and better until, in some mysterious manner, Jesus and the Kingdom eventually take over everything. Maybe others suffer through hard times, but God offers the faith-filled Christian assurance of a blessed life punctuated by the power to dispel ungodly or unpleasant circumstances.

While this concept may reflect a dimension of truth, it *must* be considered in light of other key Scriptures. All who live godly in Messiah Jesus—who tells us to take up our cross and follow Him—will be persecuted (see 2 Timothy 3:12). Every nation, declares Deity, will hate us because of Him (see Matthew 24:9). We endure afflictions, but those achieve for us an eternal weight of glory (see 2 Corinthians 4:17). Troubles befall us, but they are not synonymous with defeat: "In all things God works for the good of those who love him, who have been called according to his purpose" (Romans 8:28).

At this point, I can almost hear some of you questioning how this book is going to build your faith. I encourage you to keep reading! The Bible's message is stupendously positive. I believe the Lord is about to take your faith to dazzling new dimensions. I love and am committed to revival, the miraculous, the prophetic and especially the salvation of nations. Like you, I expect more of heaven's supernatural realm to materialize in the here and now. But I also want to see believers stay the course through birth pains. I want to see this generation fulfill its grand and unique destiny.

Paradise Restored

Deep in the genetic code of humankind resides a latent longing for something bigger—centered around Someone bigger—than ourselves. You and I were originally designed for a garden called Eden in which all our needs would be perfectly met. Every patch of soil, every living creature, was to submit peaceably and fruitfully to our dominion on the Creator's behalf. Our Maker hardwired us to walk and talk with Him just as easily and naturally as we breathe air. The fairy tales, adventure novels and redemption-plot dramas through history bespeak this insatiable yearning to fulfill our original call. Not just us, but all creation, longs for it: "We know that the whole creation has been groaning as in the pains of childbirth right up to the present time" (Romans 8:22).

God promises to answer that collective groan. His callings are irrevocable (see Romans 11:29). Deity's design for us and for our planet will not be defeated. Yeshua is returning, literally—in glorified flesh and blood—to rule and restore *everything* (see Acts 3:21). The result will resemble a return to Paradise.

Meanwhile, this present age is often described as an "in-between" time of the "already but not yet." You and I live in between the incursion of the Kingdom of heaven (Messiah's first coming) and its climactic fullness (following His Second Coming).[4] On the one hand, in this world we will have tribulation (see John 16:33, KJV). On the other hand, during this interim period, mounting supernatural blessing can be available right now to whomever will receive it.

God's glorious government *increases* through *infinity* (see Isaiah 9:7). We ought to be inspired, not inhibited, toward ever-increasing faith when, for example, some of the sick for whom we pray are marvelously healed, but not all; or some of the dead are raised, while others are buried. We are commissioned to contend with the Spirit until things on earth are "as it is in heaven." Many traditional schools of theology teach that divine blessing is not at this time attainable to its complete and totally universal extent. That need not be a statement of unbelief, but of *good* news. The closer we get to the day of His return, the greater the degree to which we will access and mediate the supernatural. Simultaneously, the more we engage with heaven, the closer the time of His return (see 2 Peter 3:12). This divine, back-and-forth synergy is escalating even now. In the process, as God's government increases, it converges more and more with Israel.

Recapturing Kingdom Revelation: Israel

So that we can track together, allow me to share a bit about my journey and how the Spirit has shifted my theological grid. My early Bible education took place in a mainstream Orthodox synagogue in the United States. There I learned the traditional Jewish approach to studying the Hebrew Scriptures, which is a straightforward and generally literal one. Words are understood at their normal face value, in their grammatical and historical context. They are given the same plain and ordinary, common-sense meaning that their original listeners or readers would have given them.[5] This is how the Bible's authors themselves typically interpreted previously penned Scriptures, in both Old and New Covenants. Yeshua and the earliest Church fathers generally followed this method of interpretation.

This general approach is called the literal-grammatical-historical method of Bible study. Its basic rationale is simple. God is a sufficiently skilled communicator to say what He means, and mean what He says, so His people can understand Him.[6] The Divine Author loves us passionately. He wants to be known intimately by ordinary human beings, not just linguistic scholars. Although there are times He occasionally employs allegory, metaphor and other literary devices, He is not tricky; it is typically not hard to tell when He uses them.

As I studied the Scriptures the way I had learned in synagogue, Yeshua gently revealed Himself to me. Then, soon after I came to faith, the Holy Spirit began speaking to my heart very personally through the Word. This was edifying and delightful! Such intimate communication remains a vital, ongoing part of our relationship. But a subtle problem arose. The more I sensed the Lord speaking personally to me, the more I started reading the Bible symbolically rather than straightforwardly.

Let me give you an example. I think many of you will relate to it. On one occasion during those early years, I was praying about whether to attend a particular Christian conference. In response the Spirit highlighted to my attention a certain verse: "Come, let us go up to the mountain of the LORD, to the house of the God of Jacob" (Isaiah 2:3). From that, I understood He was leading me to attend the event. So I went—and experienced an awesome time with Him and His people. But soon after that, I found myself referring to any potential place of awesome encounter with God as "the mountain of the Lord." This was not in itself bad or wrong, but let me explain more.

Isaiah's prophecy is one of hundreds throughout the Scriptures that foretell the future of Israel and the Davidic kingdom. In context, it objectively describes a future, decidedly material mountain of the Lord on which is located a concrete house of the God of Jacob. My subjective and limited application of the Bible passage (to any place of powerful encounter with God) was not incorrect so long as it remained just that—my subjective and limited application. It stemmed, after all, from a personal word of direction by the Holy Spirit. But it was not God's intended *fundamental* meaning of the verse. It would be a serious mistake to ignore or replace the fundamental meaning with a symbolic one.

If the fundamental meaning of the Scriptures is discounted, we miss what God is saying foundationally to us in His Word about who He is and how He operates. As a result, we can easily mistake who we are and how He has called us to live, particularly as we approach the last of these last days. We can also neglect the critical Israel component of the Kingdom, because many Old Covenant Scriptures refer fundamentally—though not exclusively—to Israel. If we forget this and interpret the Word primarily symbolically instead of more literally, we can easily, albeit unconsciously, misinterpret "Israel" to mean "the Church." Sadly, this has often been the case in Church history, giving rise to so-called replacement theology. Replacement theology is the mistaken but long-entrenched belief that God has replaced Israel in His heart and His plans with the Church. This erroneous doctrine has caused us to compromise our understanding of the Kingdom of God for nearly two thousand years.

But today is a new day.

The Presence of the Future

The Spirit is restoring an important Israel-related dimension of the Kingdom to us: the reality of the imminence of Messiah's return. Jesus' final word to us in the Bible is a prophetic statement that He is coming soon (see Revelation 22:20). This promise provides a key to unlocking revelation that is paramount to our last days destiny. Let me explain why by continuing with Isaiah 2:3 as an example.

Many of us expect Yeshua to someday appear, but only long after we expire from our own mortal house of clay. We believe He will have His literal Temple on His holy hill, and we might even get excited about it. Some of us, perhaps, hope to catch a bird's-eye view of it from our eternal, heavenly home. (However, what with heaven being heaven, it could well contain more interesting etherealities to occupy our time.) Meanwhile, God has more pressing matters for us in this brief life. The next life, we reason, will take care of itself.

But the Bible is full of specific revelation God wants us to have now of our future role as active players in the prophetic age to come, and ages beyond that. *That revelation is key to understanding our destiny in His Kingdom as we engage in it now, in this age.* Here's why:

- The literal, future fulfillment of prophecy concerning Messiah's return and establishment of His Kingdom is intensely dear to His heart, evidenced in part by the very large percentage of Bible text dedicated to it. If we love Yeshua, we want whatever is important to Him to be important to us.

- Many passages we may have assumed would be fulfilled only in heaven are actually going to materialize prophetically and tangibly here, on this earth.

- Heaven is our home—but not quite the way many of us have been taught.

- From the biblical evidence, Messiah's return is likely closer than many would think. Some of us just might be around for it. In any case, you and I are encouraged to do certain things that can hasten or expedite it (see 2 Peter 3:12a).

- Even if our earthly bodies give out before the Lord returns, we will come back with Him—not just for an instant, but for a thousand years of awesome glory—and more.

- On my watch (and yours), ancient prophetic words pertaining to Israel and the Kingdom of God are coming to pass. If we want to participate in what He is doing, we want to process these events with accuracy and integrity.

- Biblically and historically, revival is related to the Church's conscious anticipation of, and preparation for, the Second Coming of our King. Do we really want revival enough to do what it takes to get it?

From this perspective, it is not premature or irrelevant to consider the future while living wholeheartedly in the present; it is prophetic and practical. It is said that in God's Kingdom, we live in the presence of the future. The "here and now" is affected by the "there and then." Here and now, everything must be shaken that can be shaken because a Kingdom is coming that cannot be shaken (see Haggai 2:6–7; Hebrews 12:27). It can, however, be *taken*.

Love: Way of the Warrior

The Kingdom of heaven is not taken through passive inaction. Rather, Yeshua said, "The kingdom of heaven has been forcefully advancing, and forceful men lay hold of it." Or as the AMPLIFIED Bible translates, "The kingdom of heaven has endured *violent assault*, and *violent* men *seize* it by force [as a precious prize—a share in the heavenly kingdom is sought with most ardent zeal and intense exertion]" (Matthew 11:12, emphasis added).[7]

Realities shake in spiritual and natural realms when, to any extent, heaven's Kingdom is magnetized to earth. The Son of God came to destroy the works of the devil (see 1 John 3:8). That process is inherently violent. Sweet, gentle Jesus spent His life demolishing demonic clutches on humanity. There was nothing passive on the part of our tenderhearted, merciful Savior, also known as Captain of the Armies of Heaven (see Joshua 5:14). His valiant life and death embodied love's most aggressive assault ever executed. Yeshua instigated whole-scale war, it cost Him His life, and He won.

The same Messiah who ascended to the Father as Suffering Servant will most certainly descend as Conquering King. Meanwhile, the war, though already won, is not over. You and I still contend against rulers, powers and spiritual forces of wickedness in heavenly places (see Ephesians 6:12). Our stance is offensive rather than defensive in nature, but the weapons we wield are not of this world (see 2 Corinthians 10:4). We brandish a message of fiery love not just in word, but in demonstrable deed. We take that message, through every mode and means, into a world dying without God. In Holy Spirit *dunamis* power (see Acts 1:8), we invade darkness with light, following in, mediating and inheriting Messiah's life by loving, if need be, even unto death. The way of God's warrior is the way of love. How could it be otherwise? He who *is* the Way is *Himself* Love (see 1 John 4:16). We war because of love, energized by love, for the sake of love. Unassailable, all-consuming ardor for the Bridegroom-King fuels our authority in Him. It is destined to connect us like never before to the people of Zion.

Convergence with Israel

Those of us who were not alive when Israel became a recognized, modern nation in 1948 can sometimes take her existence for granted. Never have we known a world without a Middle Eastern Jewish State. But if we take a step back in history, our view adjusts, and we gain perspective. We can better appreciate the profound majesty of this hour. By standards of human history, it was but a moment ago that God reestablished the Jews in their ancestral homeland. The majority of them do not yet know their Messiah is Yeshua of Nazareth, but a good many do. Messianic Jewish believers in Jesus are growing around the world in both numbers and maturity. Salvations and dramatic miracles are not the extreme rarity they were for over 1,500 years in the Holy Land. Fulfillments of ancient biblical prophecies about Israel in the past century would have boggled the minds of many of our most august Church fathers.

Even among Jews who do not worship Yeshua, an unprecedented trend toward camaraderie with Christians is undeniable. Many freely express, for the first time, both affection and appreciation for believers. While writing this book, for instance, I happened across an article published in a respected international news periodical, written by a deputy director of communications under a former Israeli prime minister. Says the writer, who is *not* a follower of Yeshua:

> Israeli officials have at last begun to appreciate . . . evangelical support. What was once unthinkable has now become routine, as leading Christian pastors and Israeli government representatives regularly confer . . . on the principal issues of the day. [Read between the lines: God is raising up prophets from the nations for Israel.] . . . It is this genuine affection that contains the potential to forge an historic alliance.[8]

The writer goes on to suggest that Israel organize prayer battalions for the Jewish State in Christian churches.

Organized by the Holy Spirit, however, prayer battalions for Israel are already in place in congregations worldwide. From far-flung villages in rural China to tundra-laced towns in icy Siberia, I have witnessed believers passionately petition heaven's throne of grace for the salvation of the Jewish people. Represented by this interceding remnant, the global Body of Messiah is hearing God's heart for His ancient covenant people as never before. As a result, more and more descendants of Abraham, Isaac and Jacob are coming to faith in Yeshua. In the not-too-distant future, revival will sweep across Israel. In the process, the Messianic Warrior Bride will comprise that glorious convergence of Jew and Gentile as one in Christ—a convergence that crescendos when, as promised, "all Israel will be saved" (Romans 11:26).

All Israel Will be Saved

The promise of Israel's salvation is given in response to questions that arose in the early Church. As fewer Jewish people came to faith in Yeshua, some Christians wondered if the biblical promises to them were now null and void. Was God finished, they asked, with Israel? If so, that was worrisome. If He had revoked His covenant with the Jews, could He not also revoke His word to the Gentiles? If He had replaced Israel with the Church in His heart and plans, could He not someday replace the Church? The apostle Paul speaks to this issue in his letter to the Romans:

> Did God reject his people? By no means! I am an Israelite myself, a descendant of Abraham, from the tribe of Benjamin. God did not reject his people, whom he foreknew. . . . There is a [Jewish] remnant chosen by grace.
>
> Romans 11:1–2, 5

Paul adamantly affirms God's continuing covenant with the Jewish nation. Our ever-faithful Father has reserved for Himself a remnant chosen by grace, including the apostle himself. In the Bible, a remnant serves as a basis on which God preserves a whole people. The continued existence of a faithful remnant in Israel assures He will fulfill His plans for the nation's collective spiritual restoration. Today's remnant of Israel is found in her body of faithful Messianic Jewish believers. This remnant reminds us that, for His glory, Israel will yet be saved—"And so all Israel will be saved, as it is written: 'The deliverer will come from Zion; he will turn godlessness away from Jacob'" (Romans 11:26, amplifying Isaiah 59:20).

Does this promise mean that every Jew who ever lived gets saved? Of course not. Yeshua Himself told the Jewish people of His day that He alone is the way to salvation and that *nobody* comes to the Father except through Him (see John 14:6). The "all Israel" passage does not suggest a special route to redemption available to the bloodline of Abraham, Isaac and Jacob. It does not imply Jews get any unique, second chance to be saved.[9] Those who wishfully think so, even if out of sincere compassion, run the serious risk of neglecting the biblical mandate to share the Gospel with their Jewish friends (see Romans 1:16; 11:11, 31).

The best interpretation of the "all Israel" passage refers to the day of Yeshua's return, when His Messiahship is openly revealed in a singular manner. The Jewish leaders alive at that time, representing the nation as a whole, will call upon Him, and Israel will be saved.[10] The immediate context of the passage helps clarify the issue, because the same verse also contains a prophecy about the Second Coming: "The deliverer will come from Zion; he will turn godlessness away from Jacob" (Romans 11:26).

The first time Yeshua came, Israel's leaders rejected Him as their King, despite His popularity with the common folk. But someday Israel's future leaders will reverse their former decision and invite Him back as King. This will inaugurate Messiah's return to earth (see Matthew 23:39). Untold blessing will be unleashed not only to the Jews, but to the nations. As we will see later, in a very real sense, all nations will be saved after Yeshua returns (see Daniel 7:27; Psalm 67:5–7; Isaiah 2:3–4; Zephaniah 2:11).

Standing with Israel: Common Ground

Meanwhile, the Church today is repositioning with Israel, for we stand on common ground. Both peoples are in covenant relationship with Yahweh. His enemies are well aware of this fact, and they target us together. *"First the Saturday people, then the Sunday people!"* resounds the jihadist cry.[11] The Saturday people are the Jews, observing the Sabbath on Saturday; the Sunday people are the Christians. Radical Islam aims to destroy us both. It interweaves with secular humanism and materialism, emerging in a knot tied to Middle Eastern oil reserves. These combined forces target not only Judeo-Christian values, but Jews and Christians. The Church is awakening to this reality and learning to wield new weapons of love, as Christian author Lela Gilbert suggests:

> The sword of Islam . . . is wielded by devotees of death. We who have chosen life must do more than pray. We must fight for our children, our nations, our faith, our future. . . . Thankfully, with entwined roots planted in common ground, neither Christians nor Jews need fight the battle alone.[12]

As global conflict escalates, bear in mind that mounting enmity against the Church is not primarily backlash for standing with Israel. Consciously or unconsciously blaming the Jews for persecution against Christians can lead to a subtle, anti-Jewish deception. All who live godly in Messiah Jesus will be persecuted (see 2 Timothy 3:12). Those who love Him passionately also love the people He loves. True, sometimes there can be temporary trouble for believers willing to identify with His "kinsmen according to the flesh" (Romans 9:3, KJV). But the Bible says even worse troubles await those who will not stand with them (see Genesis 12:3; Obadiah 1:10–11, 15).

A spirit of anti-Semitism is inevitably the flip side of an antichrist spirit. Whenever anti-Semitism flares up, if it is not quelled, anti-Christian flames are likely to be similarly stoked. Nevertheless, God is well in control. He will use the enemy's ploys to further unite His covenant peoples, purifying and empowering us in love and war (see Daniel 11:35). For He has "created the destroyer to work havoc [for His good purposes]; no weapon forged against you will prevail" (Isaiah 54:16–17). The Messianic Warrior Bride will not be deterred by the devil, but will stand firm.

Standing with Israel does not mean agreeing with all her policies and practices, assuming one is able to discern through the media and rumor swirl what the country is in fact doing. Bible-based love for Israel should not limit love and blessing toward the Arabic peoples. Indeed, if our hearts' position regarding Israel results in lovelessness toward Palestinians, Arabs, Muslims or others, I daresay something is not quite right with our hearts' position for Israel.

To stand with Israel as a believer is to cooperate with her as God's covenant nation. It involves ministering the reality of His unconditional love through global birth pains that particularly shake the Jewish nation posted at earth's spiritual epicenter. Standing with Israel takes the form of fervent prayer[13] and practical aid at all levels. Sharing the good news of eternal life in Messiah is a priority transcending all others.

A Test of Faith

World pressure to disassociate with Israel will intensify in these last days. If we do not engage with God's heart for her now, we may find ourselves ill-prepared to align with His Kingdom purposes for the Jewish people in the future. As the love of many grows cold, we may unwittingly position ourselves against God and His Word. Jesus' striking parable about sheep and goats in Matthew 25:31–46 cautions us concerning this last days phenomenon.

The events in the parable take place in the context of worldwide judgment: "When the Son of Man comes in his glory . . . All the nations will be gathered before him" (Matthew 25:31–32). At that time, Messiah will separate the righteous, or those who feed, clothe, nurse and care for His needs, from the unrighteous, or those who do not. The righteous (sheep) receive their inheritance in the Kingdom of God; the unrighteous (goats) are forever cast from His presence. At that time, you and I will ask when it was that we saw and cared for Him—or did not. He will reply, "I tell you the truth, whatever you did for one of the least of these brothers of mine, you did for me" (Matthew 25:40).

Christian commentators in recent centuries have interpreted "these brothers of mine" specifically as referring to the Jews. States an *NIV Study Bible* note, "Ultimately, how a person treats the Jewish people will reveal whether or not he is saved."[14]

To be sure, this parable refers and applies, in a broader sense, to other people groups in other situations. Its foundational meaning, however, relates to Jesus' physical brothers during the time of tribulation associated with the last days. Israel remains near and dear to His heart, and He eternally rewards those who embrace her.

The Big Picture

The relationship of Israel and the Church is ultimately about something much bigger than Israel or the Church, or even the

Kingdom age to come. It derives from a stupendous eternal plan, one proclaiming God's praises for His unsearchable, manifold wisdom (see Romans 11:33–36). The bigger picture is that of God Himself and His overarching design for all creation:

> He made known to us the mystery of his will according to his good pleasure, which he purposed in Christ, to be put into effect when the times will have reached their fulfillment—to bring all things in heaven and on earth together under one head, even Christ.
>
> Ephesians 1:9–10

All things in heaven and on earth will magnificently converge under the Person of the Son of Man/Son of God. Yahweh's mysterious will, from before the creation of the world, is to gather a redeemed created order under Messiah's government of love (see Ephesians 1:4, 11; Colossians 1:19–20). His plan is stellar: "That in the coming *ages* he might show the incomparable riches of his grace . . . in Christ Jesus" (Ephesians 2:7, emphasis added). Deity's dominion, which knows no end, showcases His unparalleled, rich grace forever, to His good pleasure.

Would you let the Holy Spirit soak you for a moment—or longer—in that reality? Through *ages yet to come*, His splendor saturates everything. You and I will never cease to marvel in wonder and worship at the brilliance of God's blueprints for eternity, and at our unending, active role in their unfolding.

It is in the context of this larger, matchless plan that we are "God's workmanship," joined together as Jew and Gentile in Christ "to do good works" (Ephesians 2:10). To show us why and how, and the boundless blessing that results, He gives us a beautiful, tangible tale in His Word. A prophetic glimpse of Israel and the Church in their intertwined last days destiny pops alive for us in the book of Ruth, reflecting and revealing God's mystery of one new man in Messiah.

3

The Mystery of Jew and Gentile in Messiah

For he himself is our peace, who has made the two one and has destroyed the barrier, the dividing wall of hostility. . . . His purpose was to create in himself one new man out of the two, thus making peace, and in this one body to reconcile both of them to God through the cross.

Ephesians 2:14–16

An unprecedented move of the Spirit, destined to increase in coming years, is the global rejoining of Gentile to Jewish believers in Messiah. When I came to faith in Yeshua in 1975, only a dozen or so Messianic congregations existed in the world. A few decades later, at this writing, some estimate that up to half a million Jews presently follow Jesus.[1] Of these, most are in mainstream churches. Others affiliate either with Messianic congregations or house-type fellowships. Some undoubtedly keep their faith secret.[2]

Like estranged family members reunited after too many years apart, Gentile and Jewish believers are at long last becoming reacquainted—joyously, but not without occasional stretch or strain. Each is restoring to the other essential dimensions of the Kingdom of God and the knowledge of His ways. In the process, the whole Body is being given opportunity to mature in love.

The concept of Jews and Gentiles together in Christ as "one new man" is articulated in the book of Ephesians. In context, it flows from the broad description of God's redemptive plan from before creation. The one new man is not an isolated phenomenon. We exist and function within a much larger Kingdom reality than simply Jews and Gentiles getting along well together—though that is an important start. God's plan is to bring *all things* in heaven and on earth together under the dominion of Christ. Within this larger Kingdom context, non-Jewish believers are "no longer foreigners and aliens, but fellow citizens with God's people." They are "heirs together with Israel, members together of one body" (Ephesians 2:19; 3:6). In this chapter, we look at the blessing and glory that results.

One New Humanity in the Book of Ruth

Throughout the Bible, people from all nations are invited to worship Israel's God. We learn of Abraham's servant Eliezer; a "mixed multitude" leaving Egypt in the Hebrew exodus; Moses' Gentile wife Zipporah and father-in-law Jethro; Rahab of Jericho; and converts from King Xerxes's empire during Esther's day. In the New Covenant, God-fearing Gentiles worship in synagogues even before the Gospel is preached to them. Then, through Jesus, the door to the Kingdom opens even wider to whoever, wherever, believes in Him. The Scriptures refer to this transcendent phenomenon of Jew and Gentile as one new "man." (Because the meaning is identical, I often use the translation "humanity.")

The early Church, which was mostly Jewish, quickly discerned that nationality alone did not confer spiritual standing before God. There is neither Jew nor Greek, slave nor free, male nor female when it comes to partaking of the blessings of salvation (see Galatians 3:28). These distinctions, of course, still exist in the earth realm. They bear upon our daily lives and have some relevance to our redemptive destinies.[3] But they are not relevant to our sanctification or status in God's Spirit.

To help flesh out reconciliation between Jews and Gentiles in Christ, two biblical heroines of the faith, our elder sisters Ruth and Naomi, serve as vivid prototypes. The unswerving devotion of the Gentile Ruth to the Jewish Naomi, together with Naomi's sacrificial deference to Ruth, shines as a revelatory glimpse into the matchless mystery of one new humanity. The serendipitous tale demonstrates how Jew and Gentile together, serving one another in a relationship of mutual love, proved instrumental to Yeshua's first coming. Assuredly, it will again take Jew and Gentile together, each preferring the other in divine reciprocity, to bring about His Second Coming.

Israel's Desolation

The book of Ruth is primarily a Spirit-breathed, literal account of historical events.[4] But it also constitutes a typology or prophetic allegory especially befitting the 21st-century Church. The narrative takes place approximately three thousand years ago. In the opening scene, an Israelite named Elimelech, his wife Naomi and their two sons leave home to escape a famine. As you may know, names in the Scriptures are significant, reflecting the characteristics and callings of persons and places. In Ruth, names bespeak much of the book's prophetic and instructive message. Allow me, therefore, to give you a fast and easy lesson in Hebrew, the language of your spiritual forebears.

The name Elimelech means "My God is King," while Naomi translates into "Pleasant." The couple has two sons, Mahlon, meaning "Weak," "Sickly" or "Afflicted," and Kilion, meaning "Wasting Away." The family belongs to the clan of Ephrathites, which means "Fruitful Ones." They come from Bethlehem, or

"House of Bread," which is located in Judah, meaning "Praise." So at the outset, we know we have met a fruitful family called to nourish others. But there is a famine in the land, and so their offspring are weak, sickly, afflicted and wasting away.

Famine in the Scriptures represents a form of judgment. We need not delve too deeply to know that the story transpired during a time of rebellion against God. The first sentence in Ruth tells us the events took place "in the days when the judges ruled" (Ruth 1:1). The book of Judges, which immediately precedes Ruth, concludes with this sorry remark: "In those days Israel had no king; everyone did as he saw fit" (Judges 21:25). The famine was deserved, and it was devastating.

Times being so trying, Elimelech and his family seek refuge in the land of Moab—Israel's longstanding enemy. Moab, meaning "From Father," was the son resulting from an incestuous union between Lot and one of his daughters (see Genesis 19:33–37). Despite their dubious ancestry, Moab's descendants grew into a prosperous nation. But they were cruel to Israel, and consequently, God cursed them:

> No . . . Moabite or any of his descendants may enter the assembly of the LORD, even down to the tenth generation. For they did not come to meet you [Israel] with bread and water on your way when you came out of Egypt, and they hired Balaam . . . to pronounce a curse on you.
>
> Deuteronomy 23:3–4

Moab was not the sort of sanctuary you would think a starving Jewish family from the Province of Praise would pick. It seemed the Moabites had forgotten that their very existence as a people, as well as their land, was due to the generosity of the progenitor of the Jews, namely Abraham. Recall that it was Abraham who ceded the lushest-looking land in Canaan to Lot. Years later, it was Abraham's relationship with him that resulted in Lot and his family's deliverance from the brimstone annihilation of Sodom and Gomorrah. But as the years passed, so did any sense of kinship on the part of Moab's descendants with Abraham's covenant children. (Could the same be said, perhaps, of some in the Church?)

Nonetheless, Moab finds itself hosting a displaced Jewish family of destiny. There the head of the household, Elimelech ("My God is King"), dies. It is as if the kingship of God is no more for this family. Sons Mahlon and Kilion marry Moabite women, but, being the weak, sickly, afflicted and wasting away souls that they are, these two young men also die, and without children. The family's attempt to escape judgment has failed, and as a result, Naomi is "Pleasant" no longer. Soon she will change her name to Mara, meaning "Bitter."

Meanwhile, news arrives that Israel's famine has come to an end. The season of judgment is over; Naomi decides to go home. She bids her two daughters-in-law a difficult farewell. Blessing them both, she tells them to stay in Moab, make new lives, find new husbands and start new families. At this, the young women are genuinely distressed. They weep together in protest and grief. But then Orpah, whose name means "Back of the Neck," says good-bye, turning the back of her neck to her mother-in-law and "going back to her people and her gods" (Ruth 1:15).

Crossroads for the Church

Ruth, however, whose name means "Friend" or "Clinging One," will not be dissuaded. Instead, she clings all the more tenaciously to Naomi. Ruth utters words that have come to represent a commitment so supreme as to find place in many marriage vows today:

> Where you go I will go, and where you stay I will stay. Your people will be my people and your God my God. Where you die I will die, and there I will be buried. May the LORD deal with me, be it ever so severely, if anything but death separates you and me.
>
> Ruth 1:16–17

At this juncture the book's allegorical symbolism sharpens into focus. We see that Naomi personifies Israel as a whole, God's "pleasant" people. But just as Naomi becomes Mara when the living presence of God as King is removed from her, so does Israel's pleasantness turn bitter without Him. Israel today, like other nations, has not collectively surrendered to the living God. Millennia of murderous persecutions, followed by a century of terror, have also taken their tragic toll. As a result, the Jewish State has endured a type of pervasive spiritual famine. But the story is not over. Israel's suffering will be used by Yahweh for something ultimately far grander than she, like Naomi, can imagine.

Ruth, meanwhile, portrays Gentile Christians from the nations who have so joined themselves to Israel and her God that they cannot, under any circumstance, return to Moab or their Moabite gods. Ruth's choice to stick with embittered Naomi, come what may, turns on two firmly resolved matters. First, she is thoroughly devoted to Yahweh. Second, because of her faithfulness to Him, she sincerely and unconditionally loves her mother-in-law. In other words, she identifies fully with the family into which she has married. In so doing, Ruth depicts Christians who fully identify with the family of their Bridegroom-King. Orpah, on the other hand, decides differently. At first, hers seems the more sensible choice. But Orpah depicts Christians who, in crisis, revert to the security and society of the world.

The opposite choices made by the two daughters-in-law portentously parallel those we will make as believers today. As with Orpah and Ruth, our decisions will affect our destinies. Like them, Gentile believers have joined themselves to faith in the God of Israel. They have reaped blessing through the Jewish Scriptures, as well as through the Jewish patriarchs, prophets, apostles and Messiah—*through whom they have married, so to speak, into a Jewish family.*

The two Moabite women come to a crossroads. To continue on with God in the totality of what He has for them, they must cling to Naomi. The alternative is not to go forward in Him at all, but to go back to familiar gods of the world. Similarly, in these last days, those who comprise His warrior bride will cling tenaciously to Israel. To go forward in God in the years ahead, we must, like Ruth, go forward with Israel—or we shall not truly go forward at all.

Those radically in love with their Bridegroom-King will love His Jewish people. Having touched the inner chambers of God's heart, their own hearts resonate to His yearning for His ancient ones. Most wholly in love with the Most Holy, the warrior bride is so resolute in courage as to advance headlong, like Ruth, into a future fraught with uncertainty. Dependent entirely on God, she is willing to be escorted by a covenant counterpart who, like Naomi, may at times prove a bit more bitter than pleasant.

Catch the full extent of young Ruth's valiant humility. From a rather sordid background and cursed family lineage, she refuses to let her past impede her future. Ruth may or may not know that God's curse on Moab—lasting ten generations—is just now at its end.[5] What she does know is that God is worth *everything*. Those of us with personal or family histories of dysfunction can take heart. The past prevails no more when He is our Chief Goal.

Here I would like to share a side note with fellow Jewish believers in Yeshua. Years ago, when preparing my first message on the book of Ruth, I realized I did not fit neatly into any category represented by the story's cast of characters. I asked the Lord, "Are Messianic Jews Ruth, or are we Naomi?" The answer came clearly: *Yes. You are Rumi.* Instantly, I knew He was saying to make room to humbly embrace and embody the exemplary characteristics of both Ruth and Naomi. He wants us joyfully appropriating and modeling His grace for roomy hearts and lives toward both covenant peoples.

Gleaning Blessings

Resuming our biblical tale, Ruth and Naomi set out for Bethlehem, where their arrival generates a veritable stir. Elimelech's widow has changed so much that she is barely recognizable to her countrymen. Plus, she has brought with her an unenviable Moabitess. Naomi bemoans, "The LORD has afflicted me; the Almighty has brought misfortune upon me" (Ruth 1:21).

In modern times, Naomi's groan has been shared by many in Israel. It echoes each time another Jewish life is ravaged by yet another violent assault, or genocidal threat, aimed at the beleaguered sliver of a State. Yet this groaning of the country's corporate soul, like Naomi's, reflects an abiding—albeit perplexed—awareness that somehow God is still involved. Israel's groan will not dissuade Christians who, in the spirit of Ruth, refuse to let go of the Jewish people because they know it is alongside them that God's greatest blessings will be found. As our destinies increasingly converge, unredeemed Israel will likewise discover that her Savior and her salvation manifest through the Body of Christ.

The last days warrior bride will be a radical firebrand that provokes many Jews to envy for her Messiah. According to Romans 11:11, "Salvation has come to the Gentiles to make Israel envious." For almost two thousand years, this mandate has gone largely unfulfilled. But when the Jewish people encounter a company of militant lovers in whose midst Yeshua awesomely dwells, many of them will see Him at last—and they will reclaim the Desired of all Nations (see Haggai 2:7).

The timing of Naomi's return home proves providential. It happens to be harvest season—and what better place to find food than in the House of Bread (Bethlehem)? Prophetically, Ruth's emergence in Israel at harvest season corresponds to the Church's embrace of the Jewish nation as part of the end times spiritual harvest. In Ruth's day, even the most needy could find food during a harvest, for with the season came the opportunity to glean. Gleaning was God's merciful form of social welfare whereby designated portions of crops were left for the poor to gather freely (see Leviticus 23:22).

So back in Bethlehem, Ruth goes gleaning. The younger and presumably physically sturdier of the two, she undertakes the taxing job to nourish and sustain both Naomi and herself. Remarkably, from this point on Naomi never again refers to her as a daughter-in-law, but as "my daughter." Ruth is blessing Naomi as typically only a daughter (or son) would bless a mother, in covenant love and faithfulness. The profound significance of Ruth's sacrifice is more fully grasped when we consider that the Hebrew root-based definition of the word *bless* means to "kneel to enrich."[6] Ruth's kneeling in the sweltering, sunbaked fields to enrich Naomi offers a poignant picture of blessing.

God promises to bless those who bless Israel (see Genesis 12:3). Ruth, therefore, is about to glean a great deal more than grain. She quickly catches the eye of a chivalrous chap named Boaz, owner of the field in which she is studiously looking for leftovers. Tenderheartedly, he tells her, "My daughter, listen to me. Don't go and glean in another field and don't go away from here. . . . I have told the men not to touch you. And whenever you are thirsty, go and get a drink from the water jars the men have filled" (Ruth 2:8–9).

Ruth is honored, but baffled. We can imagine her mopping a sweaty brow, fingering sticky strands of hair from her face. "Why have I found such favor in your eyes that you notice me—a foreigner?" she asks (verse 10).

Boaz's reply reflects his own magnanimity of spirit. "I've been told," he says, "all about what you have done for your mother-in-law since the death of your husband—how you left your father and mother and your homeland and came to live with a people you did not know before. May the LORD repay you for what you have done. May you be richly rewarded by the LORD, the God of Israel, under whose wings you have come to take refuge" (verses 11–12).

Kinsman-Redeemer Comes in Strength

The Hebrew name Boaz means "In Him is Strength" or "Come in Strength." As it happens, Boaz is one of Naomi's relatives from Elimelech's side of the family. So when Ruth comes home and reports the day's good turn of events, Naomi is elated. She exclaims, "That man is our close relative; he is one of our kinsman-redeemers" (Ruth 2:20).

The role of kinsman-redeemer was prescribed in the Old Covenant Law (see Deuteronomy 25:5–10). Certain relatives of a deceased Israelite were designated to protect the interests and inheritance of the surviving family. The kinsman-redeemer served, among other things, to father an heir for a brother who had died, thereby securing family property that would otherwise be lost due to death. But redemption by a kinsman—or his refusal to do so and his relegation of those duties to another—had to occur pursuant to specific procedures.

Naomi knows the rules. Learning of Boaz's benevolence toward Ruth, she dares to dream again. Suddenly we hear the pleasant/bitter one praising the Lord. "Could this man be the hope of our redemption?" she perhaps thinks aloud. A strange flicker of faith—ignited by her Gentile daughter—sparks her soul. That flicker is about to explode into the surprise of a lifetime for Ruth, shaping history. Similarly, as Christians today bless the Jewish people, the question will arise in Jewish hearts, *Could this Man be the hope of our redemption?* The answer will reshape the future.

Notice what has drawn this kinsman-redeemer to the practically penniless Arab widow. The Scriptures are to the point: Ruth's faithful and unconditional love for her Jewish mother, for the Jewish people and for their God wins his heart. Boaz is captivated by her clinging friendship to Yahweh and His people. As you may know, Boaz is regarded as a type or foreshadow of Messiah.[7] He prophetically depicts Yeshua as our Kinsman and Redeemer.

Like Boaz of Bethlehem, Yeshua redeems all that was lost due to sin and death. And like Boaz, Yeshua is captivated by our clinging friendship to His Old Covenant people. His heart is won by believers from the nations demonstrating loving faithfulness to Israel. To those aligned with His kinfolk—His brethren according to the flesh—He is revealed as Kinsman.

The Church's relationship with Israel, which parallels Ruth's relationship with Naomi, is ultimately about Messiah and following Him intimately. "May you be richly rewarded by the LORD, the God of Israel, under whose wings you have come to take refuge," Boaz says in blessing the Moabitess (Ruth 2:12). Ruth has sought refuge not so much with Naomi as with Naomi's God. The Hebrew word translated "wings" in this verse can also refer to the corner of a garment or *tallit* (prayer shawl). Unconditional love for the Jewish nation is associated with coming under the Kinsman-Redeemer's *tallit*-like cover (see Ruth 3:9). As warrior, we dare not battle without His covering; as bride, we cannot bear life apart from it.

Divine Reciprocity

Up until now in the drama, Ruth has been the one kneeling to enrich Naomi. As a result, she has curried unexpected favor from a man possessing the potential to alter the course of her life. This in turn quickens Naomi's soul to the present reality of God in *her* life. Now Naomi kneels to enrich Ruth—beyond imagination.

According to the Law, Naomi herself, as surviving spouse of the deceased—not Ruth—inherits the right of kinsman-redemption. Not only does Naomi have legal right to Boaz, but he is much closer in age to her than to Ruth (see Deuteronomy 25:5; Ruth 3:10). Surely he would make a terrific husband for the older, impecunious widow. Naomi has every commonsense reason to present herself to him for marriage. Only if she voluntarily sacrifices her rights, and all the restorative blessings associated with them, can Ruth be redeemed. Amazingly and without hesitation, this is precisely what she sets out to do. The matter is quickly resolved as far as Naomi is concerned. She approaches Ruth and says, "My daughter, should I not try to find a home for you, where you will be well provided for?" (Ruth 3:1).

Though embittered by life's hard blows, and perhaps all the more because of them, Naomi is extravagantly grateful for Ruth's loyalty and love. The young woman's steadfast devotion has transformed her, and she is able to reciprocate when the right time comes. With Ruth's best interest at heart, this consummate Jewish mother risks losing whatever she could possibly gain for her daughter's sake. For if Boaz redeems and marries Ruth, under normal circumstances Naomi is likely to fade from the scene. How probable is it a new bride will cling to a distressed, former mother-in-law once she has remarried into a prominent, upscale family?[8] Won't a new husband and future children eventually crowd her out? Naomi takes the chance.

In a certain sense, Israel has done the same for the Church. On a national level, she has deliberately—if unknowingly—forgone (temporarily) the blessings of redemption. As a result, salvation has come to the Gentiles. The Jewish people's corporate rejection of Kinsman-Redeemer Yeshua has meant the reconciliation of the world through Him (see Romans 11:11, 15). To the extent the Church benefits from unsaved Israel's national spurning of salvation in Messiah, the two covenant peoples of God resemble Ruth and Naomi at the deepest level of sacrifice at this juncture in the book.

Bear in mind that if Israel's recalcitrance has benefited the nations, her repentance will propel the world toward climactic blessing:

> Moreover, if their stumbling is bringing riches to the world—that is, if Israel's being placed temporarily in a condition less favored than that of the Gentiles is bringing riches to the latter—how much greater riches will Israel in its fullness bring them! . . . For if their casting Yeshua aside means reconciliation for the world, what will their accepting Him mean? It will be life from the dead!
>
> Romans 11:12, 15, CJB[9]

Israel's redemption will mean nothing less than life from the dead. At its apex, the Lord will literally come back and redeem the earth. Recall that Yeshua conditioned His return on the Jews' repentant embrace of Him (see Matthew 23:39). As today's Ruth blesses today's Naomi, Naomi will bless Ruth in return. This back-and-forth synergy of relationship will escalate until blessing crescendos in the Person of the Redeemer who, like Boaz, comes in strength. For this divine, mutual reciprocity between Jew and Gentile, this exquisite interdependence and fruit thereof, the warrior bride will love and fight—and never give up.

Threshing Floor Test

But back in the book of Ruth, matters are still at stake. If the Moabitess is to be redeemed, Naomi must carefully prepare her according to God's ways and means. She therefore instructs Ruth scrupulously according to protocol. Her advice is not just kindly and motherly; any deviation from God's Word could backfire, dashing all their hopes to bits.

At first, Naomi's advice sounds reasonable: "Wash and perfume yourself, and put on your best clothes" (Ruth 3:3). But next it gets a little quirky and even kinky: "Then go down to the threshing floor, but don't let him know you are there until he has finished eating and drinking. When he lies down . . . go and uncover his feet and lie down. He will tell you what to do" (verses 3–4). That sounds, I daresay, downright scandalous.

We can assume that Ruth, who has demonstrated nothing less than stellar character, is a chaste woman of moral purity. Could she not have balked at Naomi's "teaching"? Might she have been tempted to conclude that these Jewish ways were getting a bit too bizarre for her? ("I've gone along with this 'Israel thing' up till now, but that's just not how we Gentiles do it. . . .") But no—not missing a beat, she replies, "I will do whatever you say" (verse 5).

Naomi has surrendered her rights to Ruth; Ruth surrenders hers to Naomi. Divine reciprocity between Jew and Gentile is about mutual submission and humble service. There can be no arrogance or conceit on the part of Christians toward Israel (see Romans 11:20–21, 25). Just as certain, there is no place for Jewish pride toward Gentiles. Any sense of self-importance will find itself exposed on threshing floors made manifest through birth-pain shakings. Just as Ruth's embrace of her Jewish mother is tested on a threshing floor, there the Church's embrace of Israel will be tested, refined and rewarded (see Matthew 3:12).

Down at the threshing floor, Ruth follows through on all she was told to do. We are allowed to eavesdrop on her encounter with Boaz—one that commences almost comically. According to the narrative,

> In the middle of the night something startled the man, and he turned and discovered a woman lying at his feet.
> "Who are you?" he asked.
> "I am your servant Ruth," she said. "Spread the corner of your garment over me, since you are a kinsman-redeemer."
> "The LORD bless you, my daughter," he replied. . . . "I will do for you all you ask."
>
> Ruth 3:8–11

Like Ruth, Gentile believers will emerge from their threshing floor test lavished with favor. It is there the Kinsman-Redeemer will spread over them the corner of His garment, His *tallit*. Their relationship with Him will be taken to new levels.

Jew and Gentile Together Bring Redemption

Boaz readily fulfills all the requirements of the Law to complete Ruth's redemption, just as Jesus fulfilled all the requirements of the Law to redeem you and me. Then Boaz announces confidently to the community of Israel, "I have bought . . . all the property of Elimelech, Kilion and Mahlon. I have also acquired Ruth the Moabitess, Mahlon's widow, as my wife" (Ruth 4:9–10).

Boaz has rightfully been given all that belonged to Elimelech ("My God is King"), even as Yeshua has been given all things by our God who is King (see Ephesians 1:22). Like Yeshua, Boaz has also rightfully taken all that belonged to "Weakness, Sickliness, Affliction" (Mahlon) and "Wasting Away" (Kilion). As Israel and the Church join together in the spirit of Ruth and Naomi, they will be catapulted as one new humanity into new dimensions of life, freed from levels of weakness, sickliness, affliction and wasting away that have beset them both.

When Boaz claims Ruth as his, the whole community joyfully welcomes her in. No longer is Ruth a lowly foreigner; she is a full member of the household of Israel, the recipient of eternal esteem: "May the LORD make the woman who is coming into your home like Rachel and Leah, who together built up the house of Israel. May you have standing in Ephrathah and be famous in Bethlehem" (Ruth 4:11). Like our forebears, we Messianic Jews must rejoice over, fully welcome, honor and bless our redeemed brothers and sisters in Yeshua from the nations.

Blessings spoken over Ruth come to pass. In the closing scene of the book, she gives birth to a son named Obed ("Servant"). Obed becomes the grandfather of King David and a direct ancestor of Jesus the Messiah. Therefore, Obed's honored mother finds herself in the lineage of the Savior of humanity, her story preserved forever. She shines into infinity as the prototypical Gentile believer who partakes of all God's blessings of redemption because of her alignment with His Jewish people. She especially foreshadows redeemed Arabic peoples destined to uniquely receive and mediate those blessings back to Israel and the nations.

Baby Obed, meanwhile, is nurtured by Naomi as if he were her own son. Obed serves to revive Naomi to the extent that she becomes pleasant again, shedding her name and identity as Mara, or "Bitter" (see Ruth 4:16–17). By the fruit of Ruth's redemption, she is in a sense brought back to life from the dead.

She prophetically depicts Israel's response to Christian love in hard times. The warrior bride's relationship with the Incarnate Kinsman-Redeemer will bear fruit that serves to revive Israel, in turn unleashing blessing for the world.

God used Jew and Gentile together to bring about Messiah's first coming. So, too, it will take Jew and Gentile together, in the spirit of Ruth and Naomi, to bring about His Second Coming. Israel will not turn to Him and be saved without the love, intercession and support of the international body of believers. This exquisite interdependence plays out in the mystery of one new humanity—a mystery the Master is unraveling in our day.

The manifest reality of one new humanity is essential to the core identity of the Messianic Warrior Bride. It will represent a major last days shift in the Church, further converging heaven with earth. But it will not go unopposed. As birth pains intensify, opposition against Israel and the Jewish people will also escalate, even among Christians. Only supernatural, Christlike love will keep Jewish and Gentile believers united as one.

Accordingly, the time is ripe for ancient truths about a supernatural love relationship with our Bridegroom-King to be revived. Unshakeable love for one another will flow from the love we allow Him to first lavish on us. Deeply intimate, heart-to-heart communion with God will characterize the last days Church. According to a traditional Jewish teaching, the pinnacle relationship of God to mankind is best described in a single word as *bridal*. Therefore, we look next at the eternal, divine romance materializing today for you and me.

4

Coming for a Bride

Hear, O Israel: The LORD our God, the LORD is one. Love the LORD your God with all your heart and with all your soul and with all your strength.

Deuteronomy 6:4–5

The cornerstone Hebrew prayer of traditional Judaism, called the *Shema* (meaning "Hear"), is based on the Deuteronomy passage above. Jesus calls this Scripture "the first and greatest commandment" (Matthew 22:38). As a child, I recited it thousands of times as part of the regular synagogue liturgy—and I was left with a troubling question.

Why, I wondered, was it not possible to live the reality of the *Shema*? Nobody I knew loved the Lord with all of his or her heart, let alone soul and strength. Not even my esteemed rabbi or devout congregational elders gave evidence of an experiential love relationship with God. None of them knew Him intimately, as had our ancestors about whom we read. Our patriarchs and prophets all talked to God, and He talked back. They had encounters with the King; they connected. If my chief command was to love the Lord with all my heart, soul and strength, I was failing miserably—and obviously I was not alone. *Why?*

I spent many years searching for an answer. Never during that time did I remotely suspect it would be found in Jesus. Like many Jews, I had been taught that at best He was irrelevant; at worst, He was responsible for repeated murders and persecutions of my people. Nevertheless, Yeshua mercifully revealed Himself to me, and as a young adult I gratefully gave Him my life. From then on, the reality of the *Shema* burned in my bones. Because He first loved me, I could at last love the Lord my God, despite my weakness and sin. Today I *must*—I *want*—to love Him more and more, and then, still *more*. I want to love Him with all my heart, all my soul and all my strength. And I think you do, too.

You and I yearn to love the Lord because He has called us to be His Bride. The consummate relationship of Messiah to His Church, the Bible says, is akin to that of a husband to his wife (see Ephesians 5:32). When Yeshua returns, He is coming for a Bride—and she will intentionally have made herself ready for Him (see Revelation 19:7). This readying process revolves around intimate devotion, worshipful affection and heartfelt surrender to Yeshua. But it also requires the testing and refining of our faith through challenging times. Therefore, as the end of the age approaches, God will use mounting anti-Christian resistance against His people to purify us for His return. In this chapter we will see how, despite intensifying birth pains, the fire of our desire for Messiah as Bridegroom will be kept ablaze.

A few of my brothers in Christ may find the bridal theme a bit challenging at first, so allow me to point out that in biblical parlance, men are just as much a part of the Bride as women are a part of the collective "sons of God" (see Matthew 5:9; Romans 8:14, 19; Galatians 3:26). It may surprise you to learn that the overwhelming majority of expositors and teachers on bridal relationship with God through the millennia have been *men*, not women. The apostle Paul, himself a steely sort of guy, said this: "I promised you [the Church] to one husband, to Christ . . .

as a pure virgin" (2 Corinthians 11:2). No need, men, to picture yourselves in a wedding gown as you open your heart to Jesus in new dimensions!

Contracting Marriage with Israel

The biblical prophets vividly portray Israel as God's bride or wife:

I was a husband to them.

Jeremiah 31:32;
see also Ezekiel 16:8

As a bride you loved me.

Jeremiah 2:2

You will call me "my husband."

Hosea 2:16

Your Maker is your husband.

Isaiah 54:5

As a bridegroom rejoices over his bride, so will your God rejoice over you.

Isaiah 62:5

The prophets' words are more than poetic metaphor. They reflect a powerful transaction that took place in the Spirit with the sons and daughters of Jacob, resulting in a type of legal marriage. To better understand this truth, we need a bit of Hebraic background.

The earliest wedding practice in the Bible involved a man simply "taking" a woman as his. First he would obtain the permission of her father or male guardian, who secured the consent of the bride-to-be. Then the groom would take the young woman into his tent and consummate the union, as did Isaac with Rebecca (see Genesis 24:67). God uses this same word for "taking" when He delivers His people from Egypt. We can assume the Hebrews likely understood that He was talking of marriage when He said, "I will *take* you as my own people, and I will be your God" (Exodus 6:7, emphasis added). They also understood that to be "taken" by God required their consent. He would not force Himself on them, but wanted a willing lover.

Years later, betrothal, or what today could be called engagement, became the first phase of a formalized Jewish marriage. At betrothal, the groom-to-be presented a written proposal, which a young woman and her father (or male guardian) would either accept or reject. If accepted, the bride price would be paid at that time, and the couple was as legally bound as they would ever be.[1] In like manner, not long after God spoke of "taking" Israel, He offered her a type of written marriage contract through Moses in the desert at Sinai (see Exodus 19:5).[2] Its terms were summed up in the Ten Commandments. Most notably and primarily, the relationship was to be strictly monogamous: "You shall have no other gods before me" (Exodus 20:3).

Israel accepted the divine proposal:

> So Moses went back and summoned the elders of the people and set before them all the words the LORD had commanded him to speak. The people all responded together, "We will do everything the LORD has said." So Moses brought their answer back to the LORD.
>
> Exodus 19:7–8

Yahweh's ultimate bride price would prove staggering. Nothing less than the sacrificial death and shed blood of His Son could pay for His treasured betrothed—from *all* nations (see 1 Peter 1:18–19). The Uncreated Sovereign of the Universe had arranged a marriage with mankind in which He fully foreknew the anguished sufferings His ravished heart would undergo (see Deuteronomy 31:16, 21). What unfathomable love!

Over and again, Israel shows herself unfaithful. Repeatedly and in righteous anger, God grieves for her. "You adulterous wife!" says the spurned Sovereign Lover (Ezekiel 16:32). Sin threatens to shatter the covenant. But God remains faithful on *His* part to *His* vow. He does not void out His Word. With stunning mercy He prophesies restoration and reconciliation:

> This is what the Sovereign LORD says: I will deal with you as you deserve, because you have despised my oath by breaking the covenant. Yet I will remember the covenant I made with you in the days of your youth, and I will establish an everlasting covenant with you.
>
> Ezekiel 16:59–60

God's everlasting covenant promised to Israel is the spectacular New Covenant that offers salvation to all nations (see Jeremiah 31:31). To an extent, this New Covenant can be accurately described as a *re*newed covenant, for it does not dispense with the essence of the Old. By it we receive anointing to love the Lord with all our heart, soul and strength, fulfilling the first and greatest renewed commandment (see Mark 12:29).

New Covenant Bridegroom and Bride

In the New Covenant, Messiah's earthly ministry reflects bridal dimensions from beginning to end. At the outset, Baptizer John decrees, "I said, 'I am not the Christ but am sent ahead of him.' The bride belongs to the bridegroom" (John 3:28–29). Not coincidentally, Jesus' first public miracle takes place at a wedding. Years later, His words to the disciples before the crucifixion bespeak the heart of a departing Bridegroom, leaving to prepare a place for His betrothed (see John 2:7–11; 14:2–3).

According to ancient Hebrew custom, after an espoused groom left his intended, he zealously began preparing a place for her. A bridal chamber was usually built as part of his father's house, much as an add-on unit. The young man himself generally would not determine when it was time to return for the woman awaiting him; his father nodded off final approval. Therefore, in a sense only the father knew when his son would come for his bride. At that point the eager groom would make haste—often unannounced—to claim and carry away his beloved.

Meanwhile, the espoused bride was called in Hebrew a *kiddushin*, literally a "sanctified one" or "set apart one." She spent the waiting period of their separation meticulously preparing herself for marriage. The bride price that had been paid for her, which included monetary and other gifts, was used in part for this purpose. The set apart *kiddushin* had but one goal, to make herself ready for the groom's return. Assisting her were female friends serving as bridesmaids. Since the young man could come at any time, they were responsible together with her to watch diligently for him. To heighten the romance, he might arrive in the middle of the night. So it became customary for both bride and bridesmaids to keep oil lamps, with oil enough for the journey, beside their beds as they slept.[3]

Weddings were merry public events. When the bridegroom finally arrived, his close friends accompanied him, making for no quiet affair. Often the exuberant young men blasted trumpets to announce their arrival, shouting in whooping excitement. The bridal attendants quickly arose, dressed the sanctified *kiddushin*, and summoned her family. They made way together toward the groom's party. Many times the two groups met up before the men actually reached the girl's home. They joined to form a lively, festal procession back to the groom's father's house, where the bridal chamber awaited. There the bride and groom secreted themselves away, enjoying each other for up to several days without interruption. Outside the chamber, wedding attendants, neighbors and family spent the time feasting, singing and dancing in celebration of the happy union of their loved ones.[4]

Yeshua's disciples would have been familiar with these customs. His parting words to them, therefore, were charged with meaning and prophetic nuance. Very soon, He would pay the full price for His betrothed by hanging on a tree. Then He would leave to prepare a place for her. Without doubt He would return, but only the Father knew when. Meanwhile, the Bride, His set apart *kiddushin*, must prepare herself and keep watch. For this purpose she was to use all the gifts He had given her. Their reunion, at the appointed hour, would be rapturous and overwhelmingly worth the wait.

Oil in Your Lamp

To further illustrate the bridal principle, Yeshua tells a tale of ten virgins, half of whom are wise and half of whom are foolish (see Matthew 25:1–13). The virgins serve in one sense as bridal attendants, but in another sense, they are members of the Lord's corporate Bride. That each possesses lamps and some measure of oil indicates they are all light-bearers who serve or minister to others. They are committed to both the bride and bridegroom, and parabolically, to the Bridegroom-King and His people. In short, they symbolize us, the Body of Messiah.

While they are sleeping, a midnight cry wakens them. *The bridegroom is coming!* But only half the virgins have enough oil to journey out to meet him. Symbolically, only half the virgins, or believers, have enough of the Spirit of God to stay ignited to the end. Only these wise virgins get to participate when the wedding feast begins. The other, foolish virgins must first go and get more oil. But by the time they do so and catch up with the others, it is too late. The door to the wedding chamber has been shut. "Therefore keep watch," Yeshua urges, "because you do not know the day or the hour" (Matthew 25:13).

I admit this parable has sometimes disquieted me. I do not want to be among those shut out from the Lord's presence, and I trust you do not either. The fact that one winter's day in 1975 I knelt and opened my heart to Him as Savior does not in itself guarantee I will have oil reserves today, tomorrow or when He comes. Whatever the interpretive implications of the story,[5] let me encourage you to be wise. Stay worshipfully watchful, get filled and refilled with the Holy Spirit, and exult in loving the Lord with all you are and all you have. A timeless Jewish song can show you how.

Song of Songs

King Solomon's matchless Song of Songs describes dazzling heights and profound depths of relationship with God. Through history, Jews and Christians alike have been captivated by this incomparable allegory of divine love. They have seen in it the zenith expression of intimacy with God. Today's body of believers is rediscovering the book's sublime revelation of relationship between Yeshua as Bridegroom-King and His cherished Bride. So superlative is this masterpiece of Scripture that, if you have never read it, I encourage you to do so now. Since time and space permit us to look at only a few of its key passages, you will benefit more if you are already familiar with the story.

As we have seen, generally the Bible should not be fundamentally interpreted in an allegorical sense. The Scriptures were written to be understood in a plain and straightforward manner in their grammatical-historical context. Accordingly, in modern times the Song has been interpreted more narrowly and literally, as a picture of marital love.[6] But as we also saw earlier, when God wants His Word fundamentally understood in a symbolic way, He makes that clear from the context. In this respect, the Song of Songs is unique. Many Jewish and Christian theologians alike have concluded that a literal, grammatical-historical interpretation alone cannot by itself reasonably or sensibly account for unduly large portions of the book. The exceptional characteristics of Solomon's masterful story call, therefore, for a symbolic interpretation interwoven together with the literal. So while the Song clearly depicts the beauty of marital love, at the same time it also metaphorically portrays intimacy of relationship between Messiah and His bride.[7]

I believe Solomon's Song will prove invaluable to the last days Church. Expanded revelation of the breadth, depth and height of Jesus' heart for redeemed humanity will transform us at the core of our being. *To the extent we linger as bride in the fire of His affections, we will find ourselves launched into and sustained in the warrior dimension.*

God's Song to You

The Song of Songs has long been extolled by some Jewish scholars as "the holy of holies" of all the biblical writings.[8] Said one rabbinic sage, "The entire universe's existence was not justified until the day Song of Songs was given within it. . . . He who recites a verse of the Song of Songs and treats it as if it were a nonspiritual or secular song . . . brings evil upon the world."[9] To my thinking, if unregenerate rabbis have for thousands of years read this book with such awe, it likely offers exponential blessing for those in whom the Holy Spirit dwells.

Jewish scholars believe the Song recounts and prophetically foresees, in sparkling imagery, Israel's past, present and future relationship with God.[10] To them, the allegory signifies the nation's betrothal at Mt. Sinai, followed by sin and spurning of Yahweh, then collective repentance. Backsliding occurs again, resulting in Israel's first and second exiles. According to this interpretation, the elusive and sometimes antagonistic third parties, the "daughters of Jerusalem," represent the nations and their maligning of the Jews. The Song is said to close with a petition for Israel's anticipated national regathering, redemption and restoration by her Bridegroom-King.

To be sure, the Lord has reserved a splendorous prophetic fulfillment of this portion of Scripture when Israel as a nation is saved. Toward that end, I expect He will beautifully revive Solomon's book uniquely for Israel. The impassioned Song will strike chords deep within her slumbering soul, rouse her and woo her back to the Beloved. Because of her unique history, she will resonate and respond as no other nation can to His resumed beckoning. Israel will discover that King Solomon writes of King Yeshua, whose love for her has been "as strong as death" (Song of Solomon 8:6[11]).

Most Christian theologians who, like the rabbis, allegorically interpret the Song, have seen it as referring to Messiah's corporate Body as a whole. Jesus is the Bridegroom-King; the universal Church is His Bride. The daughters of Jerusalem personify carnal believers. Intimacy with the King on an *individual* level, however, is not stressed. This interpretation, like that of the rabbis, is certainly not incorrect, though I believe it is incomplete.

A minority of believers has always connected to a profoundly individual application of Solomon's book. In these words penned by Israel's ancient king, they have heard the Savior speak to them very personally and intimately. As a result, the Song has given them great strength to stand firm in times of trial as well as triumph.[12] Today, in this season of intensifying birth pains, I am convinced God is alluring us into an intimately personal, as well as a corporate-level, reality of His Song of Songs.

So I invite you to tune your heart with me to the romance rhythms of heaven. Hear the unique harmony He has arranged just for *you*—one blending beautifully with myriads of others filling celestial realms. Allow a new song by the Spirit to stir your soul. Sing back to Him. Engage with the exquisite orchestration of eternity as we listen together to a few key notes.

The Kiss of God

Song of Songs begins by ushering us into the blossoming relationship of King Solomon and his new bride. In contrast to Solomon, the young woman's background is simple and ordinary. So while enthralled with her new husband, she is understandably insecure in the regal marriage. Solomon, meanwhile, remains resolute throughout the story. He lovingly shepherds her heart to maturity. As we watch the lovers interact and the bride grow, we see our own relationship with the Lord mirrored by them.

When we meet the bride, she is unabashedly passionate toward her king: "Let him kiss me with the kisses of his mouth—for your love is more delightful than wine" (Song of Solomon 1:2). The Lord's kisses refer to His Word. He kisses us, so to speak, by touching our innermost being through His Holy Word. Solomon's young bride does not withhold her desire for her bridegroom's kiss, and with this he is not in the least displeased. Similarly, God wants us enamored with His affections through His truth. Our desire for more of Him pleases Him greatly.

Though zealous and sincere, the bride is young and immature. We see this from the wording of her request in verse 2 above, with its focus on getting, not giving. Self-absorbed in the delightful experience of love, she enjoys posturing herself on the receiving end of the relationship. But soon, precisely because she is self-conscious, her attention turns from the beloved to her own perceived deficiencies. "Dark am I, yet lovely," she laments. "Do not stare at me because I am dark" (verses 5–6).

The bride's darkness symbolizes areas where light does not yet shine on her. The darkness, however, is merely superficial, not penetrating to her core identity, for despite it she is lovely. Though immature, she is not given over to sin. Like you and me, she is engaged in an unending process of maturation in relationship with her king. At times we may feel inhibited or restrained in abandoning ourselves to Jesus because we feel "dark." If the issue is immaturity or weakness, and not sin, take a cue from the bride. She realizes that despite her dark areas, her espoused one sees her as lovely. She does not withhold herself from him out of shame. By giving herself to the king, the light of his love begins to change her.

God loves you—and *enjoys* you—even though you may not be fully mature in Him. He never enjoys sin, but your King does delight in you during your wholehearted process of spiritual growth. Engaging in the experience of His love is not narcissistic; it is biblical. You were created to live connected to it. When you discover God's genuine joy over you, you find you do not withhold yourself from Him. To do so would deprive Him of the unique pleasure He takes in you. You grieve at *His* grie॰ over the loss of your companionship. Quickly you give yourself back to your King—which is exactly what He wants.

"My Lover Is Mine and I Am His"

I urge you never to wait until you feel you have achieved peak performance before giving God your all. Such a delay is inevitably deceptive, based on shame or pride or both. If your will is sincerely surrendered to Yeshua, that is enough to intentionally immerse yourself in Him in the manner of the bride in the Song. When you do, He responds with joy: "How beautiful you are, my darling! Oh, how beautiful! Your eyes are doves" (Song of Solomon 1:15). At His Word, your insecurities are quelled.

The bridegroom admires his young wife's eyes as doves. Doves not only mate for life, but they possess a peculiar ability to focus their vision.[13] The Lord loves it when your eyes gaze into His despite a world of potential distraction. With your sight set on Him, you see yourself as He sees you. "I am a rose of Sharon, a lily of the valleys," declares the bride in the book (Song of Solomon 2:1). Likewise, your life surrendered to Jesus is fragrant as a flower of the field. He loves how you smell! So when the Beloved summons you to higher places in His love, let your heart soar to meet His, and though you may not be aware of it, you will mature. Like Solomon's bride, your dove-eyed focus on the King diminishes your consciousness of self. Dark areas begin to shine as you reflect His light.

At this stage of the relationship, the bride revels in romance with the king—and there are times when we should, too. She is enthralled with the delectables he lavishes on her. "I delight to sit in his shade, and his fruit is sweet to my taste. He has taken me to the banquet hall, and his banner over me is love" (verses 3–4). Messiah's bride sits at heaven's banqueting table, partaking of Him and savoring His goodness. At His table we are nourished, strengthened and refreshed (see verse 5). Sometimes this means simply soaking in His Spirit. Whatever form it may take, over and again you and I are to revisit the table of the King.

Our time at the table enables us to confidently conclude: "My lover is mine and I am his" (verse 16). With these words, the bride in the Song takes a major step toward maturity. After sitting and banqueting, she now stands secure. She knows she is loved. Similarly, the Lord desires greatly to hear our hearts beat to the settled knowledge of His love. Future progress in Him—surrender, sanctification and service—rests on the blessed assurance that Jesus is ours. Then, like Solomon's young wife, we can be taken by Him to the next level.

The Lord is committed to conforming us to nothing less than His own likeness. So while the bride has come a long way, she will be taken still further. At present, her priority remains her satisfaction in the king, not *his* satisfaction in *her*. She has announced that primarily he belongs to her, and only secondarily does she belong to him. ("My lover is mine and I am his.") She still perceives the relationship to be mostly about her—but she is to be encouraged and not criticized. Her king, like ours, knows precisely how to beckon his bride onward and upward.

Grooming the Bride

The king allures his cherished one: "Arise, come, my darling; my beautiful one, come with me" (Song of Solomon 2:13).

The destiny of the young woman is with her husband, eventually reigning at his side. Tenderly he calls her to come. But a crisis ensues. As much as she adores the lover of her soul, certain obstacles seem insurmountable. Where he would take her is dark and scary. She shrinks back, telling him to go on alone—but to please return soon. "Until the day breaks and the shadows flee, turn, my lover, and be like a gazelle or like a young stag [running and returning swiftly] on the rugged hills" (verse 17).

The bride wants her king's blessing, but she wants it on her terms. Not deliberately rebellious, she is nonetheless unwilling or unable to trust. (I think we can all relate.) In loving chastisement, her beloved temporarily withdraws his manifest presence from her. As a result, she must now be the one to take the initiative. By the power of his love, and for her own healing and growth, she must arise to seek him (see Song of Solomon 3:1–3).

Before long the bride is lovesick, lost without the presence of Solomon. Quickly she sets out to find "the one my heart loves" (verse 2). Pleased with her response, the kind king allows himself to be readily found. At that time he also reveals to her fascinating new dimensions of his sovereign power, authority and might. She sees for herself that her husband can and will protect her. He is worthy of her trust. He—like our Jesus—will keep her in his care wherever they go (see verses 7–11).

Not once does the bridegroom rebuke his bride; the separation itself has been punishment enough. Instead, he lavishes her with love:

> All beautiful you are, my darling; there is no flaw in you . . . . You have stolen my heart, my sister, my bride. . . . How delightful is your love, my sister, my bride! . . . You are a garden locked up, my sister, my bride.
>
> Song of Solomon 4:7, 9, 10, 12

In some astonishing way, you and I have "stolen" Jesus' heart. How we can *take* heart at this mind-boggling truth! Messiah has purposely left Himself vulnerable to our affections. If we connect to even a slight degree with this Word, we are infused anew with passion and strength. We will contend for His presence, desiring to follow and please Him forever. Falling more and more in love with the King, we will invite Him to do what it takes to bring us to total surrender:

> Awake, north wind, and come, south wind! Blow on my garden, that its fragrance may spread abroad. Let my lover come into his garden and taste its choice fruits.
>
> Song of Solomon 4:16

Messiah's bride invites both north and south winds to blow, rendering herself and her garden fully His. She is ready and willing to submit to hardship for Jesus' sake. North winds are typically cold and harsh, symbolizing the testing of our faith during seasons of difficulty. Now, I do not suggest we pray for hardship, but in times of testing you and I often are conformed the most to the likeness of Christ (see Romans 8:29). Through difficulty our faith is stretched, our pride pulverized. We die to self, that He would live in us, that we would carry His Presence wherever we go. Then, when the gentler south winds blow, the fragrance of our fruitfulness is released for God's pleasure and glory. He spreads that fragrance abroad, even to the nations (see 2 Corinthians 2:14–15).

The bride's request is granted, and through tribulation she is transformed. One night the king visits her unexpectedly, catching her by surprise. He knocks at her door, literally reaching out to her through the lattice of a window (see Song of Solomon 5:2–4). It seems she is perplexed momentarily, then rises to let him in. By the time she opens the door, however, her beloved is gone. She cries, "I opened for my lover, but my lover had left; he was gone. My heart sank at his departure" (verse 6). The north wind starts to kick in.

Dark Night of the Soul

What follows is an excruciating period of searching for the presence of the king. Solomon's anguished bride spends a tortuous night roaming city streets, plaintively hunting for her husband. In the process, she is terribly misunderstood. She is cruelly attacked and wounded by local authorities who themselves are subjects of the king (see Song of Solomon 5:7). Nevertheless, the bride persists, steadfastly praising her beloved despite her confusion at what he has done. To her accusers and abusers, she is never mean-spirited. She stays focused on her king, extolling his singular beauty in grand detail. In every respect, she insists, he remains altogether worthy (see verses 10–16).

Believers have long identified with this particular experience as the "dark night of the soul." Virtually all of us have felt, at different times, a sense of the withdrawal of God's manifest, personal presence—for no readily apparent reason. I have never enjoyed dark nights of the soul. Not only do I sorely miss the perceptible presence of my King, but just as in the book, even godly authorities do not always understand. I have learned my responsibility during such times is to steadfastly trust and praise the Lord. These tests, however confounding, are always temporary. My Messiah is always faithful to reveal Himself at the right time. He has merely answered my prayers for the north and south winds to blow, that He might possess me more fully. Afterward, I am always glad He did.

On another level, the dark night of the soul paints a prophetic picture of Israel in her estrangement from God. Recognizing this, one Jewish scholar goes so far as to say that in this passage of the Song, Israel in essence declares to the nations:

> When you recognize God's greatness, testify that I realize the cause of my sufferings is not due to His inability to rescue me, or because He has cast me off, never to return to me. I am fully aware my travail is because His chastisements of love are designed to awaken me to repentance.[14]

A more penetrating confession could hardly be found. Israel foresees that the Gentiles will recognize God's greatness in the future. She asks them not to regard her as cast off forever, but to testify on her behalf that she suffers only temporarily, and only because of His jealous love for her. In this poignant admission she comes so near to—yet sadly remains so far from—the genuine repentance of which she speaks.

Israel's dark night of the soul, like ours, is designed to cause her to become wholly possessed by Yeshua. Despite withdrawal of His manifest presence, He wants her (and us) faithfully declaring, "I am my lover's and my lover is mine" (Song of Solomon 6:3). Solomon's bride confidently utters these words of testimony during her difficult search. So profound is the pronouncement that it is still incorporated into many contemporary Jewish and Christian wedding vows. When stated boldly during the dark night of the soul, it shows we are nearing the climax of our spiritual journey.

"I Belong to My Lover, and His Desire Is for Me"

Solomon's bride has by now been transformed. She has given public witness of her faith through word and deed. Her season of testing finally comes to a close. With fiery affection, the royal lover appears again at her side. Delighting immensely in her, he now praises her not only as bride but as *warrior*. "You are beautiful, my darling," He says, "majestic as troops with banners" (Song of Solomon 6:4).

She has fought a good fight and she has overcome. At this juncture she so captivates the heart of the king that he tells her, "Turn your eyes from me; they overwhelm me" (verse 5). It is as if Messiah's love for His warrior bride becomes, in some astounding manner, virtually unbearable to Him.

The Lord once allowed me a peek into His captivated heart for His people and showed me the result of our eyes gazing into His. In a vision, I saw Yeshua seated on a magnificent, heavenly throne. His eyes were set intently on His beloved ones below, His Bride still on the earth. His heart pounded with passion that reverberated through the heavens. His muscles flexed as if poised for action. At the same time, all over the planet, His worshiping Bride looked up at Him with fiery passion and purity. So steadfast was her gaze that she appeared oblivious to a ferocious battle raging all around her. The irresistible power of Yeshua's heart for her, and her heart for Him, literally magnetized each to the other. This reciprocal and magnetic attraction proved so powerful as to disrupt natural laws of the physical universe. With great anticipation, the Lord began to descend toward the Bride, almost as if pulled down. As He approached, she ascended toward Him. They met together gloriously in the air.

It is possible, I suppose, that I was allowed to see the Church caught up in the clouds to meet the Lord in the air, as described in 1 Thessalonians 4:17. I do not know for sure. What I do know is that His impassioned love for His Bride "burns like blazing fire, like a mighty flame. Many waters cannot quench [this] love; rivers cannot wash it away" (Song of Solomon 8:6–7). I also know the Uncreated Sovereign of the Universe has left Himself vulnerable to the affections—or lack thereof—of flesh-and-blood human beings like you and me. His heart is enraptured by the love of His people. It is a dizzying, dazzling concept.

As a result of this amazing love, at the end of Song of Songs we hear a victorious bride sing: "I belong to my lover, and his desire is for me" (Song of Solomon 7:10). No longer is the relationship mostly about her. From her perspective, she is hardly part of the equation anymore; she belongs to the king. Love's fire has consumed self-interest and self-consciousness. Her maturation process, with all its growing pains, has been masterfully orchestrated and worth every moment. So it is with those fervently committed to Yeshua.

The Voice of Worship

Possessed perfectly by love, the bride is no longer the same. Onlookers ask, "Who is this coming up from the desert leaning on her lover?" (Song of Solomon 8:5). Similarly, once lost in Yeshua, our former self becomes unrecognizable; our identity changes. We emerge from our desert journey, our dark night of the soul, leaning on Him like never before. Something of our own strength has died and given way to the power and beauty of His life in us. We find ourselves urging others on in their own journey with the King (see Song of Solomon 8:13). We mediate His Kingdom to a world in need of it.

The Lord's final word to us in the Song resounds, "Let me hear your voice!" (8:13). He passionately desires to hear us commune with Him during our physical separation in this life. In addition to our prayers and ongoing conversational fellowship, He loves our audible *worship*. Bridal intimacy with Yeshua is expressed in the saint's song of worship like nothing else. Not only is it pleasing to His ear, but worship is warfare (see 2 Chronicles 20:20–22). Through worship our hearts stay supple in the Spirit, and the heavens around us open wide. In essence, our voice in worship cries, in the words of Solomon's bride, "Come away, my lover . . . on the spice-laden mountains" (Song of Solomon 8:14). The cry is that of the last days Church: "The Spirit and the bride say, 'Come!'" (Revelation 22:17).

Does this cry resound in you? It is not reserved solely for the apocalyptic events of the book of Revelation. It will become the invitation and intercessory call of Yeshua's people today, magnetizing Him to our side.

As we grow in intimacy with the King, we find He offers us all manner of long-lost treasures. One of these is the Sabbath. The anointing of God's holy Sabbath further converges heaven with earth. In the next chapter, we see how through the Sabbath—with its rest and restoration—we can encounter and extend His Kingdom.

5

Sabbath Rest

There remains, then, a Sabbath-rest for the people of God; for anyone who enters God's rest also rests from his own work, just as God did from his. Let us, therefore, make every effort to enter that rest, so that no one will fall by following their example of disobedience.

Hebrews 4:9–11

"Come, my beloved, let us welcome and greet the Sabbath bride." So begins the Hebrew song *Lekha Dodi*,[1] sung by Jewish families around the world for centuries to inaugurate the seventh day of the week. For observant Jews, Sabbath celebration takes on bridal undertones. A foretaste of the Kingdom of God during the Messianic age and beyond, it is a date with Deity, His set-apart time for Israel to celebrate her love relationship with the King. A type of weekly wedding chamber, the Sabbath day provides a place in time for intimate communion between Yahweh and His betrothed. In the Sabbath a dimension of heaven and earth converge.

In Messianic grace, the Sabbath is a gift of exceeding joy. A burned-out bride cannot keep extra oil in her lamp. A battle-fatigued warrior endangers not just himself, but his entire company and possibly the conquest. Lack of rest can easily mean loss of intimacy with Yeshua—and from intimacy flows true Kingdom advance. Today the Spirit is restoring God's rest with fresh anointing for the Sabbath day. Old fears about legalism are yielding to the delight of the divine romance revived through Sabbath sanctification.

Sabbath observance is not a matter of earning or keeping salvation. It has nothing to do with somber restrictions or religious rules. These inevitably convert a day of grace and joy into a work of the flesh. Sadly, some Christians and Jews throughout history have succumbed to legalism regarding the Sabbath. But that does not mean the gift no longer serves as a portal to genuine spiritual renewal.

Have you perhaps been taught that the New Covenant abolishes the set time for Sabbath rest? Bear in mind the Sabbath existed even before God's laws were given to Israel. It is one of several biblical principles so reflective of heaven as to transcend the written Law. Other examples include the ancient prohibition against human murder (see Genesis 4:10–11) and the practice of tithing (see Genesis 14:18–20). Such basic standards of human behavior were observed long before Israel came into existence, and few if any Bible believers would presume they are no longer relevant. Consider also that while the New Covenant Scriptures do not explicitly require that the Sabbath day remain hallowed, they do not suggest it be disregarded, either. It is clear from a careful reading of the Word that Jesus, the apostles and early churches kept the Sabbath. Is it possible they knew something we today have forgotten? I invite you to walk an ancient path with me and see.

He Rested

After Deity fashioned from dust the climax of His creation—mankind made in His image—the universe experienced a holy hush:

By the seventh day God had finished the work he had been doing; so on the seventh day he rested from all his work. And God blessed the seventh day and *made it holy*, because on it he rested from all the work of creating that he had done.

Genesis 2:2–3, emphasis added

Can you imagine the incomparably sublime cosmic event?

The original Sabbath, hallowed from before humankind's fall to sin, was surely a spectacular occasion, a sanctified moment between Creator and creation. Every subsequent, biblically ordained day would relate in some respect to redemption from sin. But the Sabbath stands alone, set apart notwithstanding the rebellion of the created. It becomes the first thing in the world ever declared holy, or "set apart" according to the Hebrew meaning of the word. Day Seven—in Hebrew, *Yom Shabbat*, from which the English word "Sabbath" is derived—is holy because it is uniquely set apart to, and identified with, Yahweh. Not coincidentally, the number seven in the Scriptures represents completion and wholeness.

I believe God spent the inaugural seventh day taking immense pleasure in His completed handiwork—a world, yet untainted, that intrinsically worshiped Him (see Psalm 19:1). I also believe He very much enjoyed *Himself* within the Godhead. This divine joy was shared in intimate, holy and unparalleled communion with human beings. For our progenitors Adam and Eve, the Sabbath served as a day to partake uniquely of God's delight in His majestic handiwork, ceasing from their own creative endeavors associated with subduing the earth (see Genesis 1:28). From its inception, this day of dedicated rest would comprise a memorial to creation. It would facilitate renewal of life in God through the ages.

God did not do *nothing* on the initial seventh day. He did do something—He rested. The Omnipotent One, of course, was not tired and did not need to refrain from activity. The Hebrew word for "rest" simply means that He ceased from His work of creating. In ceasing to work, however, He did not cease *being*

God Almighty. From the essential core of His being, Yahweh continued to infuse love, goodness, peace, joy, glory and His other divine attributes throughout the universe (see John 5:17). He actively imparted blessing to the day itself (see Genesis 2:3).

Most Christians through history attributed high value to the Sabbath. When I grew up in mid-20th-century America, many cities still maintained strict Sabbath laws. Virtually all businesses, shops and nonessential service providers were closed on Sunday. It was simply a fact of life, even for us Jews who observed the Sabbath on Saturday. Believers' widespread disregard of the Sabbath did not take place with the inception of the New Covenant. Rather, it evolved only in recent decades. As postmodern Western society got busier and busier, so too did many of us postmodern Western Christians. Today, the Sabbath often means merely a couple of hours at a worship service, followed by lunch with friends, then hasty preparation for the next week's round of activities.

What is the result? For many, life has become its own hard-driving taskmaster. Each day offers a steady stream of mounting complexities, stresses and strains. The bottom line is that consumption is king, compelling many of us to acquire an overabundance of everything from food to frivolous electronics to fancy homes and vehicles. Toward the end of the twentieth century, a perplexing new disease struck, called chronic fatigue syndrome. The natural speaks of the supernatural; society, including much of the Church, had grown chronically fatigued. Today, as perhaps never before, believers and nonbelievers alike are "dis-eased" and keenly aware of a clamoring need to quiet their souls. The *shalom* of true rest eludes many of us, yet we desperately desire to access and grasp hold of it. Could the Sabbath mediate that blessing we crave?

For the Rest of Us

When God created and blessed the Sabbath, it stands to reason a seventh day of rest was incorporated into the genetic structure of life on earth. Before sin infected our world, and under ideal circumstances, a weekly day of rest became part of the rhythm of life on both spiritual and natural levels. God would later tell His people to afford the animal, plant and even mineral life under their stewardship the enjoyment of His Sabbath (see Exodus 20:8–11; Leviticus 25).

Man's fall into sin soon changed everything. Not only did we lose original and ongoing connection with the Creator, but the whole earth was cursed on our account. As a result of human rebellion, the soil would yield its substance by the sweat of our brow (see Genesis 3:17–19). No longer would the Sabbath serve solely as a hallowed memorial to creation. It would become a day of much-needed rest to recover from fatigue associated with hard labor.

Following the Fall, God next speaks of the Sabbath after Israel's exodus and redemption from Egypt. Camped out in the desert, the vagabond nation is hungry and unable to find food. Graciously, the King says He will rain down bread from heaven for them to eat. Each day they need only go out and collect their manna—except on the Sabbath, when they must rest. He promises, however, to provide enough food on the sixth day to last through the seventh. "In this way," He says, "I will test them and see whether they will follow my instructions" (Exodus 16:4).

God tests the Jews regarding the Sabbath *before* giving them the Law, or even the Ten Commandments. From His perspective, the Sabbath is more fundamental than, and exists apart from, the Law of Moses. It is part of the natural rhythm of life. God is a jealous Lover wanting His people to take time to enjoy, and thereby honor, Him. So significant is the day that He does not want them preoccupied with concerns related to such bare essentials as eating. It is "to be a day of rest, a holy Sabbath to the LORD" (Exodus 16:23). The loving Creator intends to tangibly reveal Himself as faithful Provider and Sustainer. On the Sabbath, there is no need for His loved ones to try to get ahead. Instead, we get to stay and enjoy where we are:

The LORD has given you the Sabbath; that is why on the sixth day he gives you bread for two days. Everyone is to stay where he is on the seventh day; no one is to go out.

Exodus 16:29

Sadly, on the first Sabbath day in the desert, some of the Israelites disobeyed (see Exodus 16:27). Despite all God had done for them, out they went in search of more. Not trusting He would meet their needs, they spurned His good gift of rest. From that time on, the Sabbath has been associated with faith—or unbelief (see Hebrews 4:2).

What is it today that may prevent you or me from entering into weekly Sabbath rest? Is it that we have carefully studied the Scriptures and concluded the day is genuinely unnecessary to New Covenant faith? For some, perhaps. Sabbath celebration in itself is no more a matter of earning or keeping salvation than other disciplines such as prayer, Bible reading or fellowshiping with the saints. But for some of us, could it be that if we are downright honest, the reason we do not remember the Sabbath is that we do not trust God to provide all we need in just six days a week? The truth is that our King wants not merely to provide, but—according to *His* perfect standards—to abundantly bless. He wants to endow us with goodness beyond belief, or perhaps more accurately, beyond our *un*belief.

The Fourth Commandment

With a heart pulsating to bless humanity, God took His finger of fire and with it engraved His Word in stone. He included Sabbath sanctification as the fourth of ten holy commandments:

Remember the Sabbath day by keeping it holy. Six days you shall labor and do all your work, but the seventh day is a Sabbath to the LORD your God. On it you shall not do any work, neither you, nor your son or daughter, nor your manservant or maidservant, nor your animals, nor the alien within your gates. For in six days the LORD made the heavens and the earth, the sea, and all that is in them, but he rested on the seventh day. Therefore the LORD blessed the Sabbath day and made it holy.

Exodus 20:8–11

The gift of Sabbath rest is taken in the Decalogue to new dimensions. It now includes all Gentiles who are part of the Israelite community ("aliens" in the passage above). The Divine Lover wants the seventh day holy and labor-free for them, too, if they identify with His set apart ones. Everybody, regardless of ethnic lineage, gets to "remember" and enjoy Him in sanctified rest.

To "remember," according to the Hebrew concept, is to do much more than intellectually recount an event. Biblical remembrance involves engaging one's heart with the mind to reflect on, and reexperience, a dynamic truth. Israel's remembrance of the Sabbath was meant to facilitate renewal of her love relationship with Yahweh by sharing in His intimate rest. In addition, weekly reconsecration of creation to the Creator would serve as a sign and a national testimony:

> You must observe my Sabbaths. This will be a *sign* between me and you for the generations to come, so you may know that I am the LORD, who makes you holy. . . . The Israelites are to observe the Sabbath, celebrating it for the generations to come as a *lasting* covenant. It will be a *sign* between me and the Israelites *forever*.

Exodus 31:13, 16–17, emphasis added

Israel's weekly respite in the Beloved is a sign *forever*. To every generation it testifies to the nations, and internally to Israel herself, of her covenant with Deity. In a world whose false gods afford humanity no sanctity of rest, Sabbath observance is a sign of sovereign grace. It is also a banner of redemption for those delivered from bondage to freedom:

Remember that you were slaves in Egypt and that the LORD your God brought you out of there with a mighty hand and an out-stretched arm. Therefore the LORD your God has commanded you to observe the Sabbath day.

Deuteronomy 5:15

Does that include you? Have you been brought out of slavery from a metaphorical Egypt by His mighty hand?

So supreme is the Sabbath that its desecration incurs death:

Observe the Sabbath, because it is holy to you. Anyone who desecrates it must be put to death; whoever does any work on that day must be cut off from his people. For six days, work is to be done, but the seventh day is a Sabbath of rest, holy to the LORD. Whoever does any work on the Sabbath day must be put to death.

Exodus 31:14–15; see also Exodus 35:2

To the extent we reject God's Sabbath rest, I believe something in us can die. Without holy, weekly renewal (at the least) in Him, our minds, emotions and bodies can prematurely wear out. Spiritually, we can lose essential aspects of His *shalom*—the peace, wholeness and fullness of life for which Messiah died.

Wresting the Sabbath

Maybe your energy level seems just fine right now, and your connection with God quite good. Because Christ is your Sabbath rest, you may feel no need to dedicate a day a week specifically to that purpose. You spend prolonged, focused time communing with Him daily. You worship together with the saints regularly. Good for you, my friend. Might I suggest, nevertheless, that you will last even longer and serve the Lord even better if you experience His sanctified, seventh-day rest?

On the other hand, if you are like most believers, you feel a need to live more fully, moment-by-moment, in Yeshua's promised rest. In this increasingly turbulent age, stresses and strains will escalate (like labor pains) as we approach the hour of His return. But no matter what, even in days of trouble you and I are afforded a protective and empowering *shalom* (see Habakkuk 3:16, KJV). In this rest we stay soaked in Holy Spirit oil, maintaining plenty extra for our lamps.

Recently, leading prophetic revivalists have learned Sabbath rest is critical to sustaining a long-term outpouring of the Holy Spirit. Missionary Heidi Baker says a weekly, set-apart day enables us to maintain intimacy with God and engage in the rhythm of heaven.[2] Author and revivalist Jill Austin points out that rest is a form of spiritual warfare (see Isaiah 30:15; Matthew 11:28). She explains, "We . . . get our batteries charged and then go. [But often] we fail to rest, and then we break down and are forced to rest. There is a lot of exhaustion that is not from God."[3]

Sometimes believers who zealously love the Lord find it hard to cease from the work of the ministry and stop one day a week. I confess I was one of them. For many years as a believer, I did not think it particularly important to remember the Sabbath day. I dedicated intimate, devotional time *every* day to God. Ministry in the Spirit did not tire me out; it energized me. There was much Kingdom work to do—that I loved doing. The fields were ripe for spiritual harvest, and I had been called to them. Besides, none of the Christian leaders I knew talked or taught about Sabbath day celebration; resting for 24 hours straight seemed either irrelevant or outmoded or impractical. Eventually, however, I came into a season when, despite experiencing deep realms of God and waves of His renewal, I was not living regularly in His settled *shalom*. For even at harvest, God summons us to rest: "Six days you shall labor, but on the seventh day you shall rest; even during the plowing season and harvest you must rest" (Exodus 34:21).

During that same time, I happened to be teaching a series at a local church about Old Covenant roots of New Covenant

faith. The week before I was to share on the topic of the Sabbath, the Holy Spirit convicted me. How could I minister a
reality to which I did not personally connect? It seemed there
was no alternative but to observe the next Saturday as a day
of rest—gladly and wholeheartedly—in order to teach about
it with integrity the following Sunday. After seeking the Lord's
direction, I was led to observe my Sabbath according to the
Scriptures, but in a fresh, very personal manner. I was not led
to follow the Jewish traditions I grew up with, though much
beauty and blessing can be found in them. It would be for me
a unique experiment.

To my surprise, the result was glorious. I share with you
the day's events not as a formula, but as a personal testimony
of what the Spirit can do. First, I spent prolonged time with
God in the Scriptures, worship and prayer. I did not travail in
intercession; that would have been work! To celebrate Him as
Creator, I took a long, leisurely walk outdoors, admiring Him
for His creative handiwork: trees, flowers, birds, clouds, even
neighborhood dogs barking at me along the way. I entertained
no stress-generating or work-related thought, refused phone
calls and abstained from my computer. I did not cook, having
prepared meals the day before. I read an uplifting devotional
and spent peaceful, enjoyable time with my family. Toward
evening I listened to worship music and soaked in a heavenlike
presence of the Holy Spirit. By the end of the day, my heart was
soaring in God. I went to bed early, and my sleep was sweet.
This holy and jealously guarded rest in the intimate presence
of my Savior was thoroughly and wonderfully refreshing. I also
found it much easier to maintain His Sabbath rest throughout
the following week. The experiment was enough to convince
me of the transforming reality, not tiresome ritual, of God's
seventh day. It was the beginning of a Sabbath lifestyle He has
since then called me to embrace. If you find that, like me, you
have to wrest a rest, I suspect the Sabbath anointing will prove
powerful for you, too.

Sabbath in the Holy Land

My favorite Sabbaths are spent in Israel and include Yeshua-focused fellowship with the saints. If you have ever been to Israel on a Saturday, you know that certain parts of the country come to a complete, 24-hour halt. A strange but quiet calm descends over the usual clamor of life in the Middle East. It saturates my soul with a heavenly hush, perhaps reminiscent of the first Day Seven. I love *Shabbat* (Sabbath) in the Holy Land.

When God instituted Israel's Sabbath, He also provided for regular rest, rededication and renewal of the land itself. The earth and everything in it belongs to Him (see Psalm 24:1). The Creator Redeemer is our Owner; we are but stewards of what He has entrusted to our care. Accordingly, every seventh year Israeli soil was to be given a complete rest. No planting, pruning or harvesting was to take place (see Leviticus 25:2–5). During the year the land lay fallow, God would supernaturally provide. He promised to release "such a blessing in the sixth year that the land will yield enough for three years" (Leviticus 25:21).[4]

Can you connect to the awesome beneficence of our King? A whole year off for everyone! What a potential testimony to the neighboring nations—and what tragic consequences if the Israelites spurned His good gift:

> I will scatter you among the nations . . . then the land will rest and enjoy its sabbaths. All the time that it lies desolate, the land will have the rest it did not have during the sabbaths you lived in it.
>
> Leviticus 26:33–35

Sadly, there is no biblical record of the Israelites ever fully keeping a Sabbath year. Warnings of judgment came from the prophets—but to no avail. Finally, the seemingly unthinkable occurred when God's holy zeal forced temporary eviction from the land to enforce, among other things, His Sabbaths. Then "the land enjoyed its sabbath rests; all the time of its desolation it rested" (2 Chronicles 36:21).

Israel's failure to remain in her place of promise was due in part to forgetting the Sabbath. Habitual desecration of the seventh day became an important reason for her exile from the Holy Land. Since her history serves as an example for the Church, does it not speak a prophetic word to us today?

Idolatry and Unbelief

According to the Scriptures, the underlying reason Israel dishonored the Sabbath was idolatry:

> They rejected my laws and did not follow my decrees and desecrated my Sabbaths. For their hearts were devoted to their idols. . . . They had not obeyed my laws but had rejected my decrees and desecrated my Sabbaths, and their eyes lusted after their fathers' idols.

> Ezekiel 20:16, 24

To be blunt, sometimes the reason we do not sanctify the Sabbath is that, like the Israelites, we are busy worshiping other gods. Anything we might consciously or unconsciously value more than the Lord—including family, friends or future (even good) achievements—will inevitably keep us from a day of rest. Sometimes the idol is mammon and the problem, pure greed. In recent years secular sociologists have coined the term *affluenza*,[5] combining the words affluence and influenza, to describe our culture's disease of obsessively striving for more. Is the Church necessarily immune?

Serving in ministry and raising a teenager, I sometimes feel there are not nearly enough hours in the week to care for the responsibilities I juggle. But the Lord has called me to a Sabbath lifestyle, so I generally work just six days out of seven. Admittedly, I can still be tempted to forgo a Sabbath day to tackle an endless list of personal chores: grocery shopping, yard cleanup, veterinary visits—you get the picture. Early in my Sabbath experience, however, the Holy Spirit whispered a gentle rebuke that still resounds in my heart. *The reason you're so compelled to take care of things*, He said, *is that you are bowing to an idol of self-preservation.*

I was stunned. His loving words gripped me with a conviction that staked claim to my soul. At the core of my being, I was trusting myself more than Him to keep my life in order. (How embarrassing!) *You forget*, He went on to say, *that My ability to create includes My ability to sustain.*

A very real dynamic exists between idolatry and unbelief. In matters where you or I do not believe the one true God, we will bow to another.

The children of Israel did not enter God's promised rest because of idolatry and unbelief. Yet a promise remains for all who *do* believe. Jesus makes available to you and me, every moment of every day of the week, a Sabbath rest. To paraphrase, in Messiah, a dimension of this blessed and holy seventh day is available to us always, transcending time. But the Sabbath day itself is not eradicated. Rather, its scope is extended and expanded. In the Kingdom God gives us the Sabbath—and in the Sabbath He gives us the Kingdom.

Sabbath As Prophetic Intercession

The Jewish people have long regarded the Sabbath as a foretaste of the Messianic age to come. Abraham Joshua Heschel summarizes:

> The essence of the world to come is Sabbath eternal, and the seventh day in time is an example . . . given as a foretaste of that world to come; *ot hi le-o'lam*, a token of eternity.[6]

Ceasing from work, delighting in Deity and abiding in His *shalom* connects us with heaven. The manifest reality of *Shabbat* ushers in a dimension of the Kingdom of God with all the combined nuances of Day Seven—completion, wholeness, total restoration.

The Bible says a thousand years is as one day in God's view of time (see Psalm 90:4; 2 Peter 3:8). Therefore, some speculate that the inception of a seventh millennium of history will herald a seventh "day." By this reckoning, the seventh "day" ushers in the pinnacle Sabbath of all time—the rule of Messiah on earth for a thousand years. This would coincide with the thousand years of Jesus' reign, the Millennium, described in the book of Revelation (see Revelation 20:2–7).

To some Jewish scholars and rabbis, hints of the Messianic Sabbath age are disclosed by the Hebrew calendar. In their thinking, aspects of God's dealings with the world can be divided into seven increments of approximately a thousand years. The publication of this book in 2008 coincides with the Hebrew year 5769; therefore, we are nearing completion of the sixth increment, or the year 6000. At that time, some rabbinic traditionalists expect the dawning of the Messianic age, the start of the seventh increment or millenium.

This hypothesis may or may not prove correct; time will tell. In any event, it is interesting to note that six is the number representing mankind in Scriptures. From a New Covenant perspective, following man's ways apart from Messiah for six thousand years culminates in the rule and reign of the Antichrist (see Revelation 16:1). That culmination represents ripeness for the release of God's righteous judgments, heralding the Messianic age. Then the whole earth experiences its *Shabbat*—its rest and renewal, completion and wholeness—for a thousand years, its seventh "day."[7] After that comes a new heaven and earth, glorious beyond human imagination (see Revelation 21:1; 1 Corinthians 15:24).

To remember and rejoice in the Sabbath is to proclaim Yahweh as Creator and Sovereign of the Universe. This, I believe, serves as prophetic intercession for the Sabbath age to come, the Millennium. Sabbath observance in Messiah mediates and extends His Kingdom rule in the earth in a prophetic convergence with time. When we enter into the Sabbath, supernatural and natural realms are transformed. In a sense, the Spirit and the Bride together say, "Come!"

After Jesus literally comes again, the seventh day will fina
be kept according to God's design. Scriptures referring to the
Messianic Millennium point to the continued sanctity of the Sabbath: "From one Sabbath to another, all mankind will come and
bow down before me" (Isaiah 66:23). In addition, "The priests . . .
are to keep my laws and my decrees for all my appointed feasts,
and they are to keep my Sabbaths holy" (Ezekiel 44:24).

These passages do not mean that in the future we will revert
to observing or relating to the Law the same as before Yeshua
atoned for humanity's sin. But at a minimum, they reflect an
indelible importance attached to the Sabbath day from the divine
perspective. Accordingly, when our Bridegroom-King dwells in
His holy Temple in Jerusalem, the gate to its inner court will be
shut six days a week. Yet, on the special occasion of the Sabbath day, it will be opened (see Ezekiel 46:1). At that time, "On
the Sabbaths . . . the people of the land are to worship in the
presence of the LORD at the entrance to that gateway" (Ezekiel
46:3). Special entry will be afforded into the awesome presence
of Yeshua every seventh day. Sabbath in the Millennium will be
spectacular.

Jesus, Lord of the Sabbath *Now*

Jesus reminded the people of His time that the Sabbath was
made for them; they were not made for the Sabbath (see Mark
2:27). They were made for God and were to worship Him alone,
not Day Seven. The fact that Jesus had to adjust their attitudes
about the Sabbath does not mean, however, that He abolished
it altogether (see Matthew 5:17). To the contrary, by His crucifixion and resurrection, He *fulfilled* the Sabbath. In simple
terms, Messiah now fills the Sabbath full of Himself. He becomes
our Sabbath rest. In Him, a realm of seventh-day rest is now
opened to us in the other six days of the week, just as a realm
of the millennial Kingdom is now available to us in this present

age. But He does not cancel out the Sabbath any more than He cancels out the Millennium.

Yeshua and His disciples consistently celebrated the Sabbath and kept it holy.[8] At no time did they ever desecrate the day or violate the Scriptures concerning it. The King never taught His Jewish followers to abandon the Sabbath day. He did denounce man-made traditions that were hypocritical at heart, thus undermining and violating the spirit of a day of rest. The manner in which certain religious leaders were observing the day dishonored God precisely because the Sabbath still remained holy. In this context, Messiah declared He is Lord of the Sabbath (see Matthew 12:8). The goal and focus of the Sabbath is obeisant intimacy with God.

Like Yeshua, the apostle Paul was a dedicated Sabbath keeper. Though Paul never explicitly required Sabbath observance, he never taught believers to forsake it, either. The learned scholar knew the Scriptures promised blessing to Gentiles, as well as Jews, for keeping the Sabbath in the right spirit:

> And foreigners who bind themselves to the LORD [Gentiles in the Old Covenant] to serve him, to love the name of the LORD, and to worship him, all who keep the Sabbath without desecrating it and who hold fast to my covenant—these I will bring to my holy mountain and give them joy in my house of prayer. Their burnt offerings and sacrifices will be accepted on my altar.
>
> Isaiah 56:6–7

I have never met a believer, Gentile or Jewish, who chose to embrace a Sabbath lifestyle according to the Scriptures and then regretted it.

What about Sunday?

Most believers today who keep the Sabbath do so on the first rather than the seventh day of the week. (Many times I do.) The tradition is based on decisions made by early Church authorities to cut ties with Old Covenant faith and with Jewish Christians.[9] Sadly, as a result of certain decrees, Sabbath observance on the seventh day became sufficient grounds to be accused of Judaizing. Those found guilty of Judaizing were then excommunicated from the Church. In 364, for example, the Church of Rome issued this statement:

> Christians must not Judaize by resting on Saturday, the Sabbath, but must work on that day, rather honoring the Lord's Day, Sunday; and if they can, resting then as Christians. But if any shall be found to be Judaizers, let them be anathema from Christ.[10]

Ironically, by this edict believers were required to work on the seventh day.

Some have been taught that the Church started gathering on the first day of the week during New Covenant times in honor of the Resurrection. One New Covenant verse, Acts 20:7, does indicate believers gathered at least one time on the first day of the week. But the Bible gives no evidence at all that this gathering replaced the seventh day of rest.[11] The meeting was apparently held as a celebration following, and in addition to, Sabbath worship, much like a midweek church service.

Tradition notwithstanding, the question now is whether the Creator will meet you if you choose to lovingly dedicate Sunday (or any other day of the week) to worship and intimately abide in His rest. I am certain He is gracious enough to do just that, lavishing you with His loving *shalom*. You will emerge, I believe, with fresh anointing for Kingdom advance in the week ahead.

You may discover that Sabbath rest is a revived Jewish root and route to the Holy One in a whole new dimension. I suspect you may find yourself on a new, Holy Spirit–paved highway of holiness—a *high way* to heaven. As we see in the next chapter, true holiness mediates even further the Kingdom age to come. It invites the presence of the King.

6

Highway of Holiness

For it is written: "Be holy, because I am holy."

1 Peter 1:16, quoting Leviticus 11:45

The prophet Isaiah interacted dramatically with heaven, beholding God in His bedazzling and matchless glory (see Isaiah 6:1–13). Following his throne room visitation, he speaks of highways of holiness converging with earth. His heart cry becomes, "Prepare the way for the LORD; make straight . . . a highway for our God" (Isaiah 40:3; see also 35:8). The holiness of God's people creates a highway in the spirit; righteousness prepares a way for His steps (see Proverbs 15:19; Psalm 85:13).

Many years later, John the Baptizer echoes Isaiah's words: "Repent, for the kingdom of heaven is near . . . 'Prepare the way for the Lord, make straight paths for him'" (Matthew 3:2–3). John's prophetic proclamation is anointed with monumental authority, resulting in the repentance of a nation. A remnant of Israel returns to Yahweh, and a highway of holiness clears between heaven and earth. Soon thereafter, Jesus appears publicly as Messiah (see John 1:31).

The Hebrew word for "holy," as we have seen, literally means "set apart." The incomparable Holy One is quintessentially set apart from all of creation. He is set apart in the summation of His divine attributes, including His purity, perfection, sovereignty and supremacy. In a single word, His Spirit is best characterized as holy; He is God the Holy Spirit. His redeemed people are likewise set apart. "Be holy," He says, "because I am holy" (1 Peter 1:16; Leviticus 11:45). The command is the alluring invitation of a jealous Lover wanting to walk with His set apart ones in unending, unbridled intimacy. The call to holiness flows from the romance of redemption.

A Passion for Holiness

The apostle John is known as the "disciple whom Jesus loved" (John 21:20; see also 19:26; 20:2). Among the New Covenant authors, John writes supremely on love. It is John who tells us of Yeshua's tender, parting message to the disciples the night before He is crucified. The beloved apostle also records the penetrating words, "If you love me, you will obey what I command" (John 14:15). A consummate carrier of the fire of God's love, John is passionate about obedience. I think of John as a man, like David, after God's own heart. And I think he very much wants others to know and abide in God's wondrous love. So when he tells us, over and again, that this love is linked to obedience, it is good to take John at his word:

> This is love for God: to obey his commands. And his commands are not burdensome.
>
> 1 John 5:3

> And this is love: that we walk in obedience to his commands.
>
> 2 John 1:6

> We have come to know him if we obey his commands.
>
> 1 John 2:3

Is it coincidental that John receives the most profound, single-recorded prophecy in the Bible—the entire book of Revelation? God's love leads us to obedience, and obedience leads us to holiness. Love-propelled holiness, in turn, relates dynamically to spiritual discernment and a release of high-level revelation:

Without holiness no one will see the Lord.

Hebrews 12:14

We shall see him as he is. Everyone who has this hope in him purifies himself, just as he is pure.

1 John 3:2–3

Blessed are the pure in heart, for they will see God.

Matthew 5:8

Though God's gifts and heavenly deposits are dispensed freely by grace, you and I can position or ready ourselves to receive more by loving more. We can love enough to obey His commands.

In his pulsating, divine visitation, John hears this: "The wedding of the Lamb has come, and his bride has made herself ready" (Revelation 19:7). The Bride has purposefully and intentionally made herself ready. She has a free will that her Beloved King will not cross. She chooses the way of holiness, surrendering not as a burden of legalism but as a blessing of love. Her Helper, the *Holy* Spirit, fuels and empowers her. As it is said, it takes God to love God.

The Holy Spirit is committed to taking us to higher levels of holiness ignited by unquenchable love. In the past, God's Old Covenant moral commands and prophetic statutes have often been dismissed as irrelevant to New Covenant believers. The Church today, however, is beginning to gain a fresh perspective and embrace of the ancient Law thoroughly in *grace*. We will not—and must not—return to observing the Law the same as before Messiah's once-for-all atonement for sin. We will return to a passion for holiness, however, paving highways from heaven that transform earth.

The Law of Love

Believers through the ages have extolled God's holiness and His laws, not religiously, but in sweet expression of adoration for Jesus:

> How is godliness achieved? . . . [W]hen you have learned to love, you will not even desire to do those things that might offend the One you love. . . . Once you have established such a relationship with your Lord, you will soon discover that no fault in you escapes.
>
> Madame Jeanne Guyon, circa 1685[1]

> Many have maintained the Gospel has set aside the moral law, so that believers are under no obligation to obey it. Such was the doctrine of the Nicolatians, so severely reprobated by Christ [see Revelation 2:15]. . . . They suppose that Christ has delivered them from the law, and given them the Spirit, and that the leadings of the Spirit are now to be their rule of life, instead of the law of God. . . . This doctrine represents Jesus Christ and the Holy Ghost as having taken up arms openly against the government [kingdom] of God. . . . The liberty of the Gospel does not consist in being freed from doing what the law requires, but in a man's being in such a state of mind that doing it is itself a pleasure, instead of a burden.
>
> Charles G. Finney, 1837[2]

> We are justified without the works of the law, as any previous condition of justification; but they are an immediate fruit of that faith whereby we are justified.
>
> John Wesley, 1872[3]

The grace of God promotes real holiness in men.

Charles H. Spurgeon, 1883[4]

Let us remember that God's Word stands forever, and His commandments mean the same for us today.... We obey Your laws with joy, Father. Our eagerness to do so comes not from fear but from love.

Corrie ten Boom, 1977[5]

These fathers and mothers of faith walked in ways of holiness unfamiliar to most of us today. They were not somber, dour individuals but radical, crazy-for-Jesus, blazing torches to their generation. They loved God's laws because they loved the Lawgiver, unreservedly. Their passion for obedience mediated, rather than mitigated, grace through faith. Sometimes we can mistake reverence such as theirs, flowing from a life of worship, for religiosity. We then recoil from God's commands for fear of false restriction. But what proves false is the fear; we quickly discover the "restriction" only releases us deeper into the law of liberty that is love.

As the Holy Spirit converges Israel with the Church in the Messianic Warrior Bride, a passion for His laws will be restored in holy love. To reiterate, I am not suggesting we follow the Law the same as before Yeshua's fulfillment of it. I speak neither of legalism nor of "Judaizing," but of lovestruck obedience to the Bridegroom-King. If our hearts beat with His, we grieve too greatly over disobedience to choose it. From the joy we experience of His presence and pleasure in us, we cannot help but want to obey.

As believers connect more and more with redeemed Israel, over time a dynamic ministry of God's laws will be revived. According to Romans 11:29, God has irrevocable gifts and callings on Israel. These relate to His Word: "He has revealed his word to Jacob, his laws and decrees to Israel. He has done this for no other nation" (Psalm 147:19–20). The New Covenant affirms, "What advantage, then, is there in being a Jew ... Much in every way! First of all, they have been entrusted with the very words of God" (Romans 3:1–2).

Anointing to minister the Word is not limited to Israel. God called the Jewish nation to impart that anointing to the Gentiles, which she did long ago through the Messiah and her Jewish apostles. Today many of my favorite Bible teachers are Gentile, not Jewish, believers. Nonetheless, a timeless call on Israel still resonates pertaining to her entrustment, hands-on experience and relationship with the Word. In the future, she will again humbly impart deep understanding of God's laws in Yeshua-centered faith. Ancient treasures and mysteries will be unlocked for the whole Body from heavenly storerooms (see Matthew 13:52).

Fulfilling the Law

The first five books of the Bible are identified in Hebrew as the *Torah*. The word *Torah* translates into English as "instruction" or "teaching." It likely comes from a Hebrew root meaning "to aim for a mark or target." Torah is the opposite concept of sin, which means "to miss the mark." The Torah sometimes refers not just to Genesis through Deuteronomy, but to the entire Old Covenant (see John 10:34).[6] At other times, Torah designates only God's direct commands and decrees. Finally, the term *Torah* can be used to encompass all of the above at the same time, which is how I generally use it in this book.

The Jewish people regard the Torah as a matchless gift, as did the New Covenant apostles: "All Scripture is God-breathed and is useful for teaching, rebuking, correcting and training in righteousness, so that the man of God may be thoroughly equipped for every good work" (2 Timothy 3:16–17). In this passage, the words *all Scripture* refer to—and affirm the value of—all of the *Old* Covenant, including the full Law of Moses. The New Covenant Scriptures did not yet exist in canonized form, so the writer of 2 Timothy could not have referred to them. The Old

Covenant, with all its laws, equips you and me for every good work of the Kingdom.

Both Old and New Covenants are inspired, but the New Covenant completes Yahweh's written revelation of Himself. As the *Complete Jewish Bible* translates, "The covenant He [Yeshua] mediates is better. For this covenant has been given as *Torah* on the basis of better promises" (Hebrews 8:6). The New Covenant alone, by God's grace, can be sufficient for salvation and sanctification. I have ministered in nations where I was told that, under former communist rule, whole churches had available to them only a few pages of one gospel for years at a time. These persecuted saints were no less "spiritual" than those of us with bookcases full of Bibles and computers loaded with exhaustive commentaries on both Covenants.

Historically, Christians have summarily accepted the importance and relevance of the New Covenant. But the same cannot be said of the Old Covenant,[7] and in particular, of the Law, which the Church has many times tended to discount. Therefore, the remainder of this chapter is about recouping an endowment—the Torah—rightfully belonging to God's people. While it may seem to some that I overemphasize the Law a bit in the next few pages, please consider this: To restore and determine the value of a long-lost jewel that has just been unearthed, it must first be picked up, held closely, dusted off, and studied carefully. Only then can it be enjoyed as a beautiful find, sparkling with timeless value. So will it be as the Church once more accesses the treasure of Torah.

To begin, consider that the New Covenant consistently portrays a positive picture of the Old—including the Law. Jesus Himself explains:

> Do not think that I have come to abolish the Law or the Prophets [Torah]; I have not come to abolish them but to fulfill them. I tell you the truth, until heaven and earth disappear, not the smallest letter, not the least stroke of a pen, will by any means disappear from the Law until everything is accomplished. Anyone who breaks one of the least of these commandments and teaches

others to do the same will be called least in the kingdom of heaven, but whoever practices and teaches these commands will be called great in the kingdom of heaven.

Matthew 5:17–19

Messiah Yeshua marvelously fulfills the Torah; He does not abolish or render it obsolete. Because he is the Word Incarnate, in a certain sense Jesus *is* the Torah. He does not abolish Himself or make Himself obsolete. Rather, because He alone adhered perfectly to all the conditions of the Law, never once missing the mark through sin, He opened up for you and me a new and living way to holiness (see Hebrews 10:20).

The Law of Torah makes us aware of our sin and our need for a Savior. It propels us toward salvation by grace through faith in Yeshua. Once we are saved, God's laws continue to offer perfectly practical guidance for life. We can think of Torah as a moral compass enlivened by the Spirit, for righteousness' sake. In the Matthew 5 passage above, Jesus says those practicing and teaching the commands of Torah will be called "great" in the Kingdom of heaven. But those teaching others to break the commands are deemed the "least." Jesus' fulfillment of the Law does not mean it thoroughly ceases to have any application to Him or to us. To the contrary, He is its center, fixed focus, life force, purpose and goal (see John 5:46, Luke 24:27). Messiah is the only means by which we can rightly relate to the Law. We find Him at its every juncture; He *is* the "High Way" to holiness.

Divine Covenant Ketubah

In chapter 4 we looked at ancient Jewish bridal practices, where betrothal involved the signing of a formal marriage contract. This contract is called in Hebrew a *ketubah.* The signing by bride and groom of a *ketubah* remains a cherished tradition still part of Jewish weddings today. In Christian weddings, it is typically replaced by the exchange of solemn verbal vows. We saw that God has a type of *ketubah* with Israel, represented by the covenant Law given at Sinai. Through an illustration of the *ketubah* or exchange of wedding vows, we can better understand the value of Torah in our lives today.

Let us suppose a wedding has taken place, and the new marriage has just been consummated. Now that these anticipated events are past, is the couple's underlying legal covenant abolished? Of course not. That covenant is now being fulfilled. The center, focus, life force, purpose and goal of the *ketubah* or vow becomes the set apart or holy relationship with a spouse. If one truly loves his wife or her husband, legal terms regarding the sanctity of marriage will be awesomely appreciated and gladly followed for life. Those legal terms are not meant to be formally legislated and mechanically applied to every possible life circumstance. (Who would want a marriage like that?) However, human beings are frail, and so moral principles underlying those terms may at times be extrapolated and used to navigate the myriad of complexities comprising life. If hard times threaten the relationship, the vow or *ketubah* might become more, not less, important to maintaining—even reviving—the marriage. It is similar with our covenant relationship to God.

His *ketubah*-like Torah belongs not only to Israel but to His betrothed ones from all nations. Its terms, written and fulfilled by Yeshua, are meant to be followed with joy, flowing from sanctified love. The Holy Spirit empowers and guides us in all truth, extrapolating for us timeless moral principles applicable to contemporary life. By the Word in Torah that ministers God's heart, we are sanctified (see John 17:17). Torah enables the Bride to make herself ready, without spot or wrinkle, for her coming King. It represents His holy kiss, forever relevant, life-giving and passionately prized.

Torah on the Mount

Yeshua not only affirms the continued importance of the Law, but applies it to our lives at far greater levels than Moses did. Atop a grassy hill in Galilee, He amplifies God's commands in the Sermon on the Mount. "You shall not kill" now means you shall not become angry with a brother. "Do not commit adultery" morphs into an admonition not to look lustfully at another. "Do not break a sworn oath" becomes "do not swear at all." An "eye for an eye, and a tooth for a tooth" is now "turn the other cheek." "Love your neighbor" will no longer do; the goal is to "love your enemies and pray for those who persecute you." The lifestyle of prayer, fasting and giving to the needy—already dutifully undertaken by Jews of His day—is not going to be rewarded by God if done for the reward of men (see Matthew 5:21–22, 27–28, 33–39, 43–48; 6:1–7, 16–18).

Disciplines and motives of the heart, more difficult to tame than outward behaviors, are of prime concern. Thus Yeshua goes on to say that to please God, we must not worry and should not judge others. Rather than obsess with our own man-made kingdoms, we should seek His. Then He utters the summation of it all:

> "Love the Lord your God with all your heart and with all your soul and with all your mind." This is the first and greatest commandment. And the second is like it: "Love your neighbor as yourself." All the Law and the Prophets hang on these two commandments.
>
> Matthew 22:37–40, quoting Deuteronomy 6:5

Yeshua teaches that God's holy standards, impossible for man to attain except through Him, are aimed at transforming our hearts so we will desire to do what is right. By the power of the Spirit, we surrender to Him, and He lovingly changes us from the inside out (see Ezekiel 36:26–27). Holiness becomes supernaturally natural. Torah and its laws are engraved by Deity on our hearts:

> "This is the covenant I will make with the house of Israel after that time," declares the LORD. "I will put my law [the Hebrew word used is *Torah*] in their minds and write it on their hearts. I will be their God, and they will be my people."
>
> Jeremiah 31:33[8]

Legalism or Liberty?

The tempestuous times in which we live cry for a cure that comes from the Law of God. The rotten fruits of lawlessness—death, destruction and the deception of calling good evil and evil good—threaten to shred the fabric of society. Even renowned Christian leaders fall prey to material and sensual greed, casting, if it were possible, disgrace on the Holy One. To the extent we have rebelled against God's laws under the false pretense of freedom, we have reaped imprisonment to immorality. We have abused amazing grace, shirking at the prospect of "the Law" and "coming under" it. The 20th-century Christian leader Dietrich Bonhoeffer, who was martyred for his faith, called this "cheap grace," or "grace without discipleship," as opposed to "costly grace," which he described as "the sanctuary of God that must be set apart from the world."[9]

Would you allow the Lord to dispel a myth mistakenly taught about the Torah? Some have nurtured the notion that a New Covenant believer embracing the Old Covenant has automatically lapsed into legalism. In contrast to such thinking, hear how the Hebrew psalmist below exults in Torah. The fervid worshiper is far from bound up by statutory restriction. As opposed to shouldering a load of legalism, he offers free and intimate high praise flowing from grace:

> Open my eyes that I may see wonderful things in your
>   law. . . .
> I remember your ancient laws, O Lord, and I find com-
>   fort in them. . . .
> I delight in your law. . . .
> The law from your mouth is more precious to me than
>   . . . silver and gold. . . .
> Oh, how I love your law!
>
> Psalm 119:18, 52, 70, 72, 97

The psalmist extols the Law as revelation of the Lawgiver who is love, grace and truth. The Hebrew word he uses for "Law" in the preceding verses is *Torah. He cherishes the Torah because rather than constrain him, it liberates him into his destiny in God*: "I run in the path of your commands, for you have set my heart free. . . . I will walk about in freedom, for I have sought out your precepts" (Psalm 119:32, 45).

Legalism was a foreign concept to true worshipers of Yahweh. It never described the way they related to Him. When the Israelites resorted to shallow adherence to the Law from a hypocritical heart, they earned only His rebuke. Religious-spirited observance of rules saved or sanctified no one in the Old Covenant, much less in the New.[10]

In the early apostolic Church, the question arose as to whether salvation in Christ is achieved by following the Law. In response, Paul taught strongly against legalism as an attempt to earn or keep salvation by obedience to Torah. He was hampered, however, by the lack of any existing appropriate terminology in either Hebrew or Greek with which he could express himself. Neither language contained a word or even a concept for what we now call "legalism." As a result, Paul devised the terms *under the law* and *works of the law*.[11] These Spirit-inspired phrases are very helpful when their context is considered. In context, they always relate to specific misuses of the Law that Paul seeks to correct. Sadly, when context is disregarded, the mistake is often made of writing off God's laws altogether.

Christian theologian C. E. B. Cranfield comments on this issue:

> Pauline statements, which at first sight seem to disparage the law, are really directed not against the law itself, but against that misunderstanding and misuse of it for which we now have a convenient terminology.[12]

As God shifts hearts and minds to recoup ancient truths, and as we engage with Old Covenant Scriptures at new levels, questions naturally arise. To what extent, if any, do we practically live out the commands? Are all laws in Torah equally applicable to us today? I freely admit to not having all the answers. Certainly, as you have heard me say more than once, we are not to revert to observing the Law the same as before Jesus came, died and rose again. The covenant He mediates is better. However, out of passion for the King, we cannot help but want Him to restore the righteousness His Word reflects and the holiness that befits His return.

Practical Points

Below are some suggested general parameters to consider as you prayerfully reevaluate the role of God's laws in your life. I have intentionally kept these parameters to a minimum for two reasons. First, any greater detail would exceed the scope of this book. Second, I want you taking the freedom—and responsibility—to meditate on the Scriptures and engage personally with Jesus yourself. As no two individuals have the exact same life relationship with the Lord, no two will have the exact same relationship with the Law. Plenty of room is left, as a hallmark of grace, for you to journey intimately and dynamically with the Spirit on your own, as well as with others in your community of faith.

1. For nonbelievers, the primary purpose of the Law is to point to salvation by grace, through faith in Yeshua (see Romans 10:4). For believers, it is different; Messiah's atoning sacrifice for sin changes our relationship to the Law (see Hebrews 8:6–10:22). The Law no longer condemns us. It dynamically instructs us in righteousness, escorting us into God's presence. There we surrender at greater and greater levels to Him, being made holy even as He is holy. Our lives reflect "the obedience that comes from faith" (Romans 1:5; see also 16:26).

2. The New Covenant can be sufficient for both salvation and sanctification, but it is only a fraction of the full canon of Scripture. *All* of God's words, in both Old and New Covenants, are important for His people. *The laws of heaven are reflected*

in the laws He gave us for earth. When we honor the latter, the former are increasingly made manifest. His will is done; His Kingdom comes.

3. In the New Covenant, Gentile believers are never urged to follow the Law the same as Jews—though they are not told to disregard it entirely, either. This is not because Gentile believers are either spiritually superior or inferior to Jewish believers, but is mostly a matter of Israel's unique, irrevocable calling. Bear in mind that the New Covenant is "better" than the Mosaic covenant.

4. The New Covenant never requires Jewish believers to stop following the Law of Moses with a clear focus on Yeshua. The apostles, and Paul in particular, maintain an extremely Torah-observant lifestyle. They seem to simply assume Messianic Jews will continue to follow the Law. *Today, freedom to follow the Law by grace, with integrity and focus on the absolute supremacy of Yeshua, is essential for one new humanity in Messiah to fully mature.*

5. The Torah is still relevant, with varying degrees of applicability, to both Gentile and Jewish believers. *Especially valuable to us are God's moral laws.* Many civil, agricultural and ceremonial laws relating to assorted Temple practices are presently not possible to follow. Other laws are impossible to follow because they require a full operation of a rabbinic judicial system. Still others are gender-specific or applicable only to married persons, priests or other classes of individuals within the Israelite community. But Messiah-centered, moral principles underlying those same laws can continue to instruct us in righteousness and mediate the Kingdom of heaven.

6. God gives grace for any believer to embrace not only the Law, but meaningful Jewish traditions that do not violate the Scriptures or *detract from focus on Yeshua.* Similarly, there is grace for any believer—including Jews—to live holy unto the Lord in a scriptural manner that does *not* conform to extrabiblical, Jewish tradition.

7. Obedience to the Law does not mean that Gentiles seek to become, act or look Jewish, or that Jews strive to become "more Jewish." Never are we to take up following the Torah to wrongly seek an identity in Judaism (or any other "ism") rather than in Jesus! God is after an authentic expression of love for Him in integrity, consistent with who He made us to be (see 1 Corinthians 7:17–20).

Within these broad parameters, further questions and concerns often surround two issues in particular: (1) the validity today for believers of what is called a "Torah-observant lifestyle,"[13] and (2) the dangers of Judaizing.

Torah-Observant Lifestyle

Most New Covenant passages pertaining to the Law were penned by the apostle Paul, a brilliant Jewish scholar of his day. The complexity of his teaching on the Law is almost universally acknowledged. The apostle Peter, a simple fisherman, says of Paul, "His letters contain some things that are hard to understand" (2 Peter 3:16). I have to agree with Peter. Thankfully, however, Paul is not impossible to comprehend.

God is a superb communicator and ensures that ordinary folks can understand His Word. So we must keep in mind that Paul's recorded deeds are just as much a part of the inspired canon of Scripture as are his words. Although his words alone can be difficult to apprehend, if we interpret what he says in light of what he does, we discover that his actions speak as loudly as his words and clarify much of what he writes. When we also consider the context of his teaching, much confusion and controversy can be readily resolved. Acts 21 offers an outstanding example.

In Acts 21, we see how Paul himself relates personally to the Law. In that chapter, he arrives in Jerusalem and meets with local elders of the Church. They quickly inform him that all the Jewish believers in the city remain zealous for the Law.

The elders go on to say these same believers are troubled by a false rumor. The apostle, they have heard, has started instructing Jewish Christians to forsake the Law of Moses. The people are concerned that Paul is "telling them not to circumcise their children or live according to our customs" (verse 21). To quell the rumor, the elders encourage Paul to publicly witness to his own continued lifestyle of Torah observance. They suggest he ritually purify himself in the manner of a Nazirite vow (verse 24; see also Numbers 6:1–21). "Then everybody will know there is no truth in these reports about you, but that you yourself are living in obedience to the law" (Acts 21:24).

At this point, Paul has an ideal opportunity to correct both the elders and the congregations of Jerusalem for remaining zealous for the Law—but he does not. It stands to reason, therefore, that he agrees with them. Indeed, nowhere at all does he—or any other New Covenant author—instruct Jewish Christians to abandon the Law. Instead, Paul does what he can to put an end to the rumor, taking the purification vow the very next day (Acts 21:26). The apostle is not appeasing anyone here; he took the same vow previously in another city, of his own accord (see Acts 18:18). Paul does not teach Messianic Jews to do away with circumcision, the Law of Moses or even Jewish customs, if all such matters are sincerely surrendered to Yeshua.

There is more to the story. A few days later, still in Jerusalem, the apostle is arrested and brought before the Sanhedrin, the Jewish high court. At that time, he testifies that he not only follows the Law, but that he is still a Pharisee (see Acts 23:1, 6; 26:5). After this episode, he is sent to the civil authorities. There he states, "I have done nothing wrong against the law of the Jews or against the temple" (Acts 25:8). Finally, when later describing these incidents to Jewish leaders in Rome, Paul repeats, "Although I have done nothing against our people or against the customs of our ancestors, I was arrested in Jerusalem and handed over to the Romans" (Acts 28:17).

Keep in mind the apostle has had profound encounters with Yeshua and has visited heaven. The man lives in supernatural realms; he is not bound up in legalism or restrictively tied to tradition. Yet he not only follows the Law of Moses, but also the extrabiblical customs of his day. Everything Paul writes about the Law must be understood in the broader context of these actions. When we study not only what he says, but also what he does, we see that Paul never demeans the Law itself. As Bible scholar Dr. Michael L. Brown concludes, the apostle "continued to live as a Torah-observant Jew, even though his primary mission was to take the Good News to the Gentiles."[14]

Paul demonstrates that believers are free to maintain a Torah-observant lifestyle *that revolves wholeheartedly and authentically around Messiah.* Law and grace operate *together* in Him, in one new humanity, and in the Kingdom convergence of Israel and the Church, heaven and earth.

Gentile Believers and Judaizers

I do not dispute that some have taken the observance of God's laws to an extreme that is not centered on Yeshua. At the other extreme, however, many have said that any embrace at all of Torah amounts to Judaizing. (Recall as an example the early Church's decree prohibiting Sabbath observance on Saturday.) I do not want to Judaize, and trust you do not either. Because the term historically has been misused, we must go back to the Bible to define precisely what Judaizing is.

The Judaizing controversy is described and addressed in the book of Galatians and in Acts 15. To understand the stern warning against Judaizing, we must first understand the serious problem that was taking place. The Church in Galatia—which was Gentile—was being taught by false brethren that to be saved they must be circumcised, obey the laws of Moses and convert to Judaism. This was heresy that Paul needed to firmly refute. Paul's rebuttal was indeed so firm that today it is easily misunderstood apart from its historical context.

In Acts 15, the same elders of Jerusalem who in Acts 21 urge Paul to take a Temple vow come against the Judaizers. They authoritatively denounce the idea that Gentiles must be circumcised or follow the laws of Moses to be saved. We can assume the Jewish elders were familiar with the prophetic Scriptures extending salvation to the Gentiles. So in the opposite spirit of the Judaizers, they graciously open wide the doors to God's community of faith. At the same time, they do not withhold the Torah from believers from the nations (see Acts 15:20–21). The bride, Gentile as well as Jewish, must not be denied "the kisses of his mouth" (Song of Solomon 1:2). No dimension of the Kingdom must be kept from them.

Through Church history, a minority of Gentile believers has maintained, to varying degrees, a Torah-honoring lifestyle. Today their numbers are growing. Regrettably, too many are erring toward unscriptural excess. But others, who have a solid sense of their identity in Christ, are joyfully reconnecting with their Old Covenant roots in Holy Spirit anointing. They are not trying to act like Jews or follow laws applicable only to Israel. They love the Law simply because they love the Lord. In coming years, this restorative move of the Spirit will balance out, mature and find greater place in the Body. This will produce a level of holiness that serves as a protective stance and proactive assault against the iniquitous spirit of the world in these last days.

That spirit is lawlessness, which the Bible equates with Antichrist.

Lawlessness

When Yeshua speaks of the end of this age, He characterizes it as a time when more and more people reject God's laws. Because of the increase of lawlessness, He says, the love of most— even believers—grows cold (see Matthew 24:12). Lawlessness becomes so rampant that some who are given over to it have also performed miracles in His Name. Nevertheless, they are ultimately and woefully cast from His presence (see Matthew 7:23; 2 Thessalonians 2:9).

According to 1 John 3:4, lawlessness is sin. The Church is soberly warned to be on guard against "the error of lawless men" and those teaching against God's laws (2 Peter 3:17). So serious is this phenomenon of lawlessness that another name for the Antichrist is "man of lawlessness":

> For (that day will not come) until the rebellion occurs and the man of lawlessness is revealed, the man doomed to destruction . . . proclaiming himself to be God. . . . For the secret power of lawlessness is already at work . . . then the lawless one will be revealed, whom the Lord Jesus will overthrow . . . and destroy by the splendor of his coming. The coming of the lawless one will be in accordance with the work of Satan.
>
> 2 Thessalonians 2:3–4, 7–9

This man of lawlessness will be recognized, in part, by his blasphemous attempts to change God's laws (see Daniel 7:25).

You and I are commissioned to strategize and stand against lawlessness in the opposite spirit—law-loving and abiding, holy obedience that comes from faith. While holiness is an act of love, at the same time it is also a weapon of spiritual warfare. As spiritual warfare heightens in the form of birth pains heralding Jesus' return, an anointing for holy obedience will also increase. Messiah's Bride will be a warrior ablaze in holiness, made perfectly legal by His righteousness. She will be groomed for the honor of great Kingdom battle. In the next chapter, we see how that uniquely relates to Israel's anointing.

7

Messianic Justice

With justice he judges and makes war.

Revelation 19:11

Across the globe, Jesus is revealing Himself to His Church as Commander of the Armies of Heaven. A fresh warrior anointing is imbuing the Messianic Bride. She is being fashioned to fight with new nobility, in the zeal of the Lord of Hosts. She is attuned to the Spirit's battle cry signaling the enemy's defeat—souls redeemed from hell, righteousness on earth and the coming of her King. Confrontation for the collective Body of Christ is not military in nature, but the battle—a contention for justice—is quite real.

Not long ago I was given life-altering insight into Kingdom warfare. I had been praying at the Western Wall in Jerusalem, adjacent to the Temple Mount. It seemed I could taste a tangible glory of God that resided long ago at this very site.[1] A cry arose from within me for an impartation of any ancient and residual—or future—anointing at this incomparable place. I was not thinking at all, however, about war.

That same night, I received a dream of the armies of heaven. The dream began with a wide, open field offering an unhindered view in every direction. In it I stood scanning the horizon when a peculiar sight caught my attention. Off in the distance, tiny golden trumpets slowly materialized in the sky. At first, only a handful were visible. Then, as I continued to watch, more and more trumpets formed, seemingly from nowhere. Soon there were dozens, and they sharpened into focus. Eventually I could tell that each trumpet was held by an angel. The angels and trumpets shined a brilliantly clear, golden white. The scene was electrifying.

As I kept watching, hundreds of angels with trumpets in hand, dazzling in beauty and palpable authority, gradually appeared. Their numbers multiplied before my eyes, until there were thousands—then tens of thousands, then myriads beyond number. The celestial glory overwhelmed me in my sleep; the splendor of the sight was breathtaking. Eventually this heavenly host joined together so as to form what resembled a hurricane. It was gargantuan in size, formidable yet captivatingly beautiful. The hurricane swirled in every direction due to the intensity of angelic activity comprising it. God's troops were amassing (see Joel 2:11).

Gaping at the scene, I felt energizing power surges, like windblasts of boldness, penetrate through my eyes and into my spirit. Then I awoke, with new strength and expectation coursing through my body. I somehow knew that a fresh warrior spirit was about to infuse the Church. In valiant nobility of love-fueled righteousness, this generation would contend with and prevail against evil as never before. Many angels had been commissioned to assist God's emerging champions of faith in this fight. But victory would require anointings revived from Israel of old, represented by the Temple's Western Wall. These anointings would be released to the Body as Israel herself was revived. In this chapter, we look at vital dimensions of this dynamic synergy.

Enjoying the Fight?

In the dream described above, I did not visibly see God's enemies at work. Rather, He was the One initiating Kingdom battle (see Nahum 1:3; Proverbs 10:25). For the King is never on the defensive. The omnipotent, omniscient One is always on the glorious offensive. This does not mean that He is not our Defender and Protector. But He is all-powerful; His defense is a proactive response of love aimed at Kingdom advance. In His earthly ministry, Yeshua never allowed Himself to be put on the defensive. The Savior took only the offensive posture of aggressive love (see Matthew 11:12). When we connect to the power of this truth, we will drip with anointing for battle.

Certainly there are times when God's people are called to defend, in the sense of protecting, our people and principles—or ourselves. Indeed, most of the spiritual weaponry He gives us, as we will see later, is defense and not offense related. But the King wants to shift our understanding or paradigm of warfare. *Because of the nature of His ever-increasing Kingdom, any posture of defense is really one of offense from the larger, eternal perspective.* Yeshua's ultimate victory is inevitable. So attack by the enemy presents opportunity for aggressive yet meek Kingdom conquest, a chance to smell blood—and even, at times, to enjoy a good fight.

What do I mean by such seemingly scandalous terms as *a chance to smell blood* and *enjoy a good fight*? This chapter does not concern military force. I do *not* refer to carnage or suffering associated with violence, destruction or death, especially on the part of innocent victims. I speak instead of the power of the blood of Yeshua to overcome the life-force "blood" of a supernatural enemy, according to Ephesians 6:12: "For our struggle is not against flesh and blood, but against the rulers, against the authorities, against the powers of this dark world and against the spiritual forces of evil in the heavenly realms."

We are meant to rejoice in the good fight of faith through the blood of the Lamb that assures us of Kingdom victory (see

Philippians 2:16–18; 3:1; Colossians 1:24; 1 Peter 4:13; Romans 5:3; Luke 6:22–23). The joy of the Lord sustains us in battle (see Nehemiah 8:10). For His own future joy, Yeshua endured the cross (see Hebrews 12:2). The Messianic Warrior Bride "enjoys a good fight" when she wholeheartedly surrenders to God and trusts in His victory. She revels in the execution of His righteous judgments, His justice that glorifies her King.

The Lord first confounded my understanding of spiritual warfare and rejoicing in its spoils when I ministered in Eastern Europe not long after the collapse of the former Soviet Union. For several years, I served as part of a team of Jewish and Gentile believers—a small army—sharing with ex-Soviet Jews the good news that Messiah had come.[2] Without consciously realizing it, we were declaring war:

> For though we live in the world, we do not wage war as the world does. The weapons we fight with are not the weapons of the world. On the contrary, they have divine power to demolish strongholds. We demolish arguments and every pretension that sets itself up against the knowledge of God.
>
> 2 Corinthians 10:3–5

God's enemies, it turned out, were far more aware of the declaration of war we had unwittingly released than we were. The battle that followed makes for a vivid account of deliverance, judgment unto justice and city gates unlocked—with a surprising Jewish key. So let's shift at this point from our previous focus on Jewish truths to focusing on God's Jewish people, and discover the plunder He has planned.

Unlocking City Gates: A Jewish Key

When the Union of Soviet Socialist Republics dismantled in 1989, its doors suddenly swung open to the Gospel. Together with other Messianic believers in the West, I jumped at the opportunity to take the good news of salvation to the millions of

Jews still living there. To reach them, stadium meetings were organized in numerous cities with large Jewish populations. Not just Jews would be invited; whole cities were welcomed. The Gospel is the power of God for salvation "first for the Jew, then for the Gentile" (Romans 1:16).

In that window of time, and before Islamic terror became a global concern, Westerners generally encountered little resistance to evangelism in Eastern Europe. Decades of atheism had spiritually starved the masses. They were voraciously hungry for Jesus, and amazingly, most authorities were eager to see them get fed. But when Jewish believers came to town, it was quite another matter. We were stunned to find ourselves facing mind-boggling cadres of spiritual enemies all operating in cahoots against the spread of the Gospel to the Jews. I take time here to describe the litany of opposition in order to illustrate some of the challenges—and exhilarating last days victories—ahead for the Church. To access Israel's anointing, similar battles will be fought in the future.

First we faced the usual resistance of religious Jews who call themselves "anti-missionaries." These are well-organized, ultra-Orthodox Jewish brethren fervently dedicated to keeping Jews from coming to faith in Yeshua. Not unlike their predecessors who opposed the first-century apostles, anti-missionaries from the U.S. and Israel flew all the way to ex-Soviet tundra-lands to warn local Jewish leaders not to go near the Gospel. Invoking sundry Jewish regulations, they forbade their co-religionists not only from attending the outreaches, but from accepting the desperately needed humanitarian aid we also had brought. (These prohibitions, thankfully, were rarely heeded by the locals.) Eventually, Israeli foreign ambassadors got involved. One disconcerted diplomat even phoned the president of Belarus to warn of outright war erupting if Messianic Jews were permitted to preach the Gospel in that nation.[3]

Joining the anti-missionaries were culturally Christian, fascist-oriented nationalists. Many of the extreme nationalists openly claimed a longstanding tradition of anti-Semitism.[4] They were incensed that Jews had come to sponsor a Jewish event—even though it was also quite Christian. The nationalists were not always content to lodge their complaints with government authorities. Occasionally, they physically assaulted members of our team, women as well as men.

State-affiliated and institutionalized Orthodox churches joined in the fray, outraged that we were representing Jesus as a Jewish Messiah. Aligning with the Orthodox churches were irate atheist-communists of the former Soviet regime. Neo-Nazi groups also objected fiercely—the issue being, again, the Jewish nature of it all. Local Satanists would not be left out of the mêlée, attempting (unsuccessfully) to burn down a stadium in which an outreach was held. Then came a string of bomb threats, forcing some stadiums to be evacuated in the middle of the Gospel message. Meanwhile, witches tried to cast spells not only from behind the scenes, but right in front of us. We were told that somehow even the Russian mafia got involved.

We had come humbly—in compliance, by the way, with local laws—merely to offer Jews as well as Gentiles eternal life. Yet our little band of brothers and sisters, compelled by the love of Christ, had apparently stirred up a hornet's nest. How, we wondered, had we managed to incite and unite so many frenzied splinter groups—normally all preoccupied with assailing each other? The answer, the Lord reminded us, was simple. Large-scale salvation of the Jewish people terrifies the demonic because it heralds Jesus' return. Jewish evangelism reflects a dimension of the apocalyptic battle over Jerusalem, which spells Satan's ruin.

Battle over Jerusalem

The battle for Jerusalem strategically impacts last days Kingdom warfare at many levels. The Scriptures tell us heaven's Kingdom on earth climaxes only after Yeshua's Second Coming. His return is intimately and inextricably tied to the salvation of Israel, and in particular, to Jerusalem. Israel's faith in Messiah, therefore, signals the devil's demise. So while God's enemies viciously oppose the salvation of any human being created in His image, they are uniquely threatened by the salvation of the Jews.

Insight into the battle over Jerusalem is essential for the Church to prayerfully formulate and execute its end times battle strategies. We have previously alluded to how, by His own Word, Jesus tied His return to Jerusalem's leaders welcoming Him back:

> O Jerusalem, Jerusalem, you who kill the prophets and stone those sent to you, how often I have longed to gather your children together, as a hen gathers her chicks under her wings, but you were not willing. Look, your house is left to you desolate. For I tell you, you will not see me again until you say, "Blessed is he who comes in the name of the Lord."
>
> Matthew 23:37–39

As we saw in chapter 2, over two thousand years ago, Israel as a nation rejected her Messiah by judicial decree of her spiritual leaders. But someday, that decree will be legally reversed. The reversal occurs in the context of a massive, international military invasion targeting Jerusalem. The invasion in turn relates to the heinous rule of a global dictator known as the Antichrist. At Jerusalem's plaintive cry, Yeshua returns to vanquish the foe, deliver His people, judge the wicked and rule as King (see Zechariah 12:2–3; 12:9–13:1; 14:2–9; Matthew 24:15; Daniel 9:25–27; 11:31; 2 Thessalonians 2:4; Revelation 13:14–15). At that time, Satan is locked in a bottomless pit (see Revelation 20:2–3). God's glorious Kingdom is established across the earth, headquartered in Messiah's holy Temple in Jerusalem, centered on today's Temple Mount.

Meanwhile, like a trapped and frenzied beast, Satan is scrambling to prevent the above scene from ever materializing. Our last days battles, including but not limited to Islamic terror, can be fully understood only in the larger context of this raging battle for Jerusalem, capital city of a Jewish State. Its final outcome will determine whom the nations worship as king.

God's Word assures that Satan is destined for certain defeat. Therefore, despite a plethora of opposition in the former Soviet Union, an estimated 25,000 Jews professed faith in Messiah during the outreaches of the 1990s. Many of them immigrated to Israel with their newly found faith. They have significantly changed the spiritual climate of the Jewish nation, bringing her closer to welcoming Jesus back. At the same time, many more Gentiles than Jews came to Jesus through the outreaches. Included among them were government officials we were forced to deal with because of the flurry of opposition. Over and again, we watched the Commander of the Armies of Heaven, the Just Judge, work all things for good, orchestrating details to achieve the humanly impossible. I learned to enjoy the good fight and, metamorphically, to love the smell of blood. Nothing compares to plundering the enemy's camp by saving souls and ministering God's Kingdom!

Messianic War Room Strategy

The pattern of evangelism we followed in Eastern Europe is based on a strategy that unfolds in the New Covenant. Wherever Jesus, Paul and the other apostolic evangelists go, they seek out and speak to the Jews first, and then the Gentiles.[5] The design has nothing to do with racial preference or prejudice. Greater blessing, not lesser, flows to Gentiles when God's pattern is honored (see Romans 1:16; 2:9–10). Not surprisingly, this biblical protocol still carries breakthrough anointing today, even though we live in an age of great favor on the Gentiles. Regardless of the geographic area, outreach to Jewish people first—if there are reasonable numbers of them in the population involved—means the salvation of many others. Israel's salvation unleashes blessing for the nations *already*—even though the climactic, prophetic phenomenon of Matthew 23:37–39 is *not yet*.

The Body of Christ will gain strategic insight and direction for the last days harvest as this pattern is restored in future years. This restoration by the Spirit will involve Jewish and Gentile believers coming together in mutual humility and collaborating in unprecedented anointing. It will evolve from the love and support for Israel demonstrated in recent years by "Christian Zionists," or Gentile Christians actively dedicated to the support of the Jewish nation.

I am deeply grateful for the way God has opened the hearts of Christian Zionists toward His ancient covenant people. At present, most of that love is directed toward expressing support for unsaved Israel, or for Jews who do not worship Jesus. On the one hand, it is good and right that unconditional Christian love be expressed toward sons and daughters of Jacob who do not yet—and may never—know Messiah. On the other hand, many times thorny issues are raised in the process. Because these issues impact the core identity and formation of God's one new humanity, it is time to look at them in wisdom and grace.

Israel, together with the international Jewish community, welcomes and genuinely appreciates Christian support—as long as mention is not made of their need for Yeshua. Therefore, as a general rule, major organizations dedicated to publicly blessing Israel must deliberately refrain from sharing the Gospel.[6] Often, only leaders at the top are fully aware of the scope of concessions that have been made. Messianic believers, especially Israelis, are aware of the dilemma because of the repercussions that result.

Please let me explain. For a Christian Zionist organization to maintain good standing with Israel on an official level, it typically cannot associate formally or publicly with Jews who believe in Jesus. To the mainstream Jewish world, Jews who worship Jesus as Messiah are no longer deemed Jews, but are deemed so-called traitors, allegedly dangerous to the Jewish State.[7] It is therefore politically risky for believers (and any others) who relate to Israel to give credence to Messianic Jews, or to Jewish Christians. Consequently, Jewish followers of Yeshua are rarely, if ever, permitted to overtly participate in, or derive direct benefit from, ministries seeking to bless Israel or the mainstream Jewish community.

As an example, while writing this book, I was invited to a large-scale Christian Zionist rally in Southern California. But when I spoke directly with the event's coordinator, I was told the situation regarding Jewish believers was "still too sensitive" to allow for an open presence of Messianic leaders. Therefore, I would have to do my very best to stay hidden. I was assured, however, that the evening would be lovely and enjoyable: A prominent Israeli diplomat, highly anointed worship leader and several acclaimed Christian speakers would all be there. I was warmly—and sincerely—invited to come and hide. I did not attend the event, and to my knowledge, no other Messianic leaders were present. Afterward, the unsaved Jewish community once again breathed its collective sigh of relief. These Christians, said Jewish news reports, were safe: They did not advocate Jews believing in Jesus, and they did not believe in sharing the Gospel. Plus, they had backed up their words with a large sum of money, none of which they had let go to Messianic Jews.

Believers Blessing Israel: Dual Covenants?

I sincerely rejoice and praise God for how Christian Zionist strategies have helped quell fears that many Jews have harbored toward the Church. Through events like the one above, the majority of Israelis now understand that true believers love them. In the process, some forerunning Christian leaders have personally sacrificed a great deal. From the foundations these pioneering saints have set in place, we can enter a new phase of relationship between Israel and the Church.

Today the Spirit is releasing fresh, alternative approaches to carry us to the next level. We must not stagnate, lest we fall prey to enemy traps threatening to undermine the good that has been done. Is it not possible, for example, that to the extent

Messianic Jews are denied participation in or normal entry to Christian gatherings, Jesus Himself, the consummate Messianic Jew, may also in some way be denied participation and entry? Were they alive, Paul and the other New Testament authors would have been excluded from, or carefully hidden at, the rally to which I was invited. The issue is not insult, pride or pain; it is about God's Messianic Presence. If an anti-Messianic spirit is endorsed, does that not carry an undertone of antichrist? Or, to the extent believers are unwilling to relate to other believers solely because those other believers are Jewish, could that not suggest an undertone, however unintended, of anti-Semitism?

To be fair, Gentile Christian reluctance to openly identify with Jewish Christians can stem from godly sensitivity toward unsaved Jews. It is right and commendable to be sensitive to the historical fact that Jews have suffered much anti-Semitism through institutionalized Christianity. It is appropriate to be aware of their need to build positive experiences with Christians. So at the outset of believers' interactions with Jewish people, most have good intentions. After relationships are established, they reason, doors will open to minister the Gospel without causing offense. But in reality, this rarely occurs. More often, fear of offense quietly morphs into a permanently silent "witness."

In other cases, well-meaning saints eventually conclude that Jews do not really need the New Covenant. They align with Israel's mistaken belief that they can be saved through the Old Covenant Law. The fact that Yeshua is the only Way, Truth and Life, and that no one comes to the Father but by Him (see John 14:6) is compromised, then flatly denied. To be sure, not all Christian Zionists take this position, which is formally known as dual covenant theology. Nevertheless, the doctrine is gaining increased popularity throughout the Christian world. According to the Bible, however, such thinking is heresy. I ache over the fate of Jewish souls interacting with Christians who never verbally share the way of salvation with them, and therefore remain eternally separated from God (see John 8:24; Romans

10:14–15). I also grieve over my brothers and sisters who have lost passion for the power of the Gospel.

Is it not possible that the most offensive and unloving thing we can do to the Jews is to withhold the truth of Yeshua from them when we have opportunity to share it? This might represent the deadliest form of anti-Semitism ever. Recall how hard the devil fights to keep Israel from acknowledging her Messiah, and recall the battle for Jerusalem, and I think you will better understand the strategic warfare involved.

Biblical Protocol

As we enter the next season, new alignments will form in the Body of Christ.[8] In the future, more and more Gentiles who radically love the Lord Jesus will cast their lot with Jews who also worship Him. This does *not* mean that Christian love for the lost sheep of the house of Israel will or should be diminished (see Matthew 10:6; 15:24). In the end, this added dimension of Christian love for *all* Israel, saved as well as lost, will help provoke many of the lost to jealousy for their King (see Romans 11:11). For the first time in two thousand years, unsaved Israel will witness Messiah's love unifying believing Jews and Gentiles as one new man. The result will answer Jesus' impassioned prayer: "May they be brought to complete unity to let the world know that you sent me and have loved them even as you have loved me" (John 17:23; see also verses 11, 21–22).

Out of this we will witness a fresh stirring of biblical protocol in other related spheres. One such sphere concerns the release of resources for Israel's restoration—including practical, material aid. Of this the Scriptures say:

> For if the Gentiles have shared in the Jews' spiritual blessings, they owe it to the Jews to share with them their material blessings.
>
> Romans 15:27

As we have opportunity, let us do good to all people, especially to those who belong to the family of believers.

Galatians 6:10

Poverty has long beset the believing community in Israel. Though Israel is a freedom-loving democracy, anti-missionary opposition works through political institutions so as to effect serious discrimination, sometimes violent, against Jewish believers. Israeli Messianics may endure persistent injustice in most sectors of society. Places of employment are prime targets. Jobs are often lost—if they can even be obtained—on account of faith in Messiah. If the brother or sister makes an issue of it, as of this writing they may be threatened with loss of citizenship and deportation.

Jews who are known to follow Yeshua are generally precluded from receiving help from funds or donations made to mainstream Christian or Jewish organizations. So all too often, needy brethren never receive the Romans 15 material blessings intended for them. As a matter of fact, much of this money is funneled into Jewish organizations that stand in direct opposition to Jewish evangelism. In many instances, these funds end up supporting institutions that actually persecute Jewish believers in Israel.[9] Therefore, sharing material blessings with those who belong to the Galatians 6 "family of faith" meets a critical need.[10]

I am not leveling criticism against well-meaning organizations or beloved Christian friends ablaze with God's heart. Nor do I castigate His ancient covenant people, my own countrymen, about whom He says this: "As far as the gospel is concerned, they are enemies on your account; but as far as election is concerned, they are loved on account of the patriarchs, for God's gifts and his call are irrevocable" (Romans 11:28–29).

However, I am not willing to tacitly watch a wily enemy sabotage the blessing of Israel and the building up of the Church. I want to see God's fresh fire impart new ways and means by which we can align with His last days purposes. With Gentile believers' prayers and practical collaboration, Messianic Jews will surely become much more effective in preparing the way of the Lord among their own people. The faithful remnant of Israel holds keys that cannot be turned without Gentile believers' help. When that happens, doors will open wide that bless not just Israel, but the whole Body. Referring to this phenomenon, Christian author and prophetic teacher Chuck Pierce notes:

> When we see the Messianic Jewish Church arising and coming into proper apostolic/prophetic/intercessory alignment, we will see a sweeping move of God across the earth. This should be one of our key prayer points as we pray for God's covenant people.[11]

Do you desire, along with me, to be one He can mold and mature, commission and consign in this season? Will you embrace the adventure of following Him from glory to ever-increasing glory (see 2 Corinthians 3:18) on these strategic points? To understand the implications, we next visit the Hebrew notion of war.

War in Hebrew

Traditional Judaism offers an intriguing perspective into the biblical concept of war. Some rabbis teach a dimension of the glory of God shines through each individual letter of each word in the Old Covenant. Since Hebrew is the original language in which the Master Communicator speaks to His people, every letter of every Hebrew word communicates something of His nature. The full meaning of any word, therefore, can be seen in the composite definition of its individual letters.[12] The scrolls of Scripture contain scrolls within scrolls, so to speak, of prophetic revelation. According to this theory, I researched each letter in the word "war," and the result proved surprisingly insightful.

The Hebrew word for war generally used in the Scriptures is pronounced *mil-kha-ma*. *Milkhama* can refer to a single battle, recurrent fight or full-scale military campaign.[13] It is used, for instance, in Psalm 18:34: "He trains my hands for battle," and in Isaiah 2:4: "Neither shall they learn war any more" (KJV). *Milkhama* derives from the root *la-kham*, meaning to feed on, consume or devour. According to its dictionary definition, to devour is "to destroy as if by eating." Not surprisingly, then, the Bible says the enemy prowls around "looking for someone to devour" (1 Peter 5:8). He is obsessed with destroying God's created order, then he feeds on that very destruction. By no coincidence, his first battle on earth inspired man's illegal act of feeding from the tree of life, and in his final *milkhama*, Satan himself is devoured by a lake of fire (see Revelation 20:10).

Look with me next at the meaning associated with the individual letters in *milkhama*. The first letter, *mem*, represents waters. Water is the primary physical substance of the created earth realm (see 2 Peter 3:5; Genesis 1:1–2, 6–10). The Hebrew word for "heavens" contains within it the word for waters, suggesting the heavens were also formed mostly from water. Water is used frequently in the Bible as a metaphor not just for life, but for death by divine judgment. The second letter of *milkhama*, which is *lamed*, means teaching and learning. The Hebrew concept of teaching and learning involves more than mental activity; the educational process itself impacts reality. The next letter, *khet*, refers to an enclosed or defined area. Then comes *mem* again, symbolizing waters; followed by *hey*, which denotes an opening or open window. *Hey* is also used to represent God's name.[14]

Putting these letter concepts together in the same order as they appear in *milkhama*, we view war from a certain prophetic perspective. By this reasoning, *war is used by God to release life (waters) for the sake of His teaching and mediating, in a defined sphere and through an open window of time and space, more of Himself*. In connection with its root definition, war is God's means of devouring the devourer. To a fallen world, therefore, war becomes necessary for ultimate justice and good. The goal is always the reality of greater life in Him and His ever-expanding Kingdom.

Spiritual Plunder

Keeping these nuances in mind, return again with me to the spiritual *milkhama* of Jewish evangelism in the former Soviet Union. Recall that at one point a high-ranking Israeli foreign ambassador phoned the president of Belarus to warn of war erupting in his nation if we publicly preached the Gospel there. Here is what, in fact, happened after that particular outreach.[15]

Several thousand Belarussian Jews and Gentiles found eternal life in Messiah, together as one new man. Himself touched, the president communicated to us his sincere "congratulations on the success" of the endeavor. He was especially grateful, he said, for the unity he felt it had brought to the country. Despite a regrettable history of anti-Semitism, Gentiles in Belarus were now feeling a new warmth toward Jews. Since local Jewish leaders were enjoying this new warmth, they broke rank with the anti-missionaries and gave up the fight. However, the anti-missionaries had already made such a fuss that the national media was hot on the story. For many days before, during and afterward, an unusual question was top news: Is Jesus the Jewish Messiah?

Formal expressions of gratitude came not only from the president, but from many other high-ranking political posts. Several government officials professed first-time faith in Yeshua. The small church that graciously served as our local sponsor—which was initially threatened by state authorities as a result—now received unprecedented favor from those same authorities.

I share the story because it illustrates valuable last days battle principles from a Hebraic perspective:

- A key to unlocking city gates rests in taking the Gospel "to the Jew first."
- The release of justice often involves God's judgment against the source of injustice, calling for a confrontational contention in love and faith.

- The degree of opposition to advancing His Kingdom determines the potential scope of victory and plunder of the enemy's camp. Recall that war (*milkhama*) is the release of many waters to teach, in a defined sphere of time and space, about God. Sometimes the waters come as a flood, but ultimately the Kingdom is brought to bear.

Spoils of war in the former Soviet Union were immediately and joyfully apparent. Sometimes, however, the manifestation of victory is not quite as quick. Then we are given grace to persevere in faith for the final outcome, reveling in fighting a good fight, fearing not even death. In such a season, and with staunch devotion, the Messianic Warrior Bride will overcome "by the blood of the Lamb and by the word of their testimony . . . not lov[ing] their lives so much as to shrink from death" (Revelation 12:11).

Blood of the Lamb, Word of Our Testimony

The single most significant battle on earth was fought, I believe, in the Garden of Gethsemane the night before Jesus' crucifixion. There our Savior, sweating blood, was sorely grieved and tempted to say no to the cross (see Matthew 26:39, 42; Luke 22:42–44). Imagine the flooding torment that must have caused Holy God Incarnate to utter the crushing words, "My soul is overwhelmed with sorrow to the point of death" (Matthew 26:38). I suspect the only worse horror for our King was the unresolved, agonizing dilemma of human sin (see Genesis 6:6). I believe He carried that worse horror in His heart from the moment it materialized in another garden, the one called Eden, at the Fall of man. The only way to reverse its curse was through the sacrificial shedding of His blood; love compelled Him to war.

According to God's just laws of life and death, atonement for sin requires the shedding of blood (see Hebrews 9:22). This spiritual principle gave rise to His gracious and elaborate system of sacrifice in the Old Covenant: "For the life of a creature is in the blood, and I have given it to you to make atonement for yourselves on the altar; it is the blood that makes atonement for one's life" (Leviticus 17:11).

The offering of a perfect, unblemished male lamb, goat or other creature was necessary for the remission of sin—until the time was ripe for the perfect Son of Man who offered Himself unblemished to God (see Hebrews 9:14). "The blood of Jesus" is not a magical phrase to invoke or mindlessly toss about. His holy blood is the most potent overcoming reality in the universe. Deep insights into the mystery of the blood of Jesus will be given to the Church in the days and years ahead.

Sometimes the power of bloodshed is better understood and appreciated by spiritualists in the occult than by us Christians. Throughout human history, blood by animal or human sacrifice has been spilled to appease and empower the demonic. Through blood, life or death transfers in some mysterious manner from material to spiritual realms.[16] Thus the blood of Abel cried to God from the dirt it drenched, the Israelites were forbidden from consuming blood (even as gravy with meat), and the prophetic act of Communion is much more than mere ceremony. Based on objective history, it is often said that the blood of the martyrs is the seed of the Church.[17] Spilt blood can serve as a pinnacle form of spiritual warfare. Believers who are called to martyrdom leave behind blood that continues to battle, in a sense, until Jesus returns.

The last days saints overcome Satan by the blood of the Lamb, but also required is the word of their testimony. In this context, the word of their (or our) testimony is much more than the story of how they (or we) got saved a decade ago. It is our verbal and nonverbal proclamation of, and witness to, Truth. The word of our testimony overcomes Satan to the extent that it is founded on, filled with and focused upon *God's* Word of testimony.

Our weaponry consists of wielding God's Word. The Word possesses divine power to demolish works of darkness. In it lie all our battle strategies. To prepare to engage the enemy, we are told to put on the full armor of God, meaning, in essence, we wear the Word (see Ephesians 6:11–17). The belt of truth is the Word; the breastplate of righteousness is the Word; the Gospel of peace fitted on our feet is, again, the Word. In like manner, the shield of faith is founded on the Word (see Romans 10:17). The helmet of salvation is nothing apart from the Word. Our unequivocally offensive weapon is "the sword of the Spirit, which is the word of God" (Ephesians 6:17; see also Matthew 4:1–11). Climactically, when Yeshua leads the armies of heaven at the end of the age, His name is the "Word of God" (Revelation 19:13).

The word of our testimony, together with the blood of the Lamb, carries us to the place of loving not our lives to the death. We discover that to the extent that we lose ourselves, we gain *Him*. Messiah is coming for a pure and spotless Bride whose love for Him is stronger than death; many waters cannot quench it (see Song of Solomon 8:7). We will gladly, for the joy set before us, lay down our lives for the One who offered Himself up for us. We will not run from the cross; in fiery love we will embrace that altar of atonement that binds our hearts to His. This will be our most intimate identification with the Infinite One. To wholly love is to be compelled, like Jesus, to holy war.

In this last days holy war, heaven's strategic plans and purposes unfold for us, as they did long ago, in the battlegrounds of Zion. We visit some of them in the next chapter.

8

From Zion's Battlegrounds

Then the dragon was enraged at the woman and went off to make war against the rest of her offspring—those who obey God's commandments and hold to the testimony of Jesus.

Revelation 12:17

Israel's modern-day military inductions are like those of no other nation. Whenever I watch one at the Western Wall, I am reminded that the spirited young men and women before me, consigning themselves to service, are the tangible descendants of those warriors who millennia ago beheld the unparalleled miraculous. It was their fathers and mothers who witnessed an entire Egyptian army drown in a sea, walls around Jericho tumble at trumpets, and the sun refuse to set over Canaan's hills and plains. Pages of Scripture pop alive and sweep me into the prophetic future as I witness these armies commissioned in the City of the Great King. Singing and dancing like their father David before my eyes, they ultimately fight, whether they know it or not, to defend his Messianic throne in this same place (see Luke 1:32–33; 2 Samuel 7:12–16).

For that reason, it is inevitable that the Church's warfare in the spirit converge with Israel's warfare in the natural. While we as Christians do not instigate war by military assault[1] in order to advance God's Kingdom, the battlegrounds of Zion, in the Bible and beyond, offer compelling lessons for you and me today. In this chapter we look primarily at three of them. First highlighted is the concept of military warfare. Then we move to today's critical contention over secular humanism, and lastly, we unveil a prophetic perspective on the matter of gender roles in the Body of Christ.

A Time for War

Israelis are warriors not because they like to fight, but because they desire peace. At this writing, each and every able-bodied citizen of age becomes, by law, a member of the military. They will don a uniform, submit to rugged training, learn to load and fire weapons, and prepare for battle. It is just the way it must be. It is commonly said that if Israel's enemies put down their weapons, there would be peace; if Israel laid down her weapons, there would be no Israel. Or, as one of history's most acclaimed military strategists stated, "If you want peace, prepare for war."[2] The same could be said of the Body of Christ. That assumes, however, we want *real* peace—in and by the Prince of Peace.

How does God feel about war? The Bible does not outright condone or condemn war; it assumes war as a fact of life. Certainly the Father does not enjoy watching human beings created in His image harm and destroy each other. He does not delight in the death of His enemies—and neither should we (see Ezekiel 33:11).

To some, Yahweh of ancient Israel appears much the warmonger, His wrath eventually subdued by grace through Jesus the peacemaker. But God is the same yesterday, today and forever. His character remains consistent through all of Scripture. At times His justice requires military aggression and bloodshed;

at other times, peace. Accordingly, Israel is instructed on occasion to extend peace to an enemy (see Deuteronomy 20:10),
and Christians may in certain cases take up their swords (see
Luke 22:36; Romans 13:4). As King Solomon notes, "To every
thing there is a season . . . a time of war, and a time of peace"
(Ecclesiastes 3:1, 8, KJV).

In days to come, as wars and rumors of wars increase, you and
I may be tempted to tire of the fight. Tragic suffering associated
with war—spiritual as well as military—can cause natural human
sensibilities to cringe. Then peace is craved at any price. But an
overriding desire for peace that is not Messiah-centered can
lead to a deceptive, false peace imbued with the spirit of antichrist. Then, in the end, we have no peace at all. Through birth
pains ahead, we must stand resolute in the revelation of God's
purposes. For although peace on earth is already at hand, its
time for fulfillment—which is soon—is not yet.

Why War?

War was conceived in heaven when Satan ignominiously
rebelled against the Most High (see Ezekiel 28:13–17). Adam
and Eve's subsequent sin enabled him to take his ruinous rebellion to the staging area of earth. The catastrophic result, just
one generation later, was war waged between brothers; in cold
blood Cain murdered Abel. By the time of the patriarchs, war
was very much a part of the world. Our beloved father Abraham did not refrain from violence when his family's life was at
stake. The sons of Jacob took up arms as a matter of course to
defend family honor. Centuries later, upon their exodus from
Egypt, the Hebrews were attacked and responded with force
(see Genesis 14:14–16; 34:25–31; Exodus 17:8–10). Eventually,
they undertook offensive, God-ordered territorial conquest of
the Promised Land through military means.

Thus the Creator becomes Commander over the armies of
Israel. Yahweh empowers and engineers, protects and presides
over His people in battle:

With your help I can advance against a troop; with my God I can scale a wall.... He trains my hands for battle; my arms can bend a bow of bronze. You give me your shield of victory, and your right hand sustains me.... You armed me with strength for battle; you made my adversaries bow at my feet.

Psalm 18:29, 34–35, 39

The victory is the Lord's.

When the Sovereign King summons His people to war, spiritual or natural, woe to the man or woman who recoils. One who shrinks from battle may regret it: "A curse on him who is lax in doing the LORD's work! A curse on him who keeps his sword from bloodshed!" (Jeremiah 48:10).

God's Word paints a picture of war that, if we are honest, can seem practically scandalous. His acquiescence to destruction and death is repugnant to refined society. Nevertheless, we cannot wish war away. It stares at us from our 21st-century pages of Scripture from Genesis through Revelation. If we are passionate seekers of truth consumed by His zeal, if we desire to be found unoffendable at His ways, then we must conclude Messiah's bride is a warrior because *He* is—and He says to follow Him.

The season associated with the coming of our Bridegroom-King is, in Solomon's words, a time of war. Not coincidentally, *it is also a season of unprecedented glory, supernatural power for signs and wonders, purifying of the Church, revival and Kingdom expansion.* Eventually, that stupendous time will come when we will not learn war anymore (see Isaiah 2:4; Micah 4:3). Meanwhile we watch and pray—and prepare for Kingdom conflict. Part of this preparation will come from watching and praying over Zion's battlegrounds of today and tomorrow, armed with anointing from yesterday's.

Rules of Engagement according to Torah

Every army has its written rules of engagement. Not surprisingly, God enumerates His in the Torah, teaching us His ways and disclosing a dimension of His divine personality. Issuing a minimum of rules dealing directly with war (Deuteronomy 20), God supplements them with battle-specific strategies scattered throughout the Word. In this manner, He nurtures our reliance on Him at every turn.

What are Yahweh's direct principles, relevant to us today, when His people must go out and fight? His top order is as simple to understand as it is hard to accomplish in our own strength: Do not fear. Our God who is above all others tells us why: He assures us *He* will be with us.

> When you go to war against your enemies and see . . . an army greater than yours, do not be afraid of them, because the LORD your God, who brought you up out of Egypt, will be with you. . . . Do not be fainthearted or afraid; do not be terrified or give way to panic before them. For the LORD your God is the one who goes with you to fight for you against your enemies to give you victory.
>
> Deuteronomy 20:1, 3–4

The directive recurs almost tenderly in the New Covenant in connection with the Great Commission: "And surely I am with you always, to the very end of the age" (Matthew 28:20b).

The closer the time of Jesus' return, the more His final words to His first disciples will empower His last followers in this age as well. He will be with us and fight for us, and in His presence, we will not be afraid.

I have faced some seriously scary situations in my life, including death threats, terror alerts, dangers on mission fields and a major, life-threatening illness. But in each case, the same comforting and empowering truth ultimately carried me through: God was with me. His intimate presence outweighed everything. His perfect love cast out fear.

Much as God's Kingdom is ruled by love, Satan's dominion is ruled by fear. To the extent you or I surrender to a spirit of fear, we surrender to the enemy. Our fear feeds and empowers the demonic devourer. Conversely, genuine faith leads to our surrender to the Captain of Heavenly Hosts. It empowers alliance with the angels of heaven. For this reason, Israel's battle refrain resounding through Scriptures is designed to stir up faith: "Be strong and courageous!" (see Deuteronomy 31:6–7, 23; Joshua 1:6, 9, 18; 10:25; 1 Chronicles 22:13; 28:20; 2 Chronicles 32:7). Even today, the biblical admonition serves as a watchword for the Israeli Defense Forces. Military chaplains still regularly bless their troops in the original Hebrew, "*Khazak v'amats!*"

The Hebrew motto is laden with meaning. The concept of "strong and courageous" differs much from the contemporary notion of stoic bravado. The word *strong* (*khazak*) stems from a Hebrew root that means "to cleave." Our strength derives from the Source to whom we cleave, not from mustering manly backbone. The word *courageous* (*amats*) comes from the root "to be alert," implying watchful readiness. To be strong and courageous, therefore, is to cleave to the Commander. We watch Him, and we watch what He does amid all that is happening. We stand ready to respond to His command. Israel's timeless war rally can be ours today: Be strong and courageous; *Khazak v'amats!*

God excludes from battle any soldier who is disheartened or distracted (see Deuteronomy 20:5–8). In such instances, to be excluded from battle is not a desirable, positive thing. If your passion is for Jesus, disheartenment or distraction is not much of an option. Better to repent, let Him restore your soul and throw yourself wholeheartedly back into the service of the King.

On the other hand, there may be times you or I cannot participate in one Kingdom campaign because of service in another. Deuteronomy 20:7, for example, provides a specific exemption from battle for newlyweds. The Master Strategist deploys us however He sees fit. The one sitting at His feet in a prayer closet in worshipful adoration, tending to toddlers full-time or building a righteous business can help win the war as much as the one preaching to unreached souls in a steamy jungle or serving in the military to defend Tel Aviv or Tanzania, Los Angeles or London.

Regardless of the nature of our deployment, the motive and goal is the same. We wage war out of unquenchable, holy love that compels us to mediate God's Kingdom. In the final analysis, we are gladly governed by the same overriding rule of engagement as Zion: obedience to the Bridegroom-King (see Deuteronomy 28:1).

Secular Humanism: Spirit of the Age

The Israeli Defense Forces have been called to fight battles in the natural that both prefigure and reflect battles the Church is called to fight in the supernatural.[3] In particular, Messianic Jewish soldiers prophetically link spiritually, as well as physically, not only to the nation's warriors of the past, but also to those of the future—the radically anointed zealots of the Great Tribulation. In these last days, Jesus-following Jews and Gentiles will align in warfare (see Daniel 7:21–22; Revelation 12:17). We will fight in an increasingly similar spirit, contending against overarching powers and principalities of this age.

Israel's armies are strictly defense-oriented, seeking no territorial gains, but aiming solely to protect their people.[4] The Kingdom of God, on the other hand, is lovingly offensive; it is inherently expansionist in nature. The government of God, headquartered in Jerusalem, will territorially encompass the earth after Jesus returns. Then at long last, swords will be beaten into plowshares (see Isaiah 2:2–4). This future convergence of the physical and spiritual manifests in a divine overlay of present purpose in which Israel and the Church must each access anointings of the other.

At this writing, some warn that the survival of the Jewish nation is in question. Full-blown, unconventional war and unrelenting terror threaten her existence. Nevertheless, she stands as Zion, sometimes translated "Signpost."[5] She serves as a banner to the nations of God's dealings with humanity. As we watch what He does in Zion, we discern what He will do with us. "First to

the Jew, then to the Gentile" is a principle still reflective o
ways (see Romans 2:9–11).

Signpost of Contention

To zoom in on modern-day Zion as signpost, we must first zoom out for perspective. The present international Zionist movement began toward the turn of the twentieth century. With Christian help, Jewish leaders started calling for a return to the Promised Land. After nearly two thousand years of exile, the appointed time of favor had come (see Psalm 102:13). The Zionist movement signaled God's breaking into the earth realm in a dramatic, new way. As it gained momentum, the Azusa Street Revival began, changing the course of world history. Meanwhile, God's enemies did not idly sit by in delight. Within decades, two world wars broke out, climaxing in the tragic Nazi Holocaust. Yet out of the ashes of the Holocaust the Jewish State was officially birthed.

Within hours of declaring independence in 1948, Israel was attacked by five neighboring Arab-Muslim countries, buttressed by countless hordes of irregulars. Vastly outnumbered and with an outrageously low weapons ratio, the Jews were given virtually no chance of success. But few had factored in God. Stories and accounts of miracle upon miracle abound, and to the world's surprise, Israel survived.[6] Then, with her supernatural recovery, an international revival of healing miracles soon circled the globe.

It was a season of restoration—but not without resistance. As a result of continued enemy aggression and against all odds, Israel legally gained Gaza, the Golan Heights, Judea and Samaria, including East Jerusalem, in 1967. Concomitantly and not coincidentally, the Jesus Movement exploded in the West. Internationally, supernatural Kingdom activity accelerated. *As ancient Jerusalem was restored to Israel, ancient anointing was restored to the Church through the simultaneous birth of the contemporary Messianic Jewish movement.*

In the Six Day War of 1967, Israel took a bold, biblical stance of proactive defense. When the fighting started, conquest was not her goal. It did, nevertheless, become the unforeseen, miraculous result. Sadly, however, from that point on things began to turn for her. Although murderous terror continued to beset the Jewish State, she would no longer be regarded by much of the world as brave little hero, but as unstoppable bully. The signpost message? God's people will be tolerated, even somewhat admired, as long as they present no perceptible or tangible threat to the world. However, when heaven's Kingdom breaks in with real power, world forces are threatened—and they strike back. Accordingly, after the Six Day War, Israel was soon made to face the world's chokehold of secular humanism, with its tactical force of appeasement.

Appease When There Is No Peace

Secular humanism[7] stresses mankind's capacity for his own self-realization, or total fulfillment, through human means. Rejecting God and the supernatural, humankind is extolled instead. Objective standards of morality do not exist according to humanist teaching. Moral truth is seen as merely relative to individuals and their circumstances; hence the term *moral relativism*. Under moral relativism, the Bible is no more authoritative than the *Koran*, the *Talmud*, or the *Atheist Manifesto*.[8] Humanism, with its moral relativism, amounts to creation worshiping the created instead of the Creator, and this He cannot bless (see Romans 1:25). Exalting man as god, secular humanism is destined to eventually culminate with the coronation of the Antichrist.

Humanist thought had influenced Israel, as it had other Western nations, from the inception of the modern Jewish State. Regrettably, this stronghold further entrenched when many began to attribute the stunning success of the Six Day War to the Jews' own efforts. But any rejoicing in that victory was short-lived; it soon became evident Arab-Palestinian enmity had not been quelled. (Recall Satan's ongoing battle over Jerusalem.) As a result, the international community, itself mostly humanistic, took to assailing Israel with a campaign aimed at Palestinian and Muslim terrorist appeasement. Because the philosophy of secular humanism does not possess objective moral standards of right and wrong, the logical way for it to resolve conflict is typically through appeasement. Therefore, before long the nations would collectively persuade Israel to respond to her enemies—who still sought her annihilation—by appeasing them.

Appeasement is fear-motivated compromise with evil for the sake of hoped-for relief from that evil. It is not the same as compromise. In and of itself, compromise can refer to morally positive motives, processes and results. Compromise can resolve even serious disputes through mutual concessions that do not necessarily sacrifice God's standards of right and wrong. Compromise can be undertaken in holy love, for the sake of justice, in accordance with righteousness. In contrast and by definition, appeasement as it is used today is inspired by fear of man, not God. A disguised defeat, appeasement presumes or pretends that humans can all get along without Him. In the current world war against Islamic terror, appeasement has become commonplace.

Therefore, as Israel became the first significant, modern-day target of both terror and fascist Islam, she also became the first collective entity to which the force of global appeasement was applied. Terrorists, the world maintained, could be appeased with more territory. But they were wrong. The relinquishment of territory resulted only in terror gaining steadily greater breeding ground. Assault was hatched not just against the Jewish State, but against all nations (see Genesis 12:3; Obadiah 1:10–11, 15). Israel's surrender of land to appease those still desiring her demise cannot achieve peace.

Zion stands as a sign, posting what God is doing in the world— and in us. Since Israel's Six Day War, appeasement has been used in the Church to cause compromise with sin in ways that

previously would have been unthinkable. Our grandparents—
or great-grandparents, depending on your age—would have
been appalled at the behavior characterizing today's so-called
Christian society in much of the West. They would not have
shown as much skin at a baseball game, for instance, as many
of us numbingly display in church. Saved or not, our elders at
least had the moral fiber to stand up for what was right in ways
we seldom do.

You and I are urged to appease everything from the dictates
of modern fashion to Islamofascism. But appeasement is not an
option for the Messianic Warrior Bride. Her Bridegroom-King
was tempted by it, and in His refusal to succumb (see Matthew
4:1–11), she draws strength to stand firm. She refuses to surrender to false gods and say, "'Peace, peace' . . . when there is
no peace" (Jeremiah 8:11). Unquenchable love for Yeshua and
the people for whom He died empowers her to contend for
righteousness, and to prevail.

We *must* contend in love—and *all* of us must be included.

Women at War

Women, as well as men, have from the beginning served as
warriors in the armies of Israel. In the 1940s, the Jewish nation
became the first modern military to employ female soldiers as a
matter of course. The issue was simply one of survival. The sliver
of a State, with neighboring nations all bent on its destruction,
had no choice but to conscript virtually everyone. The initia-
tion of Jewish women into active military service, including
combat duty, sparked a fire that helped raise world awareness.
Untapped talents were possibly hidden, it was realized, in half
the human race.

Not much later, Israel again raised eyebrows by electing a female prime minister, that nation's equivalent to the American
president.[9] Tongues wagged. But through the chatter, God
Himself was speaking. It was time to advance His Kingdom

purposes for women. However, as sometimes happens when Deity shakes tradition, secular society caught the message first. Not until a couple of decades later did more religious Judeo-Christian communities begin to grasp the significance of what the Spirit was saying. Regrettably, our delay came with a price.

If we the people of God do not stay, by the Spirit, on life's cutting edge and the loving offensive, we will likely find ourselves relegated to the defensive. Then, once on the defensive, we run the risk of turning altogether reactionary, easily retreating in fear to former ground. From there, advance is much more difficult. God's purposes will ultimately be achieved, but generally not without greater casualty and delay. Sadly, to a large degree this describes what happened when traditional gender roles were challenged in the Western world during the latter half of the twentieth century.

I believe God wanted His people at the helm of a life-altering shift in the Spirit. Regrettably, however, the women's liberation movement launched itself virtually void of biblical parameters. Steeped in wounds that trace back to Eden, but without the moorings of Scripture, the movement quickly radicalized into a variant of humanism called feminism. Many believers were highly offended by feminism's anti-God trappings. We defensively retreated to former ground, where advance became nearly impossible. The consequence was inevitable. To many, freedom for women became synonymous with rebellion against faith, family and the foundation of all things right and good.

In this season, however, God is giving new opportunities with a new generation. Many of the daughters and granddaughters of the former feminist movement have been apprehended by, and remain unstoppably ablaze for, their Bridegroom-King. They are returning to our congregational and ministry doorsteps—and we must welcome them back. Like Israel, we cannot win the war without them.

Feminine Mys-taque?

During my lifetime, much has changed in the Church regarding freedoms for women. Back in the 1970s, soon after surrendering my life to Yeshua, I was given a clear vision of that to which He had called me. But that calling involved the potential of at least an indirect degree of leading or teaching men. Such activity for a woman was contrary to the theology of those to whom I was submitted ecclesiastically. Puzzled, all I could do was pray.

Confident of the vision God had given, but not wanting to act contrary to the Scriptures, I undertook an intense, prayerful study of the subject. I learned an increasing number of scholars believe that many New Covenant verses about women have been taken extremely out of context for much of Church history.[10] Many passages have not been considered in light of what Jesus and the Bible authors *did* as well as what they *said*. (As a parallel, we need look only so far as traditional Church teachings on Israel or the Torah.) Finally, after a couple of decades, and with a very supportive husband, I knew I had to say yes to God and His Word.

To what extent was I wrong, and responsible to my King, for choosing to surrender to the decisions of men rather than promptly obeying Him from faith? Sometimes delays are divinely ordered. I had been taught the importance of submission to authority (see 1 Peter 2:13; Romans 13:1), even when leaders may at times be mistaken. (What human authority is always correct?)

I am certain many of you, especially women of my generation, can personally relate at least to some extent to the dilemma. If my journey reflects yours, be encouraged that in all things God works for the good of those who love Him. If your heart has been right—and you embrace a humble path of forgiveness—you lose no blessing in the end (see Romans 8:28; Joel 2:25). In my case, when I felt "all" I could do was pray, the Lord awesomely met me in intimate heart-to-heart communion. In retrospect, I would not trade that for anything. Meanwhile, for those of you sisters—especially younger generations—who cannot relate at all to my experience, may your destiny *never* be diverted by traditions that find no firm footing in God's Word!

Why has much of the Church for so long viewed women as ineligible or incapable of ministering to men? It is sometimes said that Christendom's restrictive gender-based rules trace back to extrabiblical traditions inherited from rabbinic Judaism. But as we have seen, early Church fathers systematically excised Hebraic teachings and traditions from New Covenant faith. As a result, today the Spirit is recovering and restoring severed biblical connections between Old and New Covenant truth. In reality, the Church's differential treatment of women stems not so much from Judaism as from other sociocultural factors, including ancient Greco-Roman religious traditions, having little to do with God's Word.[11] Where gender discrimination exists in the Body of Christ, the source is generally not Jewish teaching. On the other hand, Messianic faith communities that are purposefully founded on traditional Jewish tenets certainly can, to varying degrees, trace limitations on women's roles to extrabiblical rabbinic traditions.

Fearsome Female Fighters

In the beginning, God made man in His own image. God possesses both "male" and "female" traits, and it seems Adam originally did as well. In the creation account, the Hebrew word for *man*, from which the name "Adam" derives, refers to man's humanity. It does not imply gender or "maleness." Only after God fashioned Eve from Adam does the Hebrew shift to male and female.

Apparently, to provide "a helper suitable" for Adam (Genesis 2:18), God separated and took out his female nature, thus creating Eve as a perfect complement. Nothing in the Hebrew indicates Eve was subordinate to Adam. Together, both man and woman were delegated dominion over the earth (see Genesis 1:26–28). Although God cast woman in the role of helper to man, this does not suggest inferiority. The same Hebrew word for "helper" (*ezer*) in the Scriptures is frequently used in reference to Yahweh Himself as the helper. Thus the relationship of helper to the helped could not denote subjugation.

Since the curse of the Fall, a peculiar war has raged between the devil and the daughters of Eve, inspired by Deity: "I will put enmity between you and the *woman*, and between your offspring and *hers*; he will crush your head, and you will strike his heel" (Genesis 3:15, emphasis added). God did not place direct enmity between the serpent and the man, but, it seems, between the serpent and the woman. As a result, Satan has issues with us women that he does not have with men. I suspect he may hate us more; in any case, I am certain he is really quite afraid of little girls, grown-up ladies and definitely grandmas—all for good reason. Residing in our DNA is, I believe, an unconscious enmity echoing the Master's prophetic mandate. Ever since Eve, females have made for fearsome fighters destined to outmatch hell's fury.

God does not want women opting out of war because of wrong theology. Our distinct nature is not a hindrance but a help in battle. It is no secret, for example, that around the world, women as a whole tend to be regarded as more intuitive or "spiritually sensitive" than men. We often sense danger more readily, as if tuned to an internal radar. Scientists tell of more complex and interactive right and left brain functioning. Some ancient rabbis concluded women were created with an extra dose of wisdom and understanding.[12] While I must dispute any claim to superior intelligence, God certainly made us different from men on many levels. He wants His female fighters exploiting a redeemed and surrendered radar for Spirit-strategized maneuvers. (Could it be a sign of things to come that the majority of Israeli army intelligence operatives, at this writing, happen to be women?)

Healing Ancient Hatreds

If women harbor an unconscious recollection of the curse of the Fall, is it possible men also possess a type of indelible memory of the event? Could the male gender, in some manner, recall Eve's seductive proposal to partake of the fruit of the tree? If so, little appreciation is likely to be triggered for the event. More than a hint of blame-shifting can be heard by God's beloved Adam: "The woman you put here with me— *she* gave me some fruit from the tree, and I ate it" (Genesis 3:12, emphasis added). Is it not conceivable that a timeless resentment resides toward her? What about a possible simmering male guilt for succumbing to "the woman you put here with me," rather than rising to the role of interceding for her exculpation?

In this vein, social scientists note and track a troubling worldwide phenomenon. Wherever widespread human suffering exists from poverty, disease, famine or violence, a disproportionately high percentage of victims are women. In some cultures, systematic and institutionalized murderous abuse of women is commonplace.[13] This entrenched injustice is called misogyny. The dictionary definition of misogyny is, quite simply, hatred of women. In many societies, misogyny takes the form of state-sanctioned honor killing, female gender-selective abortion exclusively targeting baby girls, sex slavery, rape, legal prostitution, female genital mutilation and more. In the West, misogynous acts and abuses typically manifest more subtly—and the Church is not exempt.

A common deception about misogyny is that its victims are limited to females, when in fact it taints men at least as much. By assenting to and participating in acts that defile women, men give ground to the enemy to steal, kill and destroy *themselves*. An example that is plain to see is the deleterious effect of pornography. What is more subtle is the effect of, let's say, not getting or staying delivered from pornography through biblical teaching or deliverance because the only minister available is female. Of course, we women can perpetuate misogyny too; we cannot just blame the guys. How many of us, for instance, can still purposefully flaunt our sexuality or act out, when it seems convenient, the stereotypical "dumb blonde"? In so doing, we agree unconsciously with the same female-debasing spirit, and God grieves. (Nothing against blondes or nongeniuses intended, by the way.)

I rejoice that we are entering a season in which the truth of His Word is setting us free at new levels. As men and women genuinely become one in Christlike humility, the most fundamental reconciliation of the human race will occur. This will require and also release levels of humility, forgiveness, love and purity on the part of both men and women that, in turn, reform the fabric of Christianity. I am convinced that the Church will never be truly delivered and healed, for instance, of sexual immorality, homosexuality, abortion, child molestation and more until we repent wholeheartedly of misogyny. When we do, many Kingdom advances for which we have long prayed will explode into existence.

As the Messianic Warrior Bride lives out God's destiny for woman as suitable helper and co-regent to man, we will live out more purely and effectively our destiny as suitable helper, even co-regent, to Yeshua. Together in right relationship, man and woman will beautifully showcase the full revelation of God's personality.

My husband, Kerry, a Messianic Jewish physician and ordained pastor, has encouraged me in ministry throughout our marriage. He offers an incisive encouragement to Christian men:

> Male leaders in the Body of Messiah can now be secure enough in the Lord to receive instruction, impartation, and blessing from those God has gifted and commissioned, regardless of gender. In addition, we can empower our sisters so they know service in the Kingdom is not necessarily limited to the nursery or the kitchen. This may mean we step aside so they can rise up. When male leaders intentionally make room for women, not just in the "secular" world, but in ministerial leadership, from informal round tables to pulpits, the whole Body will be better off.[14]

A Messianic Jewish Challenge

Believers have long appreciated the great liberating truth of Galatians 3:28: "There is neither Jew nor Greek, slave nor free, male nor female, for you are all one in Christ Jesus." This concise statement teaches that Gentiles as well as Jews can receive all the blessings of salvation in Yeshua. Ethnicity does not determine spiritual status. At the same time, complementary distinctions between Jews and Gentiles are not abolished in the natural realm any more than they are abolished between men and women.

As surely as this verse liberates Jews and Gentiles into their destiny as one in Christ, it likewise illustrates that despite their natural distinctions, both men *and women* receive *all* the blessings of salvation in Messiah Jesus. Gender does not determine spiritual status any more than national bloodline. Women are not relegated to spiritual inferiority in any respect, or disqualified from serving in ministry, solely on account of being female. While I do not at all propose obliterating gender distinctives, I do suggest it is time to humbly search our hearts and ask God for fresh revelation from His Word in these last days. We must not deny the Deborahs, muzzle the Miriams (she led in more than worship), or prohibit the Priscillas (a pastoral teacher) from serving as fully as they have been called. Let us not forget that our sister Junias proved "outstanding among the apostles" (Romans 16:7).

One unique consideration in the reconciliation of male and female may relate to Messianic Jewish women. Recall the second half of Genesis 3:15 referring to the "offspring" of the woman who would crush the serpent's head. That heroic Crusher is the God-Man Messiah Yeshua. But in a broad sense, Bible scholars recognize this "offspring" pertains also to Israel, the Jewish nation through whom Yeshua was birthed. Indeed, it was the Jewish woman Miriam (Mary) whom God used to conceive a Messiah for humanity's redemption. I do not think hell has ever quite gotten over that.

From a still broader perspective, the woman's offspring includes those born anew by God's Spirit from all nations. Therefore the enemy's enmity seethes toward all Christians. It would stand to reason, then, that Jews who are also Christian and also female could be uniquely targeted by Satan. I raise the issue because, while the collective Body of Christ now includes women serving publicly to lead Kingdom advance at practically every level, Messianic Jewish women are rarely, if ever, among them. In large part, this is due to the fact that senior leadership levels in most Messianic spheres do not yet include women.[15] In future years this will change, and as God raises up female Messianic Jewish leaders, the whole Body will be blessed. The full expression of Israel's anointing—requiring both genders—will at last be restored.

Men Get Surrounded

An intriguing, yet-to-be fulfilled Old Covenant prophecy refers to the relationship between Messianic Jewish men and women, and by extension, to all believers. Jeremiah 31 is an exhilarating chapter about Israel's restoration to her land and her Lord. In this context the prophet declares, "The LORD will create a new thing on earth—a woman will surround a man" (Jeremiah 31:22). This verse baffles Bible scholars, most of whom conclude this "new thing" is so unique to the future that its meaning cannot yet be ascertained.[16] With all due respect to modern biblical scholarship, I would like to offer an interpretation.

The Hebrew word translated "surround" has a cooperative, affectionate connotation. The meaning is positive, not negative, suggesting an embrace of tender love.[17] To "surround" implies protecting another.[18] So in a sense, "surround" could relate to woman's mandate in Genesis 2:18 and 2:20 to "help" man. By this reasoning, in the context of Israel's rehabilitation, we can conclude that God establishes a new and good expression of relationship between man and woman. Israel's restoration, in the coming millennial age, catapults blessings to the nations. It reaches even to the recesses of humankind's irreducible, male-female dyad.[19]

I believe this dazzling dimension of love, reflected in woman surrounding man, is already accessible to us in the Kingdom of God. In coming years Israel's faithful remnant, together with the international Church, will begin to beautifully actualize the promise of Jeremiah 31:22. Then after Yeshua returns, the unimaginably divine will fully become tangible reality. In the remaining portion of this book, I invite you to taste that heaven on earth.

9

Messianic Millennium Coming

He will be great and will be called the Son of the Most High.
The Lord God will give him the throne of his father David, and
he will reign over the house of Jacob forever; his kingdom will
never end.

Luke 1:32–33

In every nation where I have ministered, I have found the Lord's
people eagerly anticipating His return. I have also discovered
that few have asked Him or intently prayed through what that
means personally for them. Most simply think of heaven as their
longed-for, ethereal home. They look forward to Jesus whisking
them away to be with Him there forever. But our "blessed hope"
(Titus 2:13) is actually about a great deal more.

Our Bridegroom-King is coming back to earth for a thousand years of glorious governmental, Kingdom rule. At that
time, He will restore life on earth to conditions reminiscent
of the Garden of Eden. You and I will be here with Him for
that spectacular Messianic Millennium—and beyond. He has
not consigned us to a faraway heaven for eternity. As we will

see, heaven on earth, *literally*, is ultimately better, in God's masterful design, than heaven alone. I am not saying that heaven is not unequivocally stupendous. Indeed, it is unimaginably and supremely paradisial. Nor am I saying that certain realms of heaven are not accessible to us as believers today. Yet the Bible teaches that something even more resplendent lies ahead. The Revealer of Mysteries (see Daniel 2:29, 47) is opening the eyes of His Church so we can begin to perceive it. More and more, truths are being brought into focus that have been "closed up and sealed until the time of the end" (Daniel 12:9).

Yeshua assured His disciples they would be with Him forever, and the promise applies to Christians through the ages (see Matthew 28:20; 2 Timothy 2:11–12; 1 Thessalonians 5:10). We are with Him in life and in death, when our spirits live on in heaven. Then, when He returns to the earth, believers who have died will return with Him (see 1 Thessalonians 4:14; 3:13). Included among them are those saints who will have been raptured, or caught up to meet the Lord in the air, in connection with the seven-year period of distress known as the Great Tribulation (see 1 Thessalonians 4:17). You and I will be part of that great company—and we are going to absolutely love it—if we stand firm to the end. In this chapter we see why, and delve into the future that is *now*.

Heaven on Earth

The Lord refers not just to heaven, but also to His coming Kingdom on earth, when He says, "Well done, my good servant! . . . Because you have been trustworthy in a very small matter, take charge of ten cities" (Luke 19:17; see also Matthew 25:23). He also promises, "And I confer on you a kingdom, just as my Father conferred one on me, so that you may . . . sit on thrones, judging" (Luke 22:29–30). Similarly, "At the renewal of all things, when the Son of Man sits on his glorious throne, you who have followed me will also sit on twelve thrones, judging" (Matthew 19:28).

When Yeshua spoke these words to His original disciples, they understood the beloved rabbi's words meant they would return someday to rule with Him and judge the world (see 1 Corinthians 6:2; 1 Thessalonians 4:13–14). They anticipated the King coming with "thousands upon thousands of his holy ones" (Jude 1:14). The apostle John would later see thrones on which the saints sat judging with authority over nations. He prophetically watched them serve as priests, reigning on the earth with the Lord for a thousand years as princes and kings (see Revelation 1:5–6; 2:26; 5:10; 20:4–6). The Twelve had a solid Old Covenant background and were well acquainted with the prophets' vivid descriptions of this future Kingdom.

Daniel was especially eloquent on the end times. To him it was revealed that deceased, faithful followers of Yahweh would resurrect, "shine like the brightness of the heavens," and "lead many to righteousness." They would "receive" and then "possess" the Kingdom (Daniel 12:2–3; 7:18, 22). Daniel explained that following a conflagration on earth with a ruler fitting the description of the Antichrist, "The sovereignty, power and greatness of the kingdoms *under* the whole heaven will be handed over to the saints, the people of the Most High" (Daniel 7:27, emphasis added).

In summary, Jesus comes again—to Jerusalem—together with myriads of angels and resurrected believers from all nations. At that time, He judges and vanquishes His foes. Converging heaven with earth, He rules, together with the saints, over all nations. This Messianic Millennium is followed by Satan's brief, temporary release from prison, when he is permitted to tempt humanity one last time. After that comes his swift and final demise, whereupon God's people inherit a glorious new heaven and earth. This new heaven realm is spiritual; however, the new earth realm remains material in nature. *God's consummate fullness of personality will be made manifest through the ultimate, total convergence of a perfect spiritual realm (new heaven) and perfect physical realm (new earth).* This *extremely* good news is part of the Gospel of the Kingdom for which we are to prepare, as well as to share with the whole world (see Matthew 24:14).

Davidic Covenant of the Kingdom

The Kingdom of God is based on a covenant word God gave to David three thousand years ago:

> I will raise up your offspring to succeed you, who will come from your own body, and I will establish his kingdom. . . . I will establish the throne of his kingdom forever. I will be his father, and he will be my son. . . . Your house and your kingdom will endure forever before me; your throne will be established forever.
>
> 2 Samuel 7:12–16[1]

King David took this promise literally. He understood that it referred to a physical descendant who would rule from a physical Jerusalem, *forever* (see 2 Samuel 7:18–29; 1 Chronicles 17:16–27; Psalm 89:3–4, 28–37).

Many years later, at the heaven-and-earth-shattering annunciation of Messiah's first coming, the angel Gabriel declared, "The Lord God will give him the throne of his father David, and he will reign over the house of Jacob forever" (Luke 1:32–33). From then on, Jesus is identified as inheritor of the Davidic throne, or King of the Jews. Not coincidentally, at the end of His public ministry He receives the same appellation—engraved over a cross (see Luke 23:38). Soon thereafter, the apostles relate miraculous events to the restoration of David's fallen hut or kingdom[2] (see Acts 15:16).

According to the genealogies of Luke 3 and Matthew 1, Mary and Joseph were lineal descendants of King David (see 2 Timothy 2:8).[3] Mary was familiar with the promise of the Davidic throne, and after the annunciation, burst into a song of praise. The words of her song, taken from the Scriptures, reflect an understanding of her son's appointment as royal ruler in a literal and physical sense (see Luke 1:46–55).

Yeshua's followers in the New Covenant saw Him as inheritor of a tangible Davidic throne (see Matthew 9:27; 12:23; 15:22; 20:30–34; 21:9; Acts 3:19–21; 15:13–18). Based on the biblical revelation they had, they quite logically anticipated an imminent establishment of His governmental rule.[4] The Hebrew Scriptures only hinted enigmatically at two distinct comings of Messiah. For us, the canon of New Covenant teaching clarifies that Yeshua's throne is heavenly as well as earthly, and that He is coming a second time. Yet we stand to make a mistake similar to that of the first disciples if we dismiss one reality for the other. Whereas they did not understand the heavenly dimensions of the Kingdom, believers today often do not apprehend the natural or earthly dimensions.

The Davidic Throne

Although they are on a splendid course to converge, the throne of David is not the same as the throne of God. God's throne is in heaven, where Yeshua now sits at the right hand of His Father, in full expression of His divinity (see Hebrews 8:1; 1 Peter 3:22). The Davidic throne, however, is located in Jerusalem and expresses Messiah's humanity (see Psalm 122:5). Jesus did not occupy the Davidic throne at His first coming and will not occupy it until He returns (see Isaiah 9:7; Psalm 2:6; Revelation 5:5; 22:16; Isaiah 24:21–23). He Himself differentiates between the two thrones in Revelation 3:21. There He says He will share His throne with those who overcome, just as His Father now shares His throne with Him (Jesus) because He overcame. The point is, there is no such thing as a Messianic throne not occupied by a physical Son of Man—a Jewish son of David—in a physical Jerusalem. The Gospel of the Kingdom starts with the good news of salvation through forgiveness of sin by a King who is fully God and, in Israel's ancient royal anointing, also fully human.

Why do I spend so much time on the matter? To totally spiritualize Messiah's throne is to nullify God's promise to King David and therefore to Israel—and therefore to the Church. The logical conclusion of a solely spiritual Messianic dominion removes the blessed hope of Jesus' literal return. If there is no throne of David, there is no Redeemer of Humanity ruling in Jerusalem in a resurrected body. There is only the intangible Kingdom of the spirit realm, an ethereal heaven that does not fully redeem the earth. If this is what we believe, we're not likely to connect with or access all the authority God has given us for all He has called us to be and to do.

Our ultimate destiny is to exercise dominion over the material realm fashioned for us by the Father. In the beginning, God delegated legal authority to humankind to rule the earth (see Genesis 1:28; Psalm 8:5–6). But we lost much of that authority at the Fall, tragically abdicating rights of dominion to Satan. Within the Godhead, however, a profound plan for redemption had been conceived (see Isaiah 63:5). The plan would require God's Son to live among us as a man made of flesh and blood—perfectly sinless—under the full anointing of the Spirit. Only a Jewish man would be in a position to perfectly follow and fulfill all the Law. Accordingly, the Son of Man would be a Jew, born into the Davidic lineage as legitimate heir to David's physical throne.

Yeshua would atone for the sin of all humanity (see Isaiah 53:2–12; 1 Corinthians 15:22; Romans 5:11; Hebrews 2:17). In so doing, He would legally recover all authority mankind had lost to Satan. He would then qualify to lead us in fulfilling God's mandate to subdue the earth (see Genesis 1:28). In the process, the Son of God/Son of Man would be given by His Father a Bride with whom He would intimately commune and rule forever. The implications are staggering! The Davidic nature of our King neither demeans His deity nor subtracts from His splendor; to the contrary, it magnifies His glory forever.

Good or Bad Earth?

Without this fuller revelation of Yeshua as Davidic king, key dynamic continuity between Old and New Covenants is lost. We can easily find ourselves regarding the physical realm as innately bad or hopelessly carnal. But such a perspective is not biblical. Historically, Christian reviling of the physical realm reflects pagan religions and philosophies such as Gnosticism. The apostles strenuously opposed these influences, which nonetheless wheedled their way into the early Church[5]—and as a result, many of us can still tend to see sin as having irreparably spoiled all things tangible. Yet Creator God repeatedly affirms that everything He made was good, even *very* good (see Genesis 1:31). He was pleased to create the earth realm, which expresses His character and purposes like nothing else. His intent was—and still is—for man, together with Him, to enjoy, not deny, material reality.

To be sure, following Adam and Eve's sin, God cursed the ground in Genesis 3:17. But the Hebrew word for "curse" does not mean the earth itself turned evil. The word more accurately means, as the Genesis passage goes on to describe, a diminishing of prosperity. In the end, God will not let sin have the final say; He will redeem and restore all things (see Acts 3:21; Colossians 1:19–20; Ephesians 1:9–10).

A large percentage of the Old Covenant refers to this restoration of all things during the Messianic age—as it unfolds after Yeshua returns. In the New Covenant, Messiah speaks often of the Kingdom to come. In follow-up, all the apostolic authors expound on the theme. You and I are meant to be encouraged and empowered by the blessed hope of Jesus not only returning, but also residing here. He wants us looking forward to joyful participation in His glorious, governmental, manifest presence and activity in a reformed world.

The expectation of Jesus' literal return together with the saints, and His subsequent Kingdom rule, was standard Church teaching up to the third and fourth centuries.[6] Until that time, any contradictory theology (which usually traced to pagan influence) was considered serious error. With the political institutional-ization of Christianity, however, doctrines of the faith shifted significantly. The literal-grammatical-historical approach to studying God's Word was replaced by an overall symbolic or allegoric method of interpretation.[7]

A symbolic approach clearly enjoyed the politically correct advantage over any literal interpretation of the Bible. Under an allegoric interpretation of the prophetic Scriptures, God's government rule on earth would never materialize. No King of Kings would ever return to tangibly take over the kingdoms of men. Therefore, Jesus would pose little or no threat to existing political institutions.

As time went on, much of Christendom came to focus on the symbolic, spiritual dimension of God's Kingdom, while deni-grating the physical realm. Artificial distinction was then drawn between secular and sacred spheres of life. The natural (secular) remained important insofar as it became symbolic of the spiri-tual (sacred). This thinking gave rise to an end times eschatology known as amillennialism—which had been denounced by our earliest apostolic fathers as heretical.[8]

Uh . . . Millennialism?

Today, amillennialism is one of three main eschatological views embraced by the Body of Christ. Amillennialism teaches there is no personal, literal return and rule of Messiah. His earthly reign takes place only in the hearts of men, in this pres-ent age. In contrast, "postmillennialism" holds that Jesus does return—but only after we first attain a symbolic thousand-year period of perfection. Accordingly, the Church increases in power and scope until the whole world worships Christ for a (symbolic) thousand years. Postmillennialists believe this can be achieved because, in their understanding, Satan has already been person-ally bound.[9] Some postmillennial streams believe the saints take over the governments of nations,[10] then the new heaven and earth appear. The seven-year Great Tribulation of distress is deemed either symbolic or already fulfilled.[11] A third perspective, "premillennialism," holds that Messiah's personal and literal return to earth occurs before the thousand-year Kingdom age begins. Most premillennialists believe that spectacular return follows a very real Great Tribulation lasting for seven years.

All three views contain important elements of truth.[12] My understanding of the Scriptures, however, is most consistent with a broad definition of premillennialism. To varying degrees, I also embrace perspectives traditionally associated with the other eschatological schemes. I believe, for example, that in an important—but not complete or personal—sense, Satan was bound at Yeshua's first coming. I also believe the true Church will be purified, matured and exponentially empowered by the Spirit before His Second Coming. At the same time, I am convinced Messiah really comes back for a really resplendent thousand-year reign. He displaces a very real devil who has done all he can to destroy God's people and God's purposes.

Messiah Real-ly Makes a Comeback

When Jesus was lifted to heaven, angels stood by and prophesied to His wide-eyed apostles, "Men of Galilee, . . . why do you stand here looking into the sky? This same Jesus, who has been taken from you into heaven, will come back in the same way you have seen him go into heaven" (Acts 1:11).

Messiah's return will be as tangibly real as His ascension. He Himself foretold, "They [all nations] will see the Son of Man coming on the clouds of the sky, with power and great glory" (Matthew 24:30b; see also Mark 13:26; Luke 21:27).

Every eye on earth will see Him return because He is coming back in physical form. The feet of His resurrected body will stand on the Mount of Olives in Jerusalem. Those same beautiful feet will rest in a literal geographic location, specifically Zion (see Revelation 1:7; Matthew 24:27; Zechariah 14:4; Isaiah 60:13;

Ezekiel 43:7). Yeshua's resurrected body, though in essence a natural one, will have supernatural dimensions. Recall that after He rose from the dead, the Master ate meals with His disciples. In that same body, the Lord also walked right through walls (see Luke 24:41–43; John 20:19).

Our glorified Bridegroom-King will unleash God's millennial government, a theocracy of righteousness, peace, joy and justice that you and I have never known. *The whole earth will be filled with the knowledge of the glory of the Lord, as the waters cover the sea* (see Isaiah 11:9; Habakkuk 2:14). How bedazzling is *that?!*

While I was writing this chapter, the Lord provided Kerry and me a unique opportunity to spend a week in a lovely cottage on a secluded beach in Hawaii. Just steps from the water, it was an absolutely gorgeous getaway, a delight to the senses. The cottage offered a splendid view fully overlooking the Pacific Ocean. As a result, I found myself meditating on the aforementioned verse, captivated day after day by the beauty of the sea.

The sea is majestic, interacting endlessly with light and wind to disclose ever-new wave patterns and sounds. Like the knowledge of the glory of God, it does not cease to dazzle and fascinate. As with the Kingdom, treasures hide deep beneath its surface. A colorful and adventurous world awaits those daring to dive in. The sea is a thing of joy! Yet, like the King, its ceaseless roar reminds us it is untamable. The same sparkling waters that keep us afloat can also overtake us. The sea can swallow up or pummel to pieces. It can transform dark, rugged rocks of resistance into pristine, powdery white sand.

The knowledge of God's glory will be an infinite, incomparable trove of beauty, holy awe and majesty. It will overtake the earth in righteousness, peace and justice for all.

Righteousness and Peace

Under the coming dominion of the Prince of Peace, righteousness and peace kiss each other (see Psalm 85:10; Isaiah

9:7). "Peace on earth, good will toward men" materializes on far more than Christmas cards. The nations are subdued with unprecedented peace emanating from Jerusalem, the City of Peace (see Isaiah 9:7; 57:19; 14:7). Around the world, swords are fashioned into plowshares and implements of fruitful agricultural development. People rest in peace while very much alive (see Isaiah 2:4; 54:13; 55:12).

This peace continually increases. It blankets not only humanity, but all of natural creation, even the wildest beasts (see Isaiah 9:7; Ezekiel 34:25). A dedicated animal lover, I delight to think of lambs romping with wolves, goats grazing with leopards, and calves skipping among lions, a small child taking charge of them all. Cattle will roam alongside bears while infants toy with cobras. Lions will turn vegetarian, contentedly munching straw (see Isaiah 11:6–8).

Peace saturates the planet because peace is a product of righteousness (see Isaiah 32:17). Righteousness is one of God's most essential attributes.[13] It refers to that which is pure, virtuous and correct, without fault or guilt, and in conformity to His holiness.[14] An insuppressible craving for righteousness resides, I believe, in the collective human soul, and to an extent, in all creation. With righteousness comes the settled assurance that things are as they should be; all is *right*. After Jesus returns, righteousness rains down, effecting a radical metamorphosis of the earth.[15] Righteousness beautifully characterizes the government of the Kingdom (see Isaiah 45:8; 11:4–5). Jerusalem, host city to Messiah's headquarters on earth, is reestablished in righteousness, gaining international renown as the City of Righteousness (see Jeremiah 33:16; Isaiah 1:26). Until all nations see her righteousness, we are not to cease praying for this divine covenant city (see Isaiah 62:1–2).

Righteousness impacts every element of creation and sector of society. Human interactions, from interpersonal relationships to international business deals, are characterized by righteous decisions, just dealings and peaceableness. All creation, which fell and now groans due to humanity's sin, is uplifted and restored through Christ's righteous rule (see Romans 8:19–22). In response to widespread righteousness, the ground itself heals and flourishes (see 2 Chronicles 7:14; Joel 2:21–23; Ezekiel 47:7–12).

Our house in the Negev Desert of Israel is located in a small town surrounded mostly by vast stretches of sand and stubble. Much of the time, the sun is scorching hot; water is a precious commodity in this chronically arid, thirsty environment. As a result, I have special appreciation for prophecies pertaining to streams in the desert. I revel in the reality that is coming:

> The desert and the parched land will be glad; the wilderness will rejoice and blossom. Like the crocus, it will burst into bloom; it will rejoice greatly and shout for joy. . . . Water will gush forth in the wilderness and streams in the desert. The burning sand will become a pool, the thirsty ground bubbling springs. In the haunts where jackals once lay, grass and reeds and papyrus will grow.
>
> Isaiah 35:1, 2, 6–7

Areas of the world that have experienced major spiritual revival occasionally manifest dimensions of this miraculous physical restoration of the land. Otherwise ordinary fruit and vegetable crops have, during periods of revival, spontaneously grown dramatically larger and more abundantly than normal—a foretaste of the Messianic Kingdom age.[16] The time is coming when earth's produce everywhere will be supernaturally plenteous (see Isaiah 30:23–24; 51:3; Jeremiah 31:12; Ezekiel 34:26–27; Zechariah 8:12). Nature will rejoice, bearing bountiful riches (see Joel 2:21–22; Isaiah 14:7–8; Isaiah 55:12–13; Psalm 65:13; 96:12; 98:8).

Under conditions of righteousness and peace, longevity is restored. Natural people in natural bodies (distinct from the resurrected saints) are still young at the age of one hundred. Individuals who die sooner are considered cursed. A normal lifespan equals "the days of a tree," or at least several hundred years (see Isaiah 65:20–22). Supernatural healing becomes commonplace for the sick and injured (see Isaiah 29:18–19; 35:5–6; Ezekiel 47:12). To a spectacular extent, the curse of the Fall radically reverses. Eventually creation resembles the Garden God planted in Eden (see Ezekiel 36:33–36).

Despite this amazingly great glory, the curse of the Fall is not totally revoked. Some disobedience to God still occurs during the Millennium. Natural people continue to sin and die until the time of the new heaven and earth (see Isaiah 2:4a; 54:15; Zechariah 13:3; 14:16–19). For although Satan will have been sentenced to an abyss, human nature is not. Men, women and children retain the priceless gift of free will. Even as peace and righteousness prevail, some still choose to rebel, forcing Messiah to rule by a "rod of iron" (see Psalm 2:9; Revelation 12:5; 19:15). Eventually, this rebellion culminates at the end of the thousand years, in connection with Satan's temporary return. This signals a final judgment and the devil's consignment to an eternal lake of fire (see Revelation 20:7–10). God will have allowed human nature to run its full course, and justice will have been universally served. This grand finale of divine judgment will magnificently showcase His perfect justice.

Just Judge Jesus

In our generation, many are crying out to the King to release His justice to a world (and Church) desperately in need of it. The glories of the age to come and beyond are integrally related to Messiah's manifest justice. After Jesus returns, His administration of justice reflects and mediates His perfection, love and holiness to every city and village on every continent, touching every man, woman and child. An essential attribute of the Divine Personality, justice serves as holy hallmark of the millennial Kingdom (see Isaiah 9:7; 11:3–4; 32:16; 42:1, 4; Psalm 72:1–2; 2 Thessalonians 1:6). It inspires marvel and awe in its brilliant display (see Isaiah 5:16). Together with righteousness, justice forms the foundation of His throne (see Psalm 89:14).

Justice is closely related to righteousness in both Hebrew and Greek biblical thought (see Psalm 33:5; 72:2; Isaiah 11:4; 1:27; 9:7; 32:16; 33:5). Justice is the administration or dispensation of that which is right and virtuous. In traditional Jewish theology, Yahweh's justice is inseparable from His mercy. His judgments are seen as acts of extravagant mercy to uphold righteousness and truth for mankind's own good.[17] For His people in both Old and New Covenants, the idea of judgment is positive and instructive, not negative and injurious. God's holiness and love toward humanity compel, out of mercy, His judgments. He is worshiped—on earth as well as in heaven—for His justice, or His righteous judgments, even during the Great Tribulation (see Revelation 15:3; 16:7).

God's justice is associated with His deliverance. When He judges His enemies, the righteous mercifully are set free. Enslaved Hebrews are released from Egypt, for example, in the context of judgment against their persecutors. After settling in the Promised Land, the Israelites rebel against God. Through His righteous—albeit painful—judgment of exile, they are delivered and restored to right relationship with Him. Many years later, through the crucifixion and resurrection, Yeshua pronounces judgment on His enemies, and the human race is awesomely and astonishingly delivered.

Judgment and its accompanying deliverance begins in the house of the Lord (see 1 Peter 4:17). When judgment comes to us as believers, it is to rouse us toward beneficial change. God is taking us to new levels of Himself, chastening us as a father kindly and wisely chastens his children. He is posturing us, upon our alignment with His will, for blessing (see Hebrews 12:6). Together with Him, the Messianic Warrior Bride is called to mediate justice to the nations. In response to our prayers and prophetic proclamations, He will release righteous judgments and strategies that shake the globe (see Luke 18:1–8; Revelation 5:8; 8:3–4).

Progressive Restoration

Life during the millennial rule of our Bridegroom-King decidedly will not be boring. Human intelligence is restored to pre-Fall proportions. Joy abounds, and so the joy of learning explodes (see Isaiah 12:3–6; 35:6; 55:12; 61:7; Psalm 67:4; 48:2). People from all nations eagerly travel "up to the mountain of the LORD, to the house of the God of Jacob" to be taught of Him. They thirst to learn of His ways and how to walk in them (see Isaiah 2:3; Micah 4:2). According to Isaiah 42:4, "In his law the islands [even remote reaches of the earth barely dotting the sea] will put their hope." Survivors of the Great Tribulation are sent to distant lands to impart revelation of Yeshua's fame and glory. These commissioned ones help gather others back to the King in Jerusalem (see Isaiah 66:19–20).

As humanity learns His ways, the earth is increasingly filled with the knowledge of the Lord. Creativity crescendos as the supernatural and natural, spiritual and secular, converge. No subject of study is dry and dusty, but each proves wonderfully worshipful. Yeshua's personal teachings, from the study of Scripture to the schemata of science, are infinitely more anointed, interesting and life-changing than any you have heard before. His electrifying intelligence, wisdom and understanding of all truth—for He is the Truth—are inexhaustible.

The nations must *learn* of God's ways because earth's restoration during the Millennium does not occur instantaneously. Righteousness, the knowledge of His glory, and more will progressively increase in scope and dimension as people are taught and discipled. In the past, I assumed that because Yeshua would someday descend on the global scene in a divinely sudden moment, voilà, everything would instantly change! He would speak but a word, and immediately all would be made whole. We already have instant meals, instant messaging, even instant divine healing and deliverance. Why not instant world restoration? Is anything too hard for God?

Over the years, however, I have discovered that the Scriptures do not support my rather nice and neat, instant-perfection theory. God's miracles—His sudden break-ins to the human arena that supersede natural law—do not effect widespread change apart from human cooperation. While His supernatural interventions often occur suddenly, the changes they initiate are typically progressive or gradual. Even Creation was a six-day process. The Israelites' dramatic deliverance from Egypt did not quite transpire overnight; it followed a burning bush, ten plagues and a split sea. Their inhabitation of the Promised Land took many years. The Holy Temple was built through natural processes tinged with anointing. The gospels chronicle a miraculous process of atonement for sin through Christ's birth, teachings, crucifixion, resurrection and ascension. His government continually increases; the establishment of His Kingdom on earth is a process.

Accordingly, the Bible does not teach that after Messiah returns, He repeals the natural laws He created and declared good (see Genesis 1:31). Instead, God will enjoy human beings engaging with Him in the ongoing, relational dynamic of restoring and exercising dominion over the earth. While that process began at Yeshua's first coming, it will escalate in the years ahead. After His Second Coming, new anointings and widespread miracles will punctuate the process (see Isaiah 32:15; 44:3). The millennial operation will please God greatly, as long as men submit to His leadership.

Vision for Rehabilitation

At the Second Coming most of the planet will be in tremendous need of rehabilitation. The Antichrist will have wreaked havoc with the earth during the Great Tribulation. His heinous crimes will have resulted in judgments that include perfidious plagues, decimating famines, dreadful wars, treacherous earthquakes and cosmic distresses, as well as downpours of hail, fire and blood. A third of all plant life will have burned up. Bodies of water will have spoiled or turned to blood, causing widespread devastation and death. Locusts and scorpions will have invaded whole regions (see Revelation 6:7–8, 12–14; 8:7, 8–12; 9:3). Over a third of the human population will have been wiped out (see Revelation 9:15, 18). The earth is reeling. Cities are smoldering and nations are in ghastly disarray when Messiah appears on the scene, with us at His side.

In this context the biblical prophets speak of a time of rebuilding, healing and rehabilitation. By all accounts, natural agricultural and architectural processes are involved. Formerly devastated places are rebuilt. People reconstruct cities and repopulate them. Homes are erected and enjoyed. Soils are worked. Families peaceably plant gardens and enjoy their good fruit (see Isaiah 61:4; 60:10; 62:10; 65:21; 30:23; Amos 9:14). Literal leaves from God's tree of life heal the nations (see Ezekiel 47:12; Revelation 22:2).

Meanwhile, you and I are to bear in mind that Scriptures pertaining to millennial restoration also apply, to varying degrees, to Israel and the Church today. God wants us to possess sufficient faith *now* to act on the Word; His Kingdom is *already* at hand. *The fact that pinnacle fulfillment of many prophetic promises is still ahead ought to inspire, rather than inhibit, us to believe now for the supernatural and sacred to invade the natural and secular in ever-increasing anointing.*

Training for Reigning

Resurrected saints will play a thrilling part in overseeing the millennial operation. We will have direct access to Yeshua and heavenly realms. While planetary rehabilitation takes place over time, God's manifest glory is breathtakingly visible and accessible to us from the beginning. Our resurrected bodies will resemble His, possessing both natural and supernatural traits. By delegated authority of the Bridegroom-King, we teach, judge and rule over different designated regions (see Revelation 2:26). We serve in governmental roles, directing splendid rebuilding projects and wide-scale restoration campaigns. As a kingdom of priests, we intercede on behalf of the nations, mediating to them the knowledge of God. To our delight, we continually encounter Him and gain revelation of His ways. Soaked in the anointing of an opened heaven, our hearts are exhilarated and buoyant, not burdened, in millennial ministry with our Beloved.

Meanwhile, survivors of the Great Tribulation will be living in strictly natural bodies (see Zechariah 13:2–5; 14:16–19; Joel 2:32). They will have recently witnessed the most extravagant display ever of God's deliverance at Yeshua's Second Coming. At that time, the unrepentant wicked are evicted from the earth, together with the Antichrist (see Matthew 25:41; Daniel 8:25b; Revelation 19:20–21). Then the survivors who did not align with the Antichrist begin repopulating the planet. They turn to varying levels of faith in Yahweh. The resurrected Bride disciples and advises them of the Wonderful Counselor's will and ways pertaining to every sphere of life. Nations are reestablished in justice, under righteous governments. All kings bow down to Yeshua, and all peoples serve Him. Whether the restoration of all things takes decades or centuries, of this I am certain: You and I will love it here. We will directly behold *Him.*

What should be our response today to God's awe-striking promise for tomorrow? In view of the reality that He will do "immeasurably more than all we ask or imagine," you and I are urged "to live a life worthy of the calling [we] have received" (Ephesians 3:20; 4:1). Yeshua wants us to regularly evaluate our life choices in light of that calling. Since the end of this age is near, we ought to "look forward to the day of God and speed its coming" (2 Peter 3:12). Special reward awaits those who do. The Lord will give "the crown of righteousness . . . to all who have longed for his appearing" (2 Timothy 4:8). Living in light of this blessed hope transforms us and can even expedite its arrival. As a result, greater dimensions of heaven break into earth *now.*

167

The Master took opportunity to motivate His disciples toward right living by helping them keep prophetic Kingdom goals in sight:

> I tell you the truth, at the renewal of all things, when the Son of Man sits on his glorious throne, you who have followed me will also sit on twelve thrones, judging the twelve tribes of Israel. And everyone who has left houses or brothers or sisters or father or mother or children or fields for my sake will receive a hundred times as much and will inherit eternal life.
>
> Matthew 19:28–29

When the Bridegroom-King taught about the age to come, He said we would receive different levels of rewards and positions in heaven, the Millennium and eternity (new heaven and earth). *Your assignments through eternity will be based on your heart's disposition and your deeds during your brief lifespan in this present age* (see Luke 14:14; 2 Corinthians 5:10; 1 Corinthians 3:11–15; Daniel 12:3). Love, humility, faithfulness, meekness and obedience are all key (see Matthew 5:5; 20:25–28; 25:40; Luke 22:24–30). Life here and now is training for reigning. Let us labor for eternal favor!

Prophetic insight into God's stellar plans can greatly encourage us when we undergo difficulty. Particularly at the end of the end times, He wants the Messianic Warrior Bride persevering, empowered by soul-and-spirit-saturating revelation knowledge of Kingdom joys ahead. For that reason, we have focused in this book on the ultimate glory before looking at the global tribulation that must precede it.

In the next and final chapter, we hone in on aspects of the Millennium that are specific to Israel, but already impact the Church worldwide. Following that, we speak of apocalyptic trouble. For the great and dreadful Day of the Lord is near; it is a day of trouble and who can endure it (see Joel 2:1, 11)? We shall see why and how that great, yet dreadful day is so *positively* important to you and me.

10

Standing Firm to the End

Behold, I will create new heavens and a new earth. The former things will not be remembered, nor will they come to mind. But be glad and rejoice forever in what I will create, for I will create Jerusalem to be a delight and its people a joy.

Isaiah 65:17–18

One of my personally prized, hands-on links to Jewish history is a dilapidated Hebrew prayer book printed in Russia in 1890. The timeworn volume belonged to my paternal great-grandfather. It is one of the few possessions he brought to America, before the onset of communism, from back in the days of the czars. Its pages are browned and crinkly; its fiber binding dangles together by a mere dozen or so threads. The book represents the hopes and tears of generations, and I finger through it with fondness.

Comprised mostly of Scriptures, the antique compilation contains the ancient Jewish prayer called the "Mourner's *Kaddish*."[1] This traditional invocation is offered when suffering personal bereavement. The Hebrew word *Kaddish* means "sanctification." God desires to use suffering to sanctify His people, the

Comforter wooing us deeper and deeper into the fire of His holy, jealous love.[2] The "Mourner's *Kaddish*" states, in relevant part:

> Magnified and sanctified be His great Name in the world which He created according to His will. May He establish His kingdom during your life and during your days, and during the life of all the house of Israel, even speedily and at a near time.... May He make peace for us and for all Israel, and let us say, Amen.[3]

It is a proclamation of praise and blessing, amid sorrow, for the joy of the Messianic age ahead.

For thousands of years, Christians as well as Jews have had to stand firm through suffering, just as Jesus foretold. Though times of trouble and distress in this world are inevitable, they pale in comparison to our blessings through ages to come. Many of those blessings will be unleashed, in large part, through Israel.

The Blessing of Israel

The process of earth's millennial regeneration emanates from God's promised restoration of Israel, international hub of spiritual activity. The principle of Romans 2:9–10, "first for the Jew, then for the Gentile," remains in operation. Israel's millennial restoration results from the personal presence of the King of Kings residing there, and directing every stage of its completion. As the Jewish nation is made whole, she ministers in humble service to her Maker and to the Gentile nations. Her position and role[4] do not imply narcissistic nationalism or spiritual superiority, but reflect her irrevocable calling for the benefit of others (see Romans 9:4; 11:29). God does not show favoritism (see Romans 2:11).

For the sake of King Jesus, the nations bless Israel with extravagance (see Isaiah 49:22–23; 60:14–16; 61:6–7; 45:14; 66:12; Zephaniah 3:20). Believers everywhere "sing with joy for Jacob . . . the foremost of the nations" (Jeremiah 31:7). They come to her light on account of He who is the Light (see Isaiah 60:3). They extend service to Israel in reciprocal return for her international ministry of sacrificial service to them: "The nation or kingdom that will not serve you [Israel] will perish; it will be utterly ruined" (Isaiah 60:12). The honor given her is similar to the honor we are told to have for those laboring as servant leaders in the Church (see 1 Thessalonians 5:12–13). Israel herself is never an object of worship.

At this point, perhaps some of you may be tempted to take offense at what God says about Israel's future. Please keep in mind that He uses her to test and expose the intents of the human heart. He is likely to continue to do so even during the Millennium (see Zechariah 14:17–19).

God's restoration of Israel is for the sake of His own great Name. His purpose in honoring her is to demonstrate dimensions of His faithfulness, redemptive nature and merciful justice to the world (see Ezekiel 36:22–23). Indeed, this goal forms the foundation of the Abrahamic covenant, in which Israel is identified as His channel for blessing all peoples of the earth (see Genesis 12:3). One Gentile Christian scholar has commented:

> It is through the glorification of Israel that the glorification of Yahweh is achieved. The sight of the great miracle, which He works for His people in spite of all human probability, makes the other nations submit to Him and . . . worship Him. . . . [T]he other nations share in Israel's . . . blessing.[5]

Do Gentile believers become part of Israel in the Millennium? The Bible says international communities of believers continue to exist at that time, apart from Israel, as distinct nations (see Isaiah 19:23–25; 2:3–4; Zechariah 14:16–19). They retain their own, special redemptive destinies in order to showcase God's manifold personality. However, for Gentile believers who have returned to earth with resurrected bodies, the situation appears different. Though they do not become Jewish, and most probably minister in and to the nations along with many resurrected Jewish believers, they seem to gladly make Jerusalem their home (see Hebrews 12:22; Revelation 3:12; 21:2, 10; Philippians 3:20–21).

Regathering and Revival

A dominant feature of Israel's restoration under Messiah's rule is the pinnacle regathering of Jewish people physically to the land and spiritually to the Lord. The Old Covenant Scriptures are replete with references to this phenomenon, which is affirmed in the New (see Romans 11:1–2, 11–12, 15, 28). The prophet Ezekiel foretells how the Lord lovingly searches for, assembles and heals the lost sheep of His Israeli flock. He will "gather [them] from all the countries and bring [them] back into [their] own land" (Ezekiel 36:24). He enlists the aid of Gentile nations in the operation (see Isaiah 14:2; 43:6; 49:22; 60:4, 9; 66:19–20). The promise is similar to passages of Isaiah, where the Jews are gathered "from the ends of the earth," explicitly from the north, south, east and west (see Isaiah 43:5–6; 49:12). Israel is brought back to her land, "never again to be uprooted" (Amos 9:15; see also Zechariah 9:8). Likewise, never again is Jerusalem overtaken by foreign invaders (see Jeremiah 31:40; Joel 3:17; Zechariah 14:11).

God makes a "covenant of peace" with the Jews in which their surroundings are paradisially transformed (see Ezekiel 34:11–16, 25–29). "Then they will know that I, the LORD their God, am with them and that they, the house of Israel, are my people, declares the Sovereign LORD" (Ezekiel 34:30; see also 34:28–29). Israel's hills, valleys and formerly deserted ruins are secure and abundantly fruitful (see Ezekiel 36:1–15). Speaking specifically to the mountains, the Lord says, "I will cause . . . my people Israel to . . . possess you, and you will be their inheritance; you will never again deprive them of their children" (Ezekiel 36:12).

At this writing, the same Israeli territories just referenced have either been turned over to Arabic peoples or are slated, due to international pressure, to be relinquished soon. Although geopolitical realities can change rapidly in the Middle East, the point is, the prophet speaks of a time of peace that has not been climactically fulfilled. Accompanying this peace is the promise that God will cleanse Israel from her impurities and idols, putting His Spirit in her so she faithfully keeps His laws (see Ezekiel 36:25–27).

To be sure, this last days phenomenon has already begun, and it is marvelous in our eyes. Israel's restoration is an aspect of the "already/not yet" nature of this age. We cannot deny—and should indeed bless—the current reality of Israel's regathering and revival. The Zionist movement of the past century is no mere human endeavor, but an incipient fulfillment of the prophetic Scriptures by the zeal of the Lord of Hosts. (This does not mean that everything accomplished under the rubric of Zionism in this age is in total accord with God's will. The climactic realization of these prophecies in perfect righteousness and justice awaits Messiah's return.) During this "in-between" season of birth pains, however, not all Jews return to Israel. The nation continues to be painfully uprooted, and sadly, its less-than-holy city of Jerusalem still endures division and assault.

As you and I witness and prayerfully bless the "already" dimension of Israel's physical restoration, we must never forget her need for spiritual restoration. Of critical importance to God through history is the salvation of the Jewish people. He is more than willing that all be saved, *now* (see 1 Timothy 2:4). Gentile lovers of Jesus Christ are called to provoke Jews to jealousy for relationship with the Savior (see Romans 11:11). Though Israel's collective national salvation is future, He wants us loving and praying for her, co-laboring in Jewish evangelism, and blessing the growing remnant of believers in Yeshua *now*. This remnant is essential to preparing the way for Jerusalem's future, prophetic invitation that will welcome Him back.

Amid global birth pains, God cautions the nations—including the Church and even Israel herself—not to scatter or slaughter His ancient covenant people (see Joel 3:2; Obadiah 1:10, 14; Zechariah 12:9). We are not to wrongly divide up their land, dispossess them of it or refrain from helping them in times of distress (see Ezekiel 36:4–7; Joel 3:2). When their troubles increase in years ahead, so will opportunities to extend practical aid and comfort. There will be a cost, but also a reward. The King will judge us, as we saw in chapter 2, for how faithful we have been to heed His heart for Zion (see Obadiah 1:10–15; Matthew 25:31–40; Genesis 12:3; Romans 11:20b–21).

Messiah's Millennial Temple

You and I, as regenerate believers in Jesus in whom the Holy Spirit dwells, have been given great honor. In astounding affirmation of the value He places on these mortal houses of clay, our bodies serve as temples of God's Spirit (see 1 Corinthians 6:19). At the same time, the Creator of the Universe has a holy Temple in heaven. Yet that is not all. When Yeshua returns, He takes up residence in a glorious Temple situated on Jerusalem's Mount Zion (see Ezekiel 40:2; Isaiah 2:2–3; Micah 4:1; Joel 3:17). This material Temple will be a spectacular structure, an architectural wonder beyond human imagination. It will magnificently and mysteriously converge with the Temple in heaven.

The Hebrew prophets were given resplendent revelation of the millennial Temple. They viewed a palatial compound vastly larger in size and exceedingly more majestic than either the first or second Temple. God's glory, the *Shekhinah*, returns to Israel and fills this future house (see Ezekiel 43:2–5). Says the Lord, "This is the place of my throne and the place for the soles of my feet. This is where I will live among the Israelites forever" (Ezekiel 43:7). The verse describes the literal, ruling presence of Yahweh Incarnate in the Person of Jesus. His Davidic throne is connected to the *Shekhinah* in the holy of holies. From it He reigns as King of all kings of all nations.

Because His Temple rests atop Mount Zion,[6] it becomes the "chief" mountain in the world (Isaiah 2:2). It is raised high above all others;[7] every nation streams to it. The Lord creates over

Mount Zion a thick cloud of incense-like smoke by day, and a brilliant glow of blazing fire by night. Covering this splendiferous reality is a canopy of yet still greater glory (see Isaiah 4:5).

The Temple contains a holy sanctuary and an altar at which designated Levitical priests minister directly to Yahweh (see Ezekiel 43:15–20; 44:15–16). Messiah-centered oblations take place in worshipful commemoration of His once-for-all act of redemption.[8] Flowing out from the sacred sanctuary, under the Temple and into the City of Jerusalem, then eastward, is a river reviving the region with life (see Ezekiel 47:1–12; Zechariah 14:8). Radiating from here across the earth is the wonder-stirring beauty and awe of the personal presence of Messiah Bridegroom-King. Ah, the splendor ahead!

The Bible indicates this Temple will probably not be the next, third temple that religious Jews are intent on rebuilding. Scholars agree that the biblical dimensions of the future Temple compound in Ezekiel 40–46 far exceed the geographic boundaries of Israel's Temple Mount.[9] In fact, there is not room anywhere in the modern City of Jerusalem to accommodate a temple that meets these titanic, biblical proportions. When the Lord returns, however, Israel's topography shifts significantly. Earthquakes and changes in the landscape could at that time easily provide ample space to house the prophetic superstructure.

A second reason the next temple will likely not be the millennial Temple is that the overseer of the millennial Temple's construction is described in specific Hebrew terminology used to refer to Messiah (see Zechariah 6:12–13). It seems quite a stretch for Him to occupy counterfeit quarters defiled—and possibly built by—the Antichrist (see Daniel 11:31; Matthew 24:15; 2 Thessalonians 2:4).

Millennial Jerusalem

Jesus' millennial Temple will serve as apex of a revived Jerusalem that greatly surpasses any grandeur the city has known.

God dwells in the midst of her and at the same time is a wall of fire around her (see Zechariah 2:5). The entire city is raised dramatically in elevation, reflecting her convergence with the heavenly (see Psalm 48:1–2). Sin is purged from the place; Jerusalem's residents are all holy to the Lord (see Isaiah 4:3–4). Her righteousness radiates as shining brilliance; her salvation, like a blazing torch. God is thoroughly enthralled with her. In His hand, she is transformed into a glistening "crown of splendor" (Isaiah 62:3; see also 62:2, 4–5, 7). Jerusalem is no longer the problem, but the praise and joy of all the earth (see Psalm 48:2). Formerly a war zone, she becomes the world's great comfort zone (see Isaiah 66:13). Conflict stays far from her. Jerusalem's streets bustle with dancing and laughter, the joy of brides and bridegrooms, and the exuberant worship of multitudes (see Jeremiah 33:11). Peoples of the earth organize tours to Jerusalem to entreat her King. "Let us go at once," they say to their friends. "I myself am going" (Zechariah 8:21).

The stunning character of Jerusalem is reflected in her new name, "The LORD is There" (Ezekiel 48:35). From the city a far-reaching river of revival flows, teeming with life (see Ezekiel 47:1–12; Psalm 46:4; Zechariah 14:8). The majestic beauty, love and wisdom, celebrated justice and celestial grandeur of Jerusalem's King ripples across the city and abroad to the nations. Kings and peoples of the earth are drawn magnetically to Zion to learn of Yeshua. From Him they gain grace and skill to implement earth's divinely directed, magnificent metamorphosis (see Isaiah 2:2–5).[10]

Traditional Jewish interpretation of the Scriptures identifies two Jerusalems, one above and one below (see Galatians 4:26). Jerusalem above is expected to come to earth, superimposing itself somehow upon the concrete, Middle Eastern city below. This basic rabbinic concept fits well with New Covenant eschatology.[11] As a result, Jews who do not yet know Jesus are unwittingly joining believers from the nations who do, both groups already aligning in prophetic intercession for this future city and age to come.

The present heavenly City of Jerusalem is where the spirits of deceased believers now ascend (see Hebrews 11:10; 12:22–23; John 14:2–3). There they worship, serve and await their return with Jesus to earth. At that time, which corresponds to the start of the Millennium, heavenly Jerusalem converges to a considerable (but not complete) extent with earthly Jerusalem (see Revelation 3:12; 21:9–10). Jesus' Davidic throne intersects with His heavenly throne. The holy of holies in the material Temple overlaps with the holy of holies in heaven. This intersection and overlap has been described by some contemporary Christian leaders as a "corridor of glory."

The corridor of glory encompasses Mount Zion, Jerusalem, the Temple, throne, river, smoke, fire, cloud and more. Resurrected saints will experience both heaven and earth realms (including both Jerusalems) to varying degrees, for a thousand years. After the millennial age, when the new heaven and new earth[12] are established, then the Jerusalem of above *completely* manifests and *completely* converges with the physical city below, resulting in the New Jerusalem (see Revelation 21:1–4; 2 Peter 3:13; Isaiah 65:17). It is a concept not unlike the "already/not yet" of this present age. Because of the overlapping nature of these realities, sometimes we—like the biblical prophets and Jesus' first disciples—are not able to clearly distinguish every detail between the Millennium and the new, eternal state. However, one fact is certain: It will be glory upon glory, forever and ever!

But first, there must be tribulation such as the world has never known (see Matthew 24:21; Daniel 12:1).

The Great Tribulation

The Hebrew prophets foretell a season of incomparable distress to be experienced by Israel and the nations, including the people of God. Sometimes called the Day of the Lord or the Day of Jacob's Trouble, this period is marked by unprecedented upheaval and judgment that far exceeds a single, 24-hour day.

As an observant Jew, I grew up with this concept—which always ended, thankfully, with the promise of God's eventual deliverance and blessing. When I came to faith in Yeshua many years later, I was surprised to hear that now, should it unfold in my lifetime, I would escape the whole sordid scenario. As a believer, apparently I qualified for a fast exit out of here before the apocalyptic onset of trouble. Certainly all the Christian prophecy charts pointed to it. Even my seminary professors agreed it would be so.

People are pleased to think they need not prepare for the sacrament of suffering. Who among us wants to experience pain? Problem was, the biblical facts as I read them did not line up with popular evangelical thought. Try as I might, I could find no clear guarantee against trial or tribulation in my Bible. Personally, I want to know God and the truth of His ways with integrity. As a teacher of the Word with a prophetic calling, I want to see His cherished ones fulfill their destiny with extravagant joy. As a result, I love studying Scriptures on the end times and even the Great Tribulation. I openly admit to not having a handle on every detail—who does? My worshipful study of the subject will likely prove lifelong. For now, time and space permit for only a brief glance at these unparalleled events so positively important to God's unfolding plan.[13] It is my prayer that you will approach the subject with a fresh anointing that endues you with faith-filled, forerunning vision.

Summary of Main Events

The Great Tribulation refers to the cataclysmic, seven-year period taking place at the very end of this age. It starts with a powerful global leader making a treaty with Israel involving a purported peace plan (see Daniel 9:27; 1 Thessalonians 5:3; Jeremiah 6:14). In the New Covenant, this leader is given the name Antichrist (see 1 John 2:18). The title suits him well; he is quite the opposite of, and counterfeit to, Jesus the Christ.[14] Under his auspices Israel operates—and possibly constructs—their third temple in Jerusalem. The former sacrificial system of atonement for sin according to the Law of Moses is by then reinstated. Unfortunately, these rituals deny the power of the blood of Yeshua and thereby fuel the mounting anti-Christian climate.

Halfway through the Antichrist's heinous reign, he breaks covenant with Israel and bans the Temple sacrifices. With supernatural signs and wonders, and pointing to his political, economic and military prowess—all of which are satanically inspired—he declares himself God. He demands to be worshiped and obeyed. He commits the "abomination of desolation" by desecrating the holy of holies in the third temple, possibly seating himself on a type of throne (see Matthew 24:15; Daniel 8:13; 9:27; 2 Thessalonians 2:4; Revelation 13:8–17). Outraged, the Jews reject his abhorrent claim to deity. As a result, they become the worldwide target of his unbridled, vicious fury.

Before the abomination of desolation, the Antichrist has venomously detested and murderously persecuted many Christians, Jews and others daring to oppose him. Some believers do not endure; tragically, they fall from faith (see Matthew 24:9–14; 2 Thessalonians 2:3). At this point, however ghastly things have been, matters get horrifically worse. The Antichrist now becomes fully animated and possessed by Satan. Satan, remember, is scrambling to prevent his own impending demise at Yeshua's Second Coming (see Revelation 12:7, 11–17). The result is earth's most evil of evil events—a full-blast international campaign against God and humanity that no one would survive, if not for His promised shortening of that time (see Matthew 24:22).

The second half of the Great Tribulation brings with it a unique release from heaven of God's judgments. These are signaled by seven seals, followed by seven trumpets, and finally, the outpouring of God's seven bowls of holy wrath. It is in connection with the ongoing prayers and prophetic proclamations of the saints that these judgments are released (see Revelation 5:8). Many believers are supernaturally protected during this time (see Revelation 7:2–4; 9:4; 12:6, 14; Exodus 8:22–23; Zephaniah

2:3). As 1 Thessalonians 5:9 and other Bible passages assure, God has not appointed us to suffer His wrath.

Christians are not necessarily protected, however, from the hellish fury of the Antichrist, and we should distinguish between the two. Because of his satanic rage, countless numbers of believers are martyred—and then eternally, exquisitely rewarded (see Revelation 6:11; 13:7; 16:6; 17:6). At the same time, there is a tremendous outpouring of the Holy Spirit, and multitudes come to faith in Yeshua (see Matthew 24:14; Joel 2:28–32; Revelation 7:9–14; 11:3–6; 14:6; Haggai 2:6–7; Romans 11:26). The birth pains we presently experience are related to the increase and polarization of good and evil that will crescendo in this manner in the Great Tribulation.

God is in complete control throughout these seven years (see Revelation 17:17; Matthew 28:18; Isaiah 54:16; Romans 13:1). The time is identified as the Day of the *Lord*, not the day of the devil. During this season of severest trial, the Lord is continuously worshiped in heaven—*and on earth.* The saints experience His powerful presence despite all hell breaking loose. The Great Tribulation is also the great attestation to His sovereign glory and loving justice (see Revelation 4:11; 5:9–14; 7:11–12; 11:13; 14:3, 15–18; 15:2–4; 16:5–7; 19:1–7).

The Messianic Warrior Bride trusting God will be given special grace to patiently endure. The battle will prove so fierce the Antichrist will almost overcome her (see Daniel 7:21; Revelation 13:7, 10; 14:12). Yet it is through this viperous onslaught that she is refined and purified as gold. In the Great Tribulation she is made ready for the Beloved, without wrinkle or blemish, altogether pleasing in His sight (see Revelation 19:7; Ephesians 5:26–27; Daniel 11:33–35; 1 Peter 4:1). In the crucible of her suffering, she enters into the uniquely intimate "fellowship of sharing in his sufferings" and emerges in "the power of his resurrection" (Philippians 3:10). Critical to her transformation has been her unflinching love for, and practical help to, the Jewish people (see Matthew 25:40; Isaiah 40:1–2; Genesis 12:3).

The Rap on the Rapture

Deliverance for the Church comes at a precise moment known only to the Father. At that time, those standing firm are celestially caught up in the Rapture to meet Christ Jesus in the air (see 1 Thessalonians 4:13–18; 1 Corinthians 15:51–52; Matthew 24:30–31, 39–40; 2 Thessalonians 2:1–2). In this context, the long-awaited and thrilling marriage supper of the Lamb likely takes place (see Revelation 19:7–9).

Faithful believers who do not experience physical death will enter the heavenly realm by way of the Rapture. I like to think of the Rapture in connection with the beautiful, ancient Jewish wedding traditions described in chapter 4. Recall that a betrothed young woman (*kiddushin* or "set apart one") would zealously prepare to go out and meet her beloved, together with her attendants, when he came to take her away to the place he had prepared. The bride would not know precisely when he would come, but she would eagerly anticipate his return.[15] The couple would consummate their union in a manner represented by the marriage supper of the Lamb. Then they would emerge, rejoin the larger community and function as one. So it will be with the Church that is raptured and then returns to earth with Yeshua.

In the past hundred or so years, many in the Western Church have been taught they will be evacuated in the Rapture before the onset of the Great Tribulation. Recently, however, some contemporary Christian leaders have reexamined this position. Among them is my friend Don Finto. In his popular book, *Your People Shall Be My People*,[16] Finto says the words of Scripture do not give us a guarantee of escape. He compares three different Greek words; two of them, *orge* and *thumos*, are translated "wrath," while the third, *thlipsis*, is translated "tribulation." *Thlipsis* is also translated "anguish, sufferings, distress, persecution, or trouble." The New Covenant frequently uses this third word to warn believers they are not exempt from hard times, such as in Matthew 24:29 and Revelation 7:14, both of which refer to the Great Tribulation.

For this and other reasons, Finto concludes that while the saints do not experience the outpouring of God's wrath, the period of *thlipsis* could find us still very much here. He writes:

> I could be wrong, but I would rather be prepared for the worst and be delivered than to be caught off guard. Come to think of it, if the Lord will allow me sufficient strength, I would like to be here to serve during those perilous times.[17]

After many years of prayer and study, I must agree with Don Finto. A Rapture occurring toward the close of the Great Tribulation, I am convinced, fits best with the whole canon of Scripture, and in particular, with eschatological passages in both Old and New Covenants. For these same reasons, most believers through Church history have understood, together with the Jews, that God has appointed them to stand firm in the future time of great trouble.

I expect some of you to disagree with me on this particular point. While I sincerely hope you will be challenged, I have written this chapter—and book—so that you need not agree with my timing of the Rapture to benefit greatly from *Israel's Anointing*. Regardless of your eschatology, you will gain revelation of God's heart and ways. You will be encouraged and empowered in your present, everyday life in Him. For although Jesus has overcome this world, in it we must all have *some* form of *some* tribulation (see John 16:33, KJV). Plain and simple, tribulation is an inevitable part of the Master's plan of love, for which faithful believers will ultimately be eternally grateful (see 2 Corinthians 4:17).

Israel in the Great Tribulation

During the Great Tribulation, Israel as a nation is devastatingly overrun (see Daniel 8:9; 11:45; 12:7). Most of us there will be grievously exiled and imprisoned, our lands forcibly taken and our lives sacrificed *en masse*. (As bad as this will be, it is not reason in itself for Jewish people not to live in Israel or move there in the future. During the Great Tribulation, *all* nations will suffer terribly at the hands of the Antichrist.) Through this worst genocidal attack in history, God preserves a remnant of Israel, both in the Holy Land and abroad (see Zechariah 13:8–9; 14:2; Isaiah 11:11–16; Revelation 12:13–17). Some of the saints offer loving assistance to refugee Jews, which pleases Him greatly (see Matthew 25:40). Their witness helps bring many to faith in Yeshua, including 144,000 "offered as firstfruits" (Revelation 14:4). At the Rapture, Messianic Jews are caught up together with Gentile believers. Non-Messianic Jewish leaders left behind are being prepared to call on the Name of Yeshua at a soon coming, singular moment. The staunch, prayerful support and kind witness of the Messianic Warrior Bride will have been used by God to ready Israel for this climactic event.

In the second half of the Great Tribulation, the Antichrist's fanatical focus is his military campaign at Armageddon and the battle over Jerusalem. Although his real target is not Israel, but her coming King, he has fiendishly beaten down the Jews (see Revelation 16:14; 17:14; 19:19). Desperate for deliverance, Jerusalem's leaders cry out to Yeshua to save them (see Romans 11:26).[18]

The Mighty One of Israel emerges from the sky, splendidly outfitted for this consummate battle. Declaring, "I am the Root and the Offspring of David," He has not relinquished His physical identity as a Jew (Revelation 22:16). With Him are multitudes of His holy ones, angelic hosts together with the Bride. The resurrected saints are actively alongside their King as He delivers His ancient covenant people.

The blessed hope of the Church regarding Yeshua's Second Coming is not that we are leaving, but that He is returning and Satan is leaving. Most of us are destined to depart first for the celestial paradise of heaven through the portal of physical death. But heaven is not our permanent abode. The Bridegroom-King is headed for a comeback—and therefore, so are we.

When we return with Yeshua, every eye observes the astounding, holy procession emerging from the sky. Messiah's reappearance with us from heaven is global in size and scope. This colossal company seems to circle the planet as a final witness to humanity of the Way. Amazingly, however, many people refuse to repent, following the Antichrist to the bitter end. Together with him, they persist in their rage against God. The nations are so deceived by now that they are convinced Jesus, despite His majestic, visible appearing, is the bad guy. The war of the worlds is on.

Yeshua returns to Israel, setting foot on the Mount of Olives, causing a mammoth-sized earthquake. Messiah then marches across land, delivering the Jews (see Isaiah 63:1–6; Zechariah 14:3–5; Revelation 16:18–19). He directs a spectacular defeat of the anti-God nations allied at Armageddon, and in a brilliant show of supernatural might, wins the definitive battle for Jerusalem (see Zechariah 12:2–9; 14:2–3; Joel 3:1–2, 9–17). Resurrected saints take part in this incomparable military conflagration. Yeshua then sentences Satan and his cohorts to the abyss for a thousand years (see Revelation 20:2–3). Regathering repentant, exiled Jewish survivors, Messiah proceeds to judge the nations. Using their treatment of Israel as a critical test, He casts some from His presence forever (see Matthew 25:31–46). Many individuals who come to faith after the Rapture, or who paid no homage to the Antichrist, are allowed to stay and participate in the millennial Kingdom. They are known in Scripture as "survivors" of the Great Tribulation or Day of the Lord (see Zechariah 14:16; Isaiah 4:2; 10:20; Joel 2:32). Soon they repopulate the earth with children who are also natural human beings.

Why the Tribulation?

Some have been taught that the purpose of the Great Tribulation is strictly punitive. God is angry and can no longer restrain Himself. At long last, He spews out vengeance accumulated since the Fall of mankind. But I am convinced God's purposes are much broader and grander, focused primarily on glorifying our

Bridegroom-King. We will be encouraged and empowered in the years ahead to the extent we connect to the fuller meaning of His positively good, prophetic plans through the Great Tribulation.

Pastor and author Mike Bickle sees at least seven purposes of God (there are likely more) in the Great Tribulation:

> First, God will use the Great Tribulation to purify His people, causing the Church to be as a bride prepared to walk in God's glory without any compromise. God's judgments will remove all that hinders love. . . . Second, [He] will use [it] to cause unbelievers to respond to His grace as eternity bears down on their hearts. He will usher in a great ingathering of souls and Israel's salvation. . . . Third, God will . . . vindicate the saints as He avenges their deaths. . . . Fourth, He demonstrates His power to protect His people as He did in the days of Moses in . . . Goshen. . . . Fifth, God will use the Tribulation to expose false believers within the Church. . . . Sixth, [He] allows evil to be fully manifest and then expresses His justice and righteousness in punishing people for choosing sin. . . . Seventh, God will use [the Great Tribulation] to purge and cleanse the earth from sin before the Millennial Kingdom.[19]

The Great Tribulation is therefore not only the most extensive torture, but the most excellent triumph. Those able to grasp this "divine tension" will remain at peace. During that time, they will focus on ultimate Kingdom expansion, praying forth a great harvest of souls. Ablaze in holiness, they will move under tremendous mantles for evangelism with signs and wonders. Many will be divinely protected; many will be given the blessed gift of martyrdom. In any case, the Messianic Warrior Bride will not hopelessly resign herself to a passive role. She will love to the death, if need be, knowing the former is as strong as the latter.

When the Tribulation?

A biblical perspective on the apocalyptic events associated with Yeshua's Second Coming is prophetically opened to us

Levitical fall feasts. The Hebrew word translated "feast" nically means "appointed time." The feasts are appointed nes or established dates in God's calendar as He relates to humanity. Many believers already know that pinnacle events associated with His first coming—His crucifixion, burial, resurrection and outpouring of the Holy Spirit—all perfectly coincided *to the very day* with all the Levitical spring feasts.[20] Because Yeshua fulfilled all the spring feasts the first time He came, is it not likely He will fulfill all the fall feasts the second time He comes?

Personally, I expect the events of Yeshua's return may perfectly coincide, to the very day, with the Levitical fall feasts: the Feast of Trumpets, the Day of Atonement and the Feast of Tabernacles (see Leviticus 23:23–43). Not coincidentally, these feasts all take place in the seventh month of the biblical calendar. In Scripture, the number seven, as we have seen, represents completion. Fulfillment of the fall feasts will relate to the completion of this present age.

The Feast of Trumpets (*Yom Teruah*) is occasioned by the blowing of trumpets. Occurring the first day of the seventh month, its purposes are to sound an alarm, summon God's people to attention, herald His judgments and proclaim His Kingship. Accordingly, during the Great Tribulation, angels in heaven are given seven trumpets to blow that are related to these purposes (see Revelation 8:2, 6–12; 9:1, 13; 11:15). The sound of a trumpet also heralds the Rapture and resurrection of deceased saints (see Matthew 24:29–31; 1 Corinthians 15:51–52; 1 Thessalonians 4:13–17). The Feast of Trumpets may well be fulfilled, in the context of the Great Tribulation, at the trumpet call associated with believers meeting the Lord in the air.

The Day of Atonement (*Yom Kippur*) occurs ten days after the Feast of Trumpets. The day of Israel's national repentance, judgment and salvation, *Yom Kippur* would naturally be looked to by the Jewish people as a day of deliverance. Its climactic fulfillment could prophetically take place in connection with

Jerusalem's future repentance and Israel's salvation. Five days later, the Feast of Tabernacles (*Sukkot*) represents God's final harvest. It also celebrates His provision and dwelling with His people. *Sukkot*, therefore, seems a perfectly fitting time for Yeshua's personal habitation among us to be celebrated. As earth-shaking as the fulfillments of the spring feasts were, I believe that consummation of the fall feasts will magnificently eclipse them![21]

And then . . . after all these things and the glory of a thousand years, what next?

New Heaven and New Earth

As Yeshua's thousand-year rule draws to a close, Satan is released from prison and allowed to deceive the nations one last time. Individuals born during the Millennium, under Messiah's righteous rule, will never have experienced the opportunity for evil to flourish openly. But now God gives humankind a final test. Sadly, once more an insurrection takes place against the King, led by an unrepentant Satan and his cohorts. War ensues—briefly. In a swift demonstration of supreme justice, Yeshua defeats his enemies. He casts them, together with death itself, into an eternal lake of fire (see Revelation 20:7–15; 1 Corinthians 15:26).

The scene that follows, recorded by the apostle John, is matchless in its splendor, the total climactic fulfillment of God's Kingdom:

> Then I saw a new heaven and a new earth, for the first heaven and the first earth had passed away. . . . I saw the Holy City, the new Jerusalem, coming down out of heaven from God, prepared as a bride beautifully dressed for her husband. And I heard a loud voice from the throne saying, "Now the dwelling of God is with men, and he . . . himself will be with them . . . for the old order of things has passed away."
>
> Revelation 21:1–4

If you soak in the dizzying promise of this resplendent reality, you may find that, like me, you cannot help but weep in awestruck adoration of the One Most High.

How can natural words describe a staggering, whole new order of things? Intrinsically mysterious to mere men, a stupendously distinct mode of existence has been conceived and hidden through the ages deep in the mind of the Godhead. Such is *your* destiny as Messiah's Bride.

As part of this new order, "After he has destroyed all dominion, authority and power," the Son of Man/Son of God "hands over the kingdom to God the Father" (1 Corinthians 15:24).

I invite you to meditate with me by the Spirit on what your Jewish Bridegroom-King is about to do for *you*, His prized, beloved espoused. In His own Words, you who overcome will be God's own son or daughter and inherit all this (see Revelation 21:7, 9):

- The holy, eternal city of Jerusalem, dazzling with celestial glory like a diamond the size of a continent, bedecked by twelve stunningly jeweled, gargantuan gates—with Jewish names—perpetually open to you (see Revelation 21:9–12, 16–21, 25)
- The Holy Temple that *is* Yahweh Almighty and the Lamb (see Revelation 21:22–23)
- The most excellent garden of life, surpassing Eden (see Revelation 22:1–5, 17, 19)
- The incomprehensibly magnificent *Face of God*! (see Revelation 22:4)

When the apostle John was shown these things, the beloved friend of Jesus had but one response: worship (see Revelation 22:8). Even as I write, I cannot do otherwise. Would you join me, together with "every creature in heaven and on earth and under the earth" in singing:

To him who sits on the throne and to the Lamb be praise and honor and glory and power, for ever and ever! . . . Amen.

Revelation 5:13–14

In Conclusion

It is written, "No eye has seen, no ear has heard, no mind has conceived what God has prepared for those who love him" (1 Corinthians 2:9). The fullness of God's character, conduct and creation exceeds our present physical perception and language. I have shared what has been seen only in part, heard in part and conceived in part (see 1 Corinthians 13:12). For too long, much of this partial revelation has been hidden from the Church. It is my prayer that through this book, new dimensions of heaven on earth have been opened for you. These pages have imparted keys to unlock storerooms of ancient anointings. May you run with those keys, accessing your full inheritance and destiny in God!

Perhaps some readers have never surrendered their lives to Jesus. Others may have assumed they were Christians, but now, at the end of this book, realize they are not. In any case, you can make peace with God right here and now. To follow the One who loves you more than you can possibly imagine, you need only sincerely admit to Him that you, like the rest of us, have sinned. Ask God to forgive you on account of Messiah Jesus' atonement, made once for all time, for the sin of all mankind. As an act of your will, surrender your life to Him. Ask Him to fill you with His Spirit, who will empower you to live according to *His* will. Then rejoice! According to the Scriptures, you have just been born anew (see John 3:3). Thank God for the amazing gift of salvation and eternal life! And one more thing: Please contact a local, Bible-believing congregation, a Christian friend or our ministry, to help you get off to a solid start in your relationship with the Bridegroom-King. Meanwhile, I welcome you into the family of God!

Together in the Messianic Warrior Bride company, let us covenant to give ourselves fully to the One who so extravagantly gives Himself to us. As heaven increasingly converges with earth, may we run as one body of Gentile and Jewish believers, each preferring the other above ourselves. In the fire of Messiah's affections and by the kiss of His Word, may we rest as we run in His Sabbath *shalom*. May we access heaven through highways of holiness, mediating the laws of His Kingdom. Then, through the supernaturally natural, Israel, the Church and the nations will be transformed. Birth pains preceding Jesus' return will intensify; His Kingdom does not advance without enemy opposition. But God's people will prevail. Then the greatest reformation of all will take place as the planet is restored to paradise. *Don't miss it!*

Bibliography

Alexander, Ralph H. "Ezekiel." *Expositor's Bible Commentary: Isaiah–Ezekiel.* Edited by Frank E. Gaebelein. Grand Rapids: Zondervan, 1986.

Amnesty International. *Amnesty Annual Report 2007.* http://thereport.amnesty.org.

Argyle, A. W. "Wedding Customs at the Time of Jesus." *Expository Times* 86 (1975): 214–15.

Arintero, Juan Gonzalez. *The Song of Songs: A Mystical Exposition.* Translated by James Valendar and Jose L. Morales. Rockford, Ill.: TAN Books and Publishers, Inc., 1992.

Austin, Jill. *Dancing with Destiny: Awaken Your Heart to Dream, to Love, to War.* Grand Rapids: Chosen Books, 2007.

Bacchiocchi, Samuele. *From Sabbath to Sunday: A Historical Investigation of the Rise of Sunday Observance in Early Christianity.* Rome: Pontifical Gregorian University Press, 1977.

Baron, Salo W. *The Russian Jew under Tsars and Soviets.* New York: Macmillan, 1976.

Berkowitz, Ariel, and Dvorah Berkowitz. *Torah Rediscovered: Challenging Centuries of Misinterpretation and Neglect.* Littleton, Colo.: First Fruits of Zion, Inc., 1996.

Bernis, Jonathan. "Jews Need Jesus." *Charisma*, December 2006: 14.

Bickle, Mike. International House of Prayer. http://www.ihop.org.

———. *Omega: End Times Teaching.* Kansas City, Mo.: Forerunner Books, 2006.

Bieler, Yakov. "Shir haShirim in Light of Sabbath and Yom Tov," April 2004. http://www.kmsynagogue.org/, quoting Rabbi Akiva ben Yosef.

Birnbaum, Philip. *A Book of Jewish Concepts.* New York: Hebrew Publishing Co., 1964.

Bloch, S., S. Rivaud, and C. Martinoya. "Comparing Frontal and Lateral Viewing in the Pigeon: Different Patterns of Eye Movements for Binocular and Monocular Fixation." *Behavioral Brain Research* 13, no. 2 (August 1984): 173–82.

Blood of the Martyrs. *Reformation Theology.* http://www.reformation theology.com.

Blough, Patricia M. "Cognitive Strategies and Foraging in Pigeons." *Avian Visual Cognition,* R. G. Cook. Medford, Mass.: Comparative Cognition Press, 2001. http://www.pigeon.psy.tufts.edu.

Bonhoeffer, Dietrich. *The Cost of Discipleship.* New York: Simon & Schuster, 1995.

Booker, Richard. *Here Comes the Bride.* The Woodlands, Tex.: Sounds of the Trumpet, Inc., 1995.

Bristow, John T. *What Paul Really Said about Women.* New York: HarperSanFrancisco, 1991.

Brown, Francis, S. R. Driver, and Charles A. Briggs. *A Hebrew and English Lexicon of the Old Testament.* Oxford: Clarendon Press, 1980.

Brown, Dr. Michael L. *Answering Jewish Objections to Jesus.* Vol. 1–4. Grand Rapids: Baker Books, 2007.

Bruce, F. F. *The Epistle of Paul to the Romans.* Grand Rapids: Eerdmans, 1978.

Catholic Answers. http://www.catholic.com.

Clouse, Robert G., ed. *The Meaning of the Millennium.* Downers Grove, Ill.: InterVarsity, 1977.

Coalition Against Trafficking in Women. http://www.catwinternational.org.

Cohen, Abraham. *Everyman's Talmud: The Major Teachings of the Rabbinic Sages.* New York: Schocken Books, 1995.

Cranfield, C. E. B. *A Critical and Exegetical Commentary on the Epistle to the Romans.* Vol. 2. Edinburgh: T & T Clark, 1979.

Cunningham, Loren, and David J. Hamilton. *Why Not Women? A Biblical Study of Women in Missions, Ministry and Leadership.* Seattle, Wash.: YWAM Publishing, 2000.

Curtiss, John S. *The Russian Church and the Soviet State: 1900–1917.* New York: Octagon Books, 1972.

Decker, Mike. "Messianic Jews and the Law of Return." *Israel Today,* 24 September, 2007. http://www.israeltoday.co.il.

de Graaf, John, David Wann, and Thomas Naylor. *Affluenza.* San Francisco: Berrett-Koehler Publishers, 2001.

Earhart, H. Byron, ed. *Religious Traditions of the World: A Journey through Africa, Mesoamerica, North America, Judaism, Christianity, Islam, Hinduism, Buddhism, China and Japan.* San Francisco: HarperSanFrancisco, 1993.

Edwards, Gene, ed. *Experiencing the Depths of Jesus Christ.* Goleta, Calif.: Christian Books, 1975.

Elwell, Walter A., ed. *Baker Encyclopedia of the Bible.* Grand Rapids: Baker Books, 1988.

Engelhard, Jack. "First, the Saturday People." *Arutz Sheva,* 15 September 2003. http://www.israelnationalnews.com.

Fee, Gordon D. and Douglas Stuart. *How to Read the Bible for All It's Worth.* Grand Rapids: Zondervan, 1982.

Feinberg, Charles L. *Jeremiah: A Commentary.* Grand Rapids: Zondervan, 1982.

Ferguson, E. "The Terminology of Kingdom in the Second Century." *Studia Patristica,* 17:670, edited by Elizabeth A. Livingstone. Oxford: Pergamon Press, 1982.

Finney, Charles G. "Religion of the Law and Gospel." Lecture IV, 1837. http://www.gospeltruth.net.

Finto, Don. *God's Promise and the Future of Israel.* Ventura, Calif.: Regal Books, 2005.

———. *Your People Shall Be My People.* Ventura, Calif.: Regal Books, 2001.

Frankel, Ellen, and Betsy Platkin Teutsch. *Encyclopedia of Jewish Symbols.* Northvale, N.J.: Jason Aronson Inc., 1995.

Freeman, James M. *The New Manners and Customs of the Bible.* Edited by Harold Chadwick. Orlando, Fla.: Bridge-Logos, 1998.

Freund, Michael. "In Praise of Christian Zionists." *International Jerusalem Post,* 5–11 January 2007: 23.

Friedman, David. *They Loved the Torah: What Yeshua's Followers Really Thought about the Law.* Baltimore: Lederer Books, 2001.

Fruchtenbaum, Arnold G. *Israelology: The Missing Link in Systematic Theology.* Tustin, Calif.: Ariel Ministries Press, 1989.

Gaebelein, Frank E., ed. *The Expositor's Bible Commentary.* Vol. 6. Grand Rapids: Zondervan, 1986.

Garrett, Duane. "Song of Songs." *World Biblical Commentary,* edited by Bruce Metzger, David A. Hubbard, and Glenn Barber. Nashville, Tenn.: Thomas Nelson, 2004.

Gilbert, Lela. "Natural Allies in a Dangerous World." *International Jerusalem Post,* 12 October 2007: 13.

Goll, James W. *Intercession: The Power and the Passion to Shape History.* Shippensburg, Pa.: Destiny Image, 2003.

———. *Praying for Israel's Destiny.* Grand Rapids: Chosen Books, 2005.

———. *The Prophetic Intercessor,* Grand Rapids: Chosen Books, 2007.

Grady, J. Lee. *Ten Lies the Church Tells Women.* Lake Mary, Fla.: Charisma House, 2006.

———. *Twenty-Five Tough Questions about Women and the Church.* Lake Mary, Fla: Charisma House, 2003.

Gruber, Daniel. *The Church and the Jews: The Biblical Relationship.* Hanover, N.H.: Elijah Publishing, 1997.

Guyon, Jeanne. *Le Moyen Court et Très Facile de Faire Oraison.* Grenoble, France: circa 1685.

Hayeshua, M. "Lebanon War Miracles." *Judaism—The Jewish Website.* 29 October, 2006. http://www.aish.com.

Heine, Ronald E. *Reading the Old Testament with the Ancient Church.* Grand Rapids: Baker Academic, 2007.

Henry, Matthew. *Commentary on the Whole Bible.* http://www.ccel.org.

Hertz, Dr. Joseph H., trans. *The Authorized Daily Prayer Book.* Rev. ed. New York: Bloch Publishing Co., 1975.

Herzog, Chaim. *The Arab-Israel Wars: War and Peace in the Middle East.* Updated by Shlomo Gazit. New York: Random House, 2005.

Heschel, Abraham Joshua. *The Sabbath.* New York: Farrar, Straus and Giroux, 1951.

Hjort, Maria. "Record Number of Jerusalem Marchers Despite Ban." *Jerusalem Report,* 29 October 2007: 6–7.

Intrater, Keith Asher. *From Iraq to Armageddon.* Shippensburg, Penn.: Destiny Image Publishers, 2003.

Intrater, (Keith) Asher. *What Does the Bible Really Say about the Land?* Grand Prairie, Tex.: Maoz Israel Publishing, 2006.

Israeli Defense Forces. http://www.idf.il.

Jewish Virtual Library. http://www.jewishvirtuallibrary.org.

Juster, Dan, and Keith Intrater. *Israel, the Church, and the Last Days.* Shippensburg, Penn.: Destiny Image, 1990.

Juster, Daniel C. "Israel's Restoration." *Tikkun International Newsletter*, vol. 16, no. 8 (August 2007): 1.

Kaplan, Rabbi Aryeh. *Made in Heaven.* Jerusalem: Moznaim Publishing Corp., 1983.

Keener, Craig S. *Paul, Women and Wives: Marriage and Women's Ministry in the Letters of Paul.* Peabody, Mass.: Hendrickson Publishers, 2004.

Kidner, Derek. *The Message of Jeremiah.* Downers Grove, Ill.: InterVarsity, 1987.

Kroeger, Richard Clark, and Catherine Clark Kroeger. *I Suffer Not a Woman.* Grand Rapids: Baker Books, 1992.

Ladd, George Eldon. *The Gospel of the Kingdom.* Grand Rapids: Eerdmans, 1990.

———. *The Presence of the Future.* Grand Rapids: Eerdmans, 1974.

Landman, Isaac, ed. *The Universal Jewish Encyclopedia.* Vol. 7. New York: Universal Jewish Encyclopedia Co., 1948.

Lefkovits, Etgar. "Ban on Jerusalem Christian Event Upheld." *Jerusalem Post*, 17 May, 2007. http://www.jpost.com.

———. "Evangelical Pastor Told to Leave Israel." *Jerusalem Post*, 8 August, 2007. http://www.jpost.com.

———. "HOT Wants to Pull Plug on Christian Station for Proselytizing." *Jerusalem Post*, 20 July 2007.

Longman, Tremper III, ed. *Baker Commentary on the Old Testament Wisdom and Psalms.* Grand Rapids: Baker Academic, 2005.

Martyr, Justin. *The Dialogue with Trypho.* Translated by A. Lukyn Williams. London: S.P.C.K., 1930.

McClain, Alva J. *The Greatness of the Kingdom.* Grand Rapids: Zondervan, 1959.

McGough, Richard Amiel. *The Bible Wheel.* Yakima, Wash.: Bible Wheel Bookhouse, 2006.

McKane, William. *A Critical and Exegetical Commentary on Jeremiah.* Edinburgh: T & T Clark, 1996.

Merriam Webster's Collegiate Dictionary, 10th ed. Springfield, Mass.: Merriam-Webster, 1994.

Military Quotations, Funny Quotes, Mottos and Jokes. http://www.militaryquotes.com.

Mills, Dick, and David Michael. *Messiah and His Hebrew Alphabet.* Orange, Calif.: Dick Mills Ministries, 1994.

Mowinckel, Sigmund. *He That Cometh.* Translated by G. W. Anderson. New York: Abingdon, 1954.

New Advent. http://www.newadvent.org.

NIV Study Bible. Grand Rapids: Zondervan, 1985.

Norris, Richard A., Jr., ed. *The Song of Songs Interpreted by Early Christians and Medieval Commentators.* Grand Rapids: Eerdmans, 2003.

Onfrey, Michael. *The Atheist Manifesto: The Case against Christianity, Judaism, and Islam.* New York: Arcade Publishing, 2007.

Operation World. http://www.operationworld.org.

Oren, Michael B. *Six Days of War: June 1967 and the Making of the Middle East.* New York: Random House Ballantine, 2003.

Otis, George, Jr. *Informed Intercession.* Ventura, Calif.: Renew, 1999.

"Pale of Jewish Settlement." *Encyclopedia Judaica*, 13:24–28. Jerusalem: Keter Publishing House, 1972.

Pierce, Chuck D., and Rebecca Wagner Sytsema. *The Future War of the*

Church. Ventura, Calif: Regal Books, 2007.

Pierce, Ronald W., and Rebecca Merrill Groothuis, eds. *Discovering Biblical Equality: Complementarity without Hierarchy*. Downers Grove, Ill.: Inter-Varsity, 2005.

Pinkus, Benjamin. *The Jews of the Soviet Union: The History of a National Minority*. Cambridge, Mass.: Cambridge University Press, 1988.

Quotations Page, The. http://www.quotationspage.com.

Price, Randall. *Jerusalem in Prophecy*. Eugene, Ore.: Harvest House, 1998.

Rahab, David. "The Beleaguered Christians of the Palestinian-Controlled Areas." *Jewish Virtual Library*. http://www.jewishvirtuallibrary.org.

Riasanovsky, Nicholas V. *A History of Russia*. New York: Oxford University Press, 1984.

Rich, Tracy R. *Judaism 101*. http://www.jewfaq.org.

Rosenthal, Marvin J. *Examining the Pre-Wrath Rapture of the Church*. Nashville: Thomas Nelson, 1994.

Ross, Allen P. *Creation and Blessing: A Guide to the Study and Exposition of the Book of Genesis*. Grand Rapids: Baker Books, 1988.

Saucy, Robert L. *The Case for Progressive Dispensationalism*. Grand Rapids: Zondervan, 1993.

Scherman, Nosson, and Meir Zlotowitz, eds. *Shir ha Shirim/Song of Songs: A New Translation with a Commentary Anthologized from Talmudic, Midrashic and Rabbinic Sources*. In Artscroll Tanach Series. New York: Mesorah Publications, 2004.

Silvoso, Ed. *Women: God's Secret Weapon*. Ventura, Calif: Regal Books, 2001.

Singer, Isidore, ed. *The Jewish Encyclopedia*. Vol. 8. New York and London: Funk and Wagnall's, 1904.

Sliker, David. *End-Times Simplified: Preparing Your Heart for the Coming Storm*. Kansas City, Mo.: Forerunner Books, 2005.

Spurgeon, Charles H. *Sermons*. http://www.spurgeon.org.

———. *Sermons on the Song of Solomon*. Pasadena, Tex.: Pilgrim Publications, 1974.

Stern, David H. *Complete Jewish Bible: An English Version of the Tanakh (Old Testament) and B'rit Hadashah (New Testament)*. Clarksville, Md.: Jewish New Testament Publications, 1998.

———. *Jewish New Testament Commentary*. Clarksville, Md.: Jewish New Testament Publications, 1992.

Strong, James. *The Exhaustive Concordance of the Bible, Main Concordance*. Nashville: Abingdon, 1977.

ten Boom, Corrie. *Each New Day*. Uhrichsville, Ohio: Barbour and Co., Inc., 1977.

Tenney, Merrill C., ed. *The Zondervan Pictorial Encyclopedia of the Bible*. Grand Rapids: Zondervan, 1976.

Teplinsky, Sandra. *Out of the Darkness: The Untold Story of Jewish Revival in the Former Soviet Union*. Jacksonville Beach, Fla.: Hear O Israel Publishing, 1998.

Teplinsky, Sandra. *Why Care about Israel? How the Jewish Nation Is Key to Unleashing God's Blessings in the 21st Century*. Grand Rapids: Chosen Books, 2004.

Tzu, Sun. *The Art of War*. Translated by Samuel B. Griffith. London/New York: Oxford University Press, 1963.

United Nations. http://www.un.org.

Walvoord, John F. *Israel in Prophecy.* Grand Rapids: Zondervan, 1962.

————. *The Millennial Kingdom.* Grand Rapids: Zondervan, 1959.

————. *The Prophecy Knowledge Handbook.* Wheaton: Victor Books, 1990.

Wesley, John. *The Law Established through Faith: Discourse 1.* http://www.wesley.nnu.edu.

Wigooder, Geoffrey, ed. *The New Encyclopedia of Judaism.* Washington Square, N.Y.: New York University Press and Jerusalem Publishing House, 2002.

Wilson, Marvin R. *Our Father Abraham: Jewish Roots of the Christian Faith.* Grand Rapids: Eerdmans, and Dayton, Ohio: Center for Judaic-Christian Studies, 1989.

World Health Organization. http://www.who.int.

World Holocaust Forum. http://www.worldholocaustforum.org.

Wurmbrand, Richard. *The Sweetest Song.* Bartlesville, Okla.: Living Sacrifice Book Co., 1988.

Zernov, Nicholas. *Eastern Christendom.* New York: G.P. Putnam's Sons, 1961.

Zuck, Roy B. *Basic Bible Interpretation: A Practical Guide to Discovering Biblical Truth.* Wheaton: Victor Books, 1991.

Please note: This bibliography is limited to works referenced in the main text.

Notes

Chapter 2: Kingdom Convergence

1. Certain fulfillments of Jesus' Olivet Discourse took place in the century following His resurrection, but final fulfillment is reserved for the very end of this age and has not yet come to pass.

2. *The New International Version*, *New Living Translation* and *New American Standard* are among those using "birth pains;" *The Living Bible* and others use "horrors."

3. *Merriam Webster's Collegiate Dictionary*, 10ᵗʰ ed. (Springfield, Mass.: Merriam-Webster, 1994).

4. See generally, George Eldon Ladd, *The Gospel of the Kingdom* (Grand Rapids: Eerdmans, 1990).

5. This hermeneutic was adopted by leading evangelical seminarians in the 1978 Chicago Statement on Biblical Hermeneutics. See also, Gordon D. Fee and Douglas Stuart, *How to Read the Bible for All It's Worth* (Grand Rapids: Zondervan, 1982), 16–27; see generally, Roy B. Zuck, *Basic Bible Interpretation: A Practical Guide to Discovering Biblical Truth* (Wheaton: Victor Books, 1991).

6. See, for example, 2 Corinthians 1:13; Deuteronomy 30:11; Fee and Stuart, *How to Read the Bible for All It's Worth*, 16–27; Zuck, *Basic Bible Interpretation*, 26.

7. This passage should not be misinterpreted so as to suggest or advocate any attempted imposition of faith in Jesus by militaristic or other such force.

8. Michael Freund, "In Praise of Christian Zionists," *International Jerusalem Post*, 5 January 2007, 23. Despite new openness, many Israelis still harbor varying degrees of defensiveness toward Christians and resistance to the Gospel.

9. See, for example, C. E. B. Cranfield, *The International Critical Commentary, The Epistle to the Romans*, vol. 2., ed. J. A. Emerton and C. E. B Cranfield (Edinburgh: T & T Clark, 1979), 576–77.

10. See, for example, F. F. Bruce, *The Epistle of Paul to the Romans* (Grand Rapids: Eerdmans, 1978), 222; Cranfield, *Romans*, 2:576–77; Robert L. Saucy, *The Case for Progressive Dispensationalism* (Grand Rapids: Zondervan, 1993), 255–56.

11. Jack Engelhard, "First, the Saturday People," *Arutz Sheva*, 15 September 2003, http://www.israelnationalnews.com/Articles/Article.aspx/2747; David Rahab, "The Beleaguered Christians of the Palestinian-Controlled Areas," *Jewish Virtual Library*, http://www.jewishvirtuallibrary.org/jsource/Peace/christianpal.html#56.

12. Lela Gilbert, "Natural Allies in a Dangerous World," *The International Jerusalem Post*, 12 October 2007, 13.

13. See James W. Goll, *Praying for Israel's Destiny* (Grand Rapids: Chosen Books, 2005); *The Prophetic Intercessor* (Grand Rapids: Chosen Books, 2007); and *Intercession: The Power and the Passion to Shape History* (Shippensburg, Pa.: Destiny Image, 2003).

14. *NIV Study Bible* (Grand Rapids: Zondervan, 1985), see note on Matthew 25:31–46.

Chapter 3: The Mystery of Jew and Gentile in Messiah

1. Operation World, http://www.gmi.org/ow/country/isr/owtext.html. Other estimates are much lower; precise counts are impossible. See, for example, Mike Decker, "Messianic Jews and the Law of Return," *Israel Today*, 24 September 2007, http://www.israeltoday.co.il/default.aspx?tabid=182&view=item&idx=1550.

2. Operation World, http://www.gmi.org/ow/country/isr/owtext.html.

3. Israel's redemptive destiny means, for example, that she still retains the land covenant promised to Abraham, Isaac and Jacob. All nations and people groups carry unique redemptive destinies reflecting God's glory.

4. The Scriptures are to be interpreted first and foremost in a literal manner, based on the plain meaning of the Word, wherever it is reasonable to do so. Any personal or deeper interpretation and application can then be made based on the literal interpretation.

5. The curse may have been indefinite (see Nehemiah 13:1–2), in which case Ruth's conversion and reward bear even greater weight.

6. James Strong, *The Exhaustive Concordance of the Bible, Main Concordance* (Nashville: Abingdon, 1977), see *bless* in Main Concordance and *barakh* in Hebrew and Chaldee Dictionary; Francis Brown, S. R. Driver and Charles A. Briggs, *A Hebrew and English Lexicon of the Old Testament* (Oxford: Clarendon Press, 1980), see *barakh*; Allen P. Ross, *Creation and Blessing: A Guide to the Study and Exposition of the Book of Genesis* (Grand Rapids: Baker Books, 1988), 263.

7. Romans 11:26, citing Isaiah 59:20 and 60:16; Matthew Henry, *Commentary on the Whole Bible*, http://www.ccel.org/h/henry/mhc2/Ru.ii.html.

8. Ruth's new mother-in-law may have been Rahab the harlot-turned-heroine of faith (see Matthew 1:5).

9. David H. Stern, *Complete Jewish Bible: An English Version of the* Tanakh *(Old Testament) and* B'rit Hadashah *(New Testament)* (Clarksville, Md.: Jewish New Testament Publications, 1998).

Chapter 4: Coming for a Bride

1. P. Trutza, "Marriage," *The Zondervan Pictorial Encyclopedia of the Bible*, vol. 4, ed. Merrill C. Tenney (Grand Rapids: Zondervan, 1976), 96.

2. Marvin R. Wilson, *Our Father Abraham: Jewish Roots of the Christian Faith* (Grand Rapids: Eerdmans, and Dayton, Ohio: Center for Judaic-Christian Studies, 1989), 204; Ariel and Dvorah Berkowitz, *Torah Rediscovered: Challenging Centuries of Misinterpretation and Neglect* (Littleton, Colo.: First Fruits of Zion, 1996), 12.

3. A. W. Argyle, "Wedding Customs at the Time of Jesus," *Expository Times*, vol. 86 (1975), 214–15; Trutza, "Marriage," 96; Hazel W. Perkin, "Marriage, Marriage Customs," *Baker Encyclopedia of the Bible*, vol. 2, ed. Walter A. Elwell (Grand Rapids: Baker Books, 1988), 1405–410; Philip Birnbaum, *A Book of Jewish Concepts* (New York: Hebrew Publishing Co., 1964), 423–24; "Marriage," in *The Universal Jewish Encyclopedia*, vol. 7, ed. Isaac Landman (New York: Universal Jewish Encyclopedia Co., 1948), 369–72; "Marriage," in *The Jewish Encyclopedia*, vol. 8, ed. Isidore Singer (New York and London: Funk and Wagnall's Co., 1904), 337.

4. Ibid.

5. Sincere and godly believers, including scholars, subscribe to different interpretations of this parable. Many see in it the issue of the eternal security of the believer's salvation. Others see in the story a parallel to believers prepared to meet Messiah when He comes for His Church at the end of the age, and those who, though unprepared, eventually enter His presence later on. The main point, in any case, is the same: By the power of His love, we are to stay watchful and ready.

6. R. K. Harrison, "Song of Solomon," in *Zondervan Encyclopedia*, vol. 5, ed. Merrill C. Tenney, 490–91; Richard S. Hess, "Song of Songs," *Baker Commentary on the Old Testament Wisdom and Psalms*, ed. Tremper Longman III (Grand Rapids: Baker Academic, 2005), 250–51.

7. See generally, Fr. Juan Gonzalez Arintero, *The Song of Songs: A Mystical Exposition*, trans. James Valendar and Jose L. Morales (Rockford, Ill.: TAN Books and Publishers, 1992); Charles H. Spurgeon, *Sermons on the Song of Solomon* (Pasadena, Tex.: Pilgrim Publications, 1974); and Richard A. Norris Jr., ed., *The Song of Songs Interpreted by Early Christians and Medieval Commentators* (Grand Rapids: Eerdmans, 2003). See also, Duane Garrett, "Song of Songs," *Word Biblical Commentary*, vol. 23b, ed. Bruce Metzger, David A. Hubbard and Glenn W. Barber (Nashville: Thomas Nelson, 2004), 64–67, 72–74; and Hess, "Song of Songs," *Old Testament Wisdom and Psalms*, 250–51, where the author, who adheres to a more literal interpretation, concludes the Song's consummation is reached with Christ and His Bride.

8. Nosson Scherman and Meir Zlotowitz, eds., *Shir ha Shirim/Song of Songs: A New Translation with a Commentary Anthologized from Talmudic, Midrashic and Rabbinic Sources*, Artscroll Tanach Series (New York: Mesorah Publications, 2004), 68, quoting Rabbi Akiva ben Yosef.

9. Ibid, 68–69, citing *Talmud: Sanhedrin* 101a; Yakov Bieler, "Shir haShirim in Light of Sabbath and Yom Tov," April 2004, http://www.kmsynagogue.org/Shir.html, quoting Rabbi Akiva ben Yosef.

10. "Marriage," in *The New Encyclopedia of Judaism*, ed. Geoffrey Wigooder (Washington Square, N.Y.: New York University Press and Jerusalem Publishing

House, 2002), 503; "Marriage," *The Jewish Encyclopedia*, 8:338; Garrett, "Song of Songs," 60–64.

11. In Hebrew, the book's title literally reads Song of "Songs," but I have used Song of "Solomon" to conform to the NIV and other contemporary translations.

12. See generally, Richard Wurmbrand, *The Sweetest Song* (Bartlesville, Okla.: Living Sacrifice Books, 1988). This devotional on the Song of Songs shares how bridal intimacy with Jesus sustained believers who were persecuted and martyred for their faith in the twentieth century.

13. Some currently popular interpretations of Song of Songs profess that doves, which are technically pigeons, have no peripheral vision. However, all scientific evidence is to the contrary. Doves benefit from extraordinarily wide-range, excellent peripheral vision. See, for example, S. Bloch, S. Rivaud and C. Martinoya, "Comparing Frontal and Lateral Viewing in the Pigeon: Different Patterns of Eye Movements for Binocular and Monocular Fixation," *Behavioral Brain Research* 13, no. 2 (August 1984): 173–82; Patricia M. Blough, "Cognitive Strategies and Foraging in Pigeons," *Avian Visual Cognition*, ed. R. G. Cook (Medford, Mass: Comparative Cognition Press, 2001), http://www.pigeon.psy.tufts.edu/avc/; Dr. John Fowler, American Dove Association, personal email, 26 January 2007.

14. Schermann and Zlotowitz, *Shir ha Shirim/Song of Songs*, 154, quoting Yedidiah Lipman Lipkin, *Divrei Yedidiah*.

Chapter 5: Sabbath Rest

1. The song *Lekha Dodi* reflects certain nonbiblical concepts, including the exaltation of the Sabbath as a bridal partner. I mention *Lekha Dodi* here merely to illustrate the Jewish connection of the Sabbath to bridal intimacy.

2. Heidi Baker, message at Toronto Airport Christian Fellowship in Toronto, Canada, 1 November 2007.

3. Jill Austin, *Dancing with Destiny: Awaken Your Heart to Dream, to Love, to War* (Grand Rapids: Chosen Books, 2007), 150.

4. The Torah also provides for Israel to observe a sabbatical year every fifty years, a year of Jubilee (see Leviticus 25:10ff.).

5. See generally, John de Graaf, David Wann and Thomas Naylor, *Affluenza* (San Francisco: Berrett-Koehler Publishers, 2001).

6. Abraham Joshua Heschel, *The Sabbath* (New York: Farrar, Straus and Giroux, 1979), 74, quoting Rabbi Elijah de Vidas, *Reshit Hokmah, Sha'ar ha'Kedushah*, ch. 2.

7. Jesus said we could not know the day or hour of His return, but He encouraged us to remain watchful of the season. I do not encourage specific date setting, but I do encourage awareness of Messiah's imminent return. The seven-day-millennium possibility is offered as an illustration for this purpose.

8. Time and space do not allow for discussion here of critical issues and Scriptures, such as Colossians 2:16–17. For a more thorough treatment, see David Friedman, *They Loved the Torah: What Yeshua's Followers Really Thought about the Law* (Baltimore: Lederer Books, 2001), 9–19.

9. Canon 29 of the Council of Laodicea, 364 A.D. For a more thorough treatment of this issue, see Wilson, *Our Father Abraham*, 79–84; and Samuele Bacchiocchi,

From Sabbath to Sunday: A Historical Investigation of the Rise of Sunday Obser-vance in Early Christianity (Rome: Pontifical Gregorian University Press, 1977). See also, Ronald E. Heine, *Reading the Old Testament with the Ancient Church* (Grand Rapids: Baker Academic, 2007), 73–74.

10. Catholic Answers, http://www.newadvent.org/fathers/3806.htm. See also New Advent, http://www.catholic.com/library/Sabbath_or_Sunday.asp.

11. The believers' gathering on the first day of the week could actually refer to Saturday evening, not Sunday. According to the biblical, lunar-based calendar marking days from sunset to sunset, Saturday after sunset starts the first day of the week. The believers would probably have been expected to report to work on Sunday after sunrise.

Chapter 6: Highway of Holiness

1. Jeanne Guyon, *Le Moyen Court et Très Facile de Faire Oraison* (Grenoble, France: circa 1685); Gene Edwards, ed., *Experiencing the Depths of Jesus Christ* (Goleta, Calif.: Christian Books, 1975), 45, 47, 74, 76.

2. Charles G. Finney, "Religion of the Law and Gospel," *Lectures to Professing Christians, 1836–37*, no. 4, http://www.gospeltruth.net/1836LTPC/indexltpc. htm.

3. John Wesley, "The Law Established through Faith: Discourse 1," http://www.wesley.nnu.edu/john_wesley/sermons/035.htm.

4. Charles H. Spurgeon, *Sermons*, http://www.spurgeon.org/sermons/1735. htm.

5. Corrie ten Boom, *Each New Day* (Uhrichsville, Ohio: Barbour and Co., Inc., 1977), 118.

6. *Torah* can also refer to oral laws allegedly issued by Moses, regarded by some traditional rabbis as equal in authority to the written Torah. Such usage is not included in the definitions or scope of this book.

7. Passages like Hebrews 8:6 are sometimes misunderstood to mean the whole Old Covenant is entirely superseded by the New. In context, however, such passages are explaining more specifically that God's new covenant of salvation, as described in Jeremiah 31 and that exists through Jesus as Messiah, is superior to the priestly sacrificial system of atonement under the old Mosaic covenant. See Dr. Michael L. Brown, *Answering Jewish Objections to Jesus*, vol. 4: *New Testament Objections* (Grand Rapids: Baker Books, 2007), 262–63; David H. Stern, *Jewish New Testament Commentary* (Clarksville, Md.: Jewish New Testament Publications, 1992), 683–89; *NIV Study Bible* (Grand Rapids: Zondervan, 1985), see note on Hebrews 8:7.

8. Jeremiah 31:33 contains another important truth. The New Covenant is a legal and spiritual covenant that was made with Israel. The covenant is extended so as to include believers from all nations; nevertheless, Jeremiah's word is a profound prophecy that has yet to come to pass in fullness for *Israel*.

9. Dietrich Bonhoeffer, *The Cost of Discipleship* (New York: Simon & Schuster, 1995), 45.

10. Believers not embracing the Torah can also succumb to religious legalism. Sometimes even Charismatics and Pentecostals can, for example, ritualize what

was once a spontaneous manifestation of the Spirit, turning it into an uninspired measure of holiness.

11. Stern, *Commentary*, 535–37.

12. Cranfield, *Romans*, 853.

13. There is no universal agreement on the practical definition of "Torah-observant lifestyle." Due to limitations of time and space, I use the phrase here in only a very general and broad sense to refer to any degree of Torah observance that significantly exceeds normative and contemporary Church practice.

14. Brown, in his Christian apologetic aimed at Jews, *Answering Jewish Objections*, 4:245. I attribute credit for some of the concepts in this chapter to Dr. Brown's insightful work on the Torah's relevance to believers in Jesus.

Chapter 7: Messianic Justice

1. Besides housing the manifest presence of God in the Old Covenant, the Temple compound likely served as locus of the outpouring of the Holy Spirit on Pentecost/Shavuot (see Luke 24:53 and Acts 2:1–4; 13–15). The "Upper Room" where Jesus' followers were gathered was likely located in close proximity to the Temple. The phenomenon that occurred in the Upper Room probably spilled over to the streets and climaxed at the Temple.

2. This outreach ministry to the former Soviet Union was organized and directed by Jonathan Bernis of Hear O Israel Ministries, a Messianic Jewish ministry now part of Jewish Voice Ministries International, based in Phoenix, Arizona. See generally, Sandra Teplinsky, *Out of the Darkness: The Untold Story of Jewish Revival in the Former Soviet Union* (Jacksonville Beach, Fla.: Hear O Israel Publishing, 1998).

The opposition detailed in this chapter is a composite description of actual events the Hear O Israel team experienced while engaged in Jewish evangelistic outreach in the former Soviet Union, 1994–2000.

3. These and other events are documented in Teplinsky, *Out of the Darkness*.

4. A thousand years ago, the small Slavic state in Eastern Europe that eventually mushroomed into the vast Union of Soviet Socialist Republics adopted Christianity as its official faith. See Nicholas Zernov, *Eastern Christendom* (New York: G.P. Putnam's Sons, 1961), 111; John S. Curtiss. *The Russian Church and the Soviet State: 1900–1917* (New York: Octagon Books, 1972), 6–7; Benjamin Pinkus, *The Jews of the Soviet Union: The History of a National Minority* (Cambridge, Mass.: Cambridge University Press, 1988), 4–5.

The form of Christianity adopted, however, was replete with replacement theology. As a result of politically entrenched replacement theology, both church and state came to regard the Jewish people as a divinely repudiated race. Sadly, contempt toward Jews turned to hatred and then to outright, murderous persecution. See Salo W. Baron, *The Russian Jew under Tsars and Soviets* (New York: MacMillian, 1964), 6, 17–18; Nicholas V. Riasanovsky, *A History of Russia* (New York: Oxford University Press, Inc., 1984), 394–96.

Over the next millennia, millions of Russian Jews would be exiled or exterminated. Nearly three million Soviet Jews were murdered in the Nazi Holocaust, helped by Soviet collaborators. See Baron, *The Russian Jew*, 32–33; Pinkus, *The Jews of the Soviet Union*, 13; "Pale of Jewish Settlement," *Encyclopedia Judaica*, vol. 13, (Jerusalem: Keter Publishing House, 1972), 24–28; Ilya Altman and David Poltorak, World Holocaust Forum, http://www.worldholocaustforum.org/eng/history/5/index.wbp. Meanwhile, Jews were prohibited from leaving the USSR.

5. When Paul says in the synagogue in Corinth, "We now turn to the Gentiles" (Acts 13:46), he is not announcing a policy shift to go solely to the Gentiles. He is stating that in this particular city, after first sharing with the Jews, he now turns to the Gentiles. This becomes clear because after leaving Corinth, he immediately resumes the pattern of preaching first to the Jew, then to the Gentile (see Acts 17:1–4, 10, 17; 18:4, 19; 19:8; 20:21).

6. See, for example, Jonathan Bernis, "Jews Need Jesus," *Charisma*, December 2006, 14; Don Finto, *God's Promise and the Future of Israel* (Ventura, Calif.: Regal Books, 2005), 199–200; Associated Press, "Rabbis Told Jews to Shun Evangelicals," *Jerusalem Post*, 24 September 2007; Daniel C. Juster, "Israel's Restoration," *Tikkun International Newsletter*, August 2007, stating the government-registered Christian Allies Caucus in Israel requires, at the behest of the Israeli government, that every Christian with whom they work expressly commit *not* to proselytize or evangelize Jews. (This is not to impugn the Christian Allies Caucus, which I believe reflects a powerful work of the Spirit.)

7. Decker, "Messianic Jews," *Israel Today*, describing, as an Israeli attorney, laws that prevent Messianic Jews from obtaining Israeli citizenship.

8. As this book went to its publisher, a major evangelical organization held its first large-scale event in Jerusalem in which an Israeli Messianic Jewish leader was given public platform. Another large gathering by a different Christian ministry, also involving Israeli Messianic leaders, is presently underway. See also, "Voice of the Martyrs Newsletter," 13 March 2008.

9. Bernis, "Jews Need Jesus," 14; Finto, *God's Promise*, 199–200; Sandra Teplinsky, *Why Care about Israel? How the Jewish Nation Is Key to Unleashing God's Blessings in the 21st Century* (Grand Rapids: Chosen Books, 2004), 144–46; Chuck D. Pierce and Rebecca Wagner Sytsema, *The Future War of the Church* (Ventura, Calif.: Regal Books, 2007), 245–46; see also, for example, "Ban on Jerusalem Christian Event Upheld," *Jerusalem Post*, 17 May 2007, http://www.jpost.com/servlet/Satellite?cid=1178708627502&pagename=JPost%2FJPArticle; Asher (Keith) Intrater, *What Does the Bible Really Say about the Land?* (Grand Prairie, Tex.: Maoz Israel Publishing, 2006), 40; Etgar Lefkovits, "Evangelical Pastor Told to Leave Israel," *Jerusalem Post*, 8 August 2007, http://www.jpost.com/servlet/Sattelite?cid=1186557463960&pagename=JPost%2FJArticle; Etgar Lefkovits, "HOT Wants to Pull Plug on Christian Station for Proselytizing," *Jerusalem Post*, 20 July 2007, 6; Maria Hjort, "Record Number of Jerusalem Marchers Despite Ban," *Jerusalem Report*, 2 October 2007, 6–7; Juster, "Israel's Restoration," *Tikkun Newsletter*, 1; Matthew Wagner, "Messianics: Attack One of Many," *Jerusalem Post*, 25 March 2008. http//www.jpost.com.

10. To help needy Israeli believers, our ministry, Light of Zion, collects and regularly delivers financial aid to them; see www.lightofzion.org.

11. Pierce and Systema, *The Future War of the Church*, 225–26.

12. This approach is suggested merely as a supplemental aid to solid, systematic Bible study. Linguistic and doctrinal issues involved in biblical word usage are complex and exceed the scope of this book.

13. Francis Brown, S. R. Driver and Charles A. Briggs, *A Hebrew and English Lexicon of the Old Testament* (Oxford: Clarendon Press, 1980), 535–36.

14. Dick Mills and David Michael, *Messiah and His Hebrew Alphabet* (Orange, Calif.: Dick Mills Ministries, 1994), 21–22, 35–36, 59–68; Richard Amiel McGough, *The Bible Wheel* (Yakima, Wash.: Bible Wheel Bookhouse, 2006), 183, 213, 247, 261; Ellen Frankel and Betsy Platkin Teutsch, *The Encyclopedia of Jewish Symbols*, (Northvale, N.J.: Jason Aronson, 1995), 5.

The Hebrew letters also possess numeric values, which are not discussed in this book.

15. The events recounted are detailed in Teplinsky, *Out of the Darkness*, 69–70, 77.

16. This does not speak of magic, but of realities in the spirit realm that we understand only in part (see 1 Corinthians 13:9–10, 12).

17. The quote is attributed to Tertullian, a Church father of the second century; history testifies to its accuracy. http://www.reformationtheology.com/2006/05/the_blood_of_the_martyrs.php.

Chapter 8: From Zion's Battlegrounds

1. Although this book does not directly address the subject of believers in military service in nations other than Israel, individual Christians whom God has led to join the armed forces of their nations deserve our prayers and support.

2. Flavius Vegetius Renatus, circa 390 A.D., Military Quotes, http://www.military-quotes.com/vegetius-renatus.htm. For comparative background to Israel's modern-day situation, see, for example, Nehemiah 4:1–23.

3. Hostility toward God has found expression in assailing Jews, together with Christians, off and on throughout history. With the existence of a modern Jewish State, the military locus of that hostility aimed at Jews now centers on the biblical Promised Land.

4. For an introductory study on Israel's modern wars, see generally, Chaim Herzog, *The Arab-Israel Wars: War and Peace in the Middle East*, updated by Shlomo Gazit (New York: Random House, 2005). See also, *Spirit of the IDF*, http://dover.idf.il/IDF..

5. William McKane, "A Critical and Exegetical Commentary on Jeremiah," *The International Critical Commentary*, vol. 2, ed. J. A. Emerton, C .E. B. Cranfield and G. N. Stanton (Edinburgh: T & T Clark, 1996), 803; see also Brown, Driver, and Briggs, *Hebrew and English Lexicon of the Old Testament*, 846.

6. See, for example, *Against All Odds: Israel Survives* DVD series (Chicago: American Trademark Pictures and Questar Inc., 2007); Herzog, *The Arab-Israeli Wars*; M. Hayeshua, "Lebanon War Miracles," http://www.aish.com/jewishissues/israeldiary/Lebanon_War_Miracles.asp; Michael B. Oren, *Six Days of War: June 1967 and the Making of the Middle East* (New York: Random House Ballantine, 2003); Marty Shoub, "Under the Shadow of the Almighty," *Oasis* newsletter, December 2006.

7. The postmodern philosophy of secular humanism traces its roots to the European Age of Reason that began in the 1700s.

8. Michael Onfrey, *The Atheist Manifesto: The Case against Christianity, Judaism and Islam* (New York: Arcade Publishing, 2007).

9. Golda Meir served as Israeli Prime Minister from 1969–1974. She was the third elected female head of state in the modern world, following Indira Ghandi of India and Sirimavo Bandaranaike of Sri Lanka. http://www.jewishvirtuallibrary.org/jsource/biography/meir.html.

10. A more thorough study of relevant, controversial Scriptures and biblical issues pertaining to women's roles in the Body of Christ is beyond the scope of this book. Any comprehensive treatment of the topic would easily require its own tome. At the same time, a preliminary overview runs the risk of raising more questions than could possibly be answered here and now. That a fair discussion on women in ministry would prove unwieldy in this context only underscores its critical nature. For that reason, despite inherent limitations, I have addressed it here. I provide biblical perspectives that I believe will rise to the fore in coming years.

Non-scholarly books proposing that the Scriptures permit women to potentially serve God in the same general callings as men include Cunningham and Hamilton, *Why Not Women?*; J. Lee Grady, *Ten Lies the Church Tells Women* (Lake Mary, Fla.: Charisma House, 2006); J. Lee Grady, *Twenty-Five Tough Questions about Women and the Church* (Lake Mary, Fla.: Charisma House, 2003); John T. Bristow, *What Paul Really Said about Women* (New York: HarperSanFrancisco, 1991); Craig S. Keener, *Paul, Women and Wives: Marriage and Women's Ministry in the Letters of Paul* (Peabody, Mass.: Hendrickson Publishers, 2004); Ed Silvoso, *Women: God's Secret Weapon* (Ventura, Calif.: Gospel Light, 2001); Ronald W. Pierce and Rebecca Merrill Groothuis, ed., *Discovering Biblical Equality: Complementarity without Hierarchy* (Downers Grove, Ill.: InterVarsity Press, 2005).

11. Richard Clark Kroeger and Catherine Clark Kroeger, *I Suffer Not a Woman* (Grand Rapids: Baker Books, 1992), 138–70; Loren Cunningham and David J. Hamilton, *Why Not Women? A Biblical Study of Women in Missions, Ministry and Leadership* (Seattle: YWAM Publishing, 2000), 71–92.

12. *Babylonian Talmud, Tractate Niddah* 45b; Abraham Cohen, *Everyman's Talmud: The Major Teachings of the Rabbinic Sages* (New York: Schocken Books, 1995), 161. The Talmud says women are endowed with a greater degree of *binah* (intuition, understanding, intelligence) than men. The rabbis reportedly infer this from the fact that woman was "built" (Genesis 2:22) rather than "formed" (Genesis 2:7), and the Hebrew root of "build" refers to insight. http://www.jewfaq.org/women.htm.

13. Cunningham and Hamilton, *Why Not Women?*, 17–21, 73–92; World Health Organization, "Multi-Country Study on Women's Health and Domestic Violence against Women, Initial Results, 2005," http://www.who.int/gener/violence/who_multicountry_study/en/; Amnesty International, "2007 Report: Middle East and Africa," http://thereport.amnesty.org/eng/Regions/Middle-East-and-North-Africa; United Nations, "Women at a Glance," http://www.un.org/ecosocdev/geninfo/women/women96.htm; Coalition Against Trafficking in Women, "International CATW Annual Report, 2006," http://www.catwinternational.org.

14. Dr. Kerry Teplinsky, message given in Anaheim, California, 24 November 2007.

15. Thankfully there are some exceptions. At this writing, these are mostly limited to worship leaders. On rare occasions, Messianic Jewish women—but generally Gentiles who converted to Judaism and married leading Messianic rabbis—have served as spokeswomen for the larger Messianic body.

16. McKane, *Jeremiah*, concluding the verse describes an "indeterminable new thing . . . created by Yahweh . . . all but incredible . . . in the Messianic age," 807; Frank E. Gaebelein, ed., *The Expositor's Bible Commentary*, vol. 6 (Grand Rapids: Zondervan, 1986), 571; Charles L. Feinberg, *Jeremiah: A Commentary* (Grand Rapids: Zondervan, 1982), 215, stating the verse is "beyond present solution"; Derek Kidner, *The Message of Jeremiah* (Downers Grove, Ill: InterVarsity Press, 1987), 109.

17. *NIV Study Bible* (Grand Rapids: Zondervan, 1985), study note to Jeremiah 31:22.

18. Feinberg, *Jeremiah*, 215, stating the word "surround" is an affectionate term, implying protection; see also, *Strong's Concordance, Hebrew and Chaldee Dictionary*, word 5826.

19. I have heard it said that the Bible's "irreducible dyad of human existence" is that of Jew and Gentile. I propose, however, that God's fundamental division of the human race, from creation, is between man and woman.

Chapter 9: Messianic Millennium Coming

1. David's rule is also identified with David himself resurrected during the Millennium and serving under his biological descendant, Jesus the Messiah, in whom that rule is climactically fulfilled (see Jeremiah 30:9, 15–17; Ezekiel 37:24–25; 34:23; Hosea 3:5).

2. In recent years, many believers have experienced a wonderfully revived focus on the restoration of David's tabernacle relating to worship through music, song and dance. Worship is an important component of the restoration of David's tabernacle. However, it is just one dimension of many. The restoration of David's tabernacle (or hut or booth) refers to the full earthly, governmental Kingdom of Messiah's millennial rule.

3. See also, Brown, *Answering Jewish Objections to Jesus*, 4:76–97.

4. See George Eldon Ladd, *The Presence of the Future* (Grand Rapids: Eerdmans, 1974), 64–65; Saucy, *Progressive Dispensationalism*, 242–45.

5. The apostolic authors of the New Covenant address issues pertaining to Gnosticism. *The NIV Study Bible*, 1811, 1833, 1906; A. F. Walls, "Gnosticism," in *Zondervan Encyclopedia*, vol. 2, ed. Merrill C. Tenney (Grand Rapids: Zondervan, 1976), 738.

6. Saucy, *Progressive Dispensationalism*, 242, note 52; John F. Walvoord, *The Millennial Kingdom* (Grand Rapids: Zondervan, 1959), 45–47; Justin Martyr, *The Dialogue with Trypho*, trans. A. Lukyn Williams (London: S.P.C.K., 1930), 52, 169, 172; E. Ferguson, "The Terminology of Kingdom in the Second Century," in *Studia Patristica*, vol. 17, ed. Elizabeth A. Livingstone (Oxford: Pergamon Press, 1982), 670.

7. Walvoord, *Millennial Kingdom*, 45–47; Justin Martyr, *Dialogue with Trypho*, 52, 169, 172; Dan Juster and Keith Intrater, *Israel, the Church and the Last Days* (Shippensburg, Penn.: Destiny Image, 1990), 57–60; Daniel Gruber, *The Church and the Jews: The Biblical Relationship* (Hanover, N.H.: Elijah Publishing, 1997), 24–41, 213–31.

8. Walvoord, *Millennial Kingdom*, 47; Martyr, *Dialogue with Trypho*, 169, Sec. 80.1–5.

9. The Bible indicates that Satan remains actively influential in the sphere of human activity (see Acts 5:3; 1 Corinthians 7:5; 2 Corinthians 4:3–4; 11:14; 12:7; 1 Thessalonians 2:18; 2 Thessalonians 2:8–9; 1 Timothy 1:20; 1 John 3:8, 10; 1 Peter 5:8; see also Ephesians 6:11–13).

10. Although I personally disagree with much of classic postmillennialism, I do encourage believers to actively influence human governments for good, especially through prayer (see 1 Timothy 2:1–2; Matthew 28:18–19; Acts 4:19–20; 5:28–29). God sets in place those who rule, and He has instructed us to pray for them (see Romans 13:1–6; John 19:11; 1 Peter 2:13).

11. The preterist view regards the events described in Matthew 24:3*ff.* as having been totally, climactically fulfilled in the first century A.D.

12. For a non-scholarly book contrasting these views, see generally, Robert G. Clouse, ed., *The Meaning of the Millennium* (Downers Grove, Ill.: InterVarsity Press, 1977).

13. A.H. Leitch, "Righteousness," Tenney, *Zondervan Encyclopedia*, vol. 5, 104.

14. Ibid., 105–6.

15. Alva J. McClain, *The Greatness of the Kingdom* (Grand Rapids: Zondervan, 1959), 234–41.

16. George Otis, Jr., *Informed Intercession* (Ventura, Calif.: Renew, 1999), 18–23. In a sense, modern Israel has already entered into a dimension of this prophetic reality in the present-day restoration of her land that lay desolate for virtually two millennia.

17. Cohen, *Everyman's Talmud*, 16–20.

Chapter 10: Standing Firm to the End

1. The prayer is an abridged version of a lengthier *Kaddish* that is part of the regular worship liturgy. In use in Jesus' day, the *Kaddish* would have been familiar to His disciples when they asked Him how to pray. He answered their question with what we now call the Lord's Prayer (see Matthew 6:9–13), incorporating words and concepts from the *Kaddish*. The Lord's Prayer goes on to include portions of other Jewish prayers in use at the time. See James M. Freeman, *The New Manners and Customs of the Bible*, updated by Harold Chadwick (Orlando, Fla.: Bridge-Logos, 1998), 414–15.

2. Bear in mind, however, that atonement for sin does not exist in any form other than through the crucifixion and resurrection of Jesus the Messiah.

3. Dr. Joseph H. Hertz, trans., *The Authorized Daily Prayer Book*, rev. ed. (New York: Bloch Publishing, 1975), 399.

4. Some Gentile Christian theologians use the phrase "pre-eminent role." Saucy, *Progressive Dispensationalism*, 231, 303–4; John F. Walvoord, *Israel in Prophecy* (Grand Rapids: Zondervan, 1962), 118–31.

5. Sigmund Mowinckel, *He That Cometh*, trans. G. W. Anderson (New York: Abingdon, 1954), 149.

6. Mount Zion is synonymous with the Temple Mount in this context.

7. Arnold G. Fruchtenbaum, *Israelology: The Missing Link in Systematic Theology* (Tustin, Calif.: Ariel Ministries Press, 1989), 809.

8. Based on Ezekiel chapters 40–48, some scholars believe temple sacrifices will be reinstated for this purpose—but *not* as atonement for sin.

9. John F. Walvoord, *The Prophecy Knowledge Handbook* (Wheaton: Victor Books, 1990), 200, 204; Fruchtenbaum, *Israelology*, 809; Ralph H. Alexander, "Ezekiel," *Expositor's Bible Commentary: Isaiah–Ezekiel*, vol. 6, ed. Frank E. Gaebelein (Grand Rapids: Zondervan, 1986), 943.

It is unlikely that Ezekiel's Temple describes the Temple structure as it exists in the new heaven and earth because God Himself is the Holy Temple there (see Revelation 21:22–23). It probably, however, includes dimensions of this ultimate Temple that is God Himself, and that manifest in the millennial Temple as part of the "already/not yet" phenomenon.

10. As we have seen, many of the prophetic Scriptures apply to our walk with Yeshua *today*, to varying degrees, as Gentile or Jewish believers. The primary interpretation of these passages is found in their grammatical-historical context, rendering a straightforward, generally literal understanding of the Word of God. However, believers partake *now* of increasing dimensions of the "already/not yet" nature of the Kingdom of God.

11. See also, Randall Price, *Jerusalem in Prophecy* (Eugene, Ore.: Harvest House, 1998), 304–18; Walvoord, *Prophecy Knowledge Handbook*, 635–38.

12. The Bible gives good reason to believe the new earth is the same earth we live in today, renewed and purged by fire, thoroughly transformed by its climactic and complete convergence with heaven.

13. For an introductory overview of the Great Tribulation, see generally, David Sliker, *End-Times Simplified: Preparing Your Heart for the Coming Storm* (Kansas City, Mo.: Forerunner Books, 2005); and Mike Bickle, *Omega: End Times Teaching* (Kansas City, Mo.: Forerunner Books, 2006).

14. Some, but not all, of the Antichrist prophecies found in Daniel were foreshadowed and *partially* fulfilled by Antiochus IV Epiphanes, ruler of the Hellenistic Seleucid Empire in the second century B.C. Those holding to a preterist view reject any future fulfillment of these prophecies or of related prophecies about Israel's restoration and the Great Tribulation.

15. Consistent with this understanding is the broad definition of the Greek word *paralambano*, used in reference to the Rapture in Matthew 24:39–41, and sometimes translated "taken." *Paralambano* appears in Matthew 1:20 in the angel's instruction to Joseph not to be afraid to "take" Mary as his wife.

16. Don Finto, *Your People Shall Be My People* (Ventura, Calif.: Regal Books, 2001), 170–72. For a similar view, see generally, Marvin J. Rosenthal, *Examining the Pre-Wrath Rapture of the Church* (Nashville: Thomas Nelson, 1994).

17. Finto, *Your People*, 171.

18. Please be aware that discussion of this unfolding of events can be highly offensive to many Jewish people who do not believe in Jesus. While most Jews familiar with the Old Covenant do not deny the coming Day of the Lord, or Day of Jacob's Trouble, the prospect of calling on the name of Jesus or Yeshua to save them is not part of their accepted understanding. Regrettably, many Jewish people have gotten the impression that believers actually look forward to (or are callous about) this time of Jewish suffering because they (the believers) think only of its ushering in Christ's return. This misunderstanding must be dealt with by first ensuring that our hearts are pure. While we eagerly anticipate Messiah's return and do not compromise the truth of the Gospel, we must embrace and reflect His unconditional love for Israel and the lost.

19. Mike Bickle, unpublished study notes, "Studies in the End-Times (2007): Negative Trends, People and Events in the End-Times" (Kansas City, Mo.: International House of Prayer Mission Base, 2007), 6–7, http://www.ihop.org/group/group.aspx?id=1000000379. The study notes also provide numerous Scripture references and are quoted here with permission of the author.

20. Jesus was crucified on Passover, entombed during the Feast of Unleavened Bread, and resurrected on the Feast of First Fruits. The Holy Spirit was poured out on the Feast of Weeks, otherwise known as Pentecost (see Leviticus 23:5–21).

21. Traditional Judaism also relates the fall feasts to events associated with Messiah's coming. Rabbi Yisrael Ba'al Shem Tov, as quoted in Rabbi Shlomo Riskin, "What to Ask For," *International Jerusalem Post*, 21 September 2007, 30, states:

> On Rosh Hashana we pray that God be proclaimed King over the entire world, that the Sacred Marriage . . . come about immediately. On Yom Kippur . . . the High Priest proclaims everyone purified . . . [At Tabernacles, we] pray that the Merciful One establish for us the fallen tabernacle of King David and erect the Eternal Temple to which all nations will flock.

Index

Abel, 128, 132
Abraham, 43–44
Adam, 143, 144
affluenza, 86
anointing, 97
Antichrist, 88, 117, 152, 165–66
    See also Great Tribulation
Antiochus IV Epiphanes, 208n13
anti-Semitism, 115–16, 121, 122, 126
Arabs, 18
Austin, Jill, 83
Azusa Street Revival, 137

Baker, Heidi, 83
Bernis, Jonathan, 202n2
Bible study, literal-grammatical-histori-
    cal method of, 28–29
Bickle, Mike, 185
birth pains (*odin*), 22–23
Brown, Michael L., 108

Cain, 132
Christendom, 19
Christian Allies Caucus, 203n6
Christian Zionists, 119–20, 121
Christianity, institutionalization of, 157
Christians, 180
    acceptance of the Old and New Cov-
        enants, 98–99

and Jews, 33–34, 36–37, 197n8
Church, the (Body of Christ; Body of
    Messiah), 19
as bride to Christ, 94
Cranfield, C. E. B., 103

Daniel, 152, 208n13
David, 25, 93, 130, 206nn1–2
    and the Davidic Covenant, 153–54
    and the Davidic throne, 154–55, 174,
        176
Day of Jacob's Trouble, 26

ethnicity, 24
evangelism, 118
    Jewish evangelism, 126
Eve, 143–44
Ezekiel, 172, 208n8

faith, 113–14
Fall, the, 79, 144–45, 162
false gods, 23
famine, 43
feminism/women's liberation move-
    ment, 141
Finney, Charles G., 95
Finto, Don, 181–82
free will, 162

Garden of Gethsemane, 127
Gentiles, 16, 17, 34, 39, 97, 104, 105, 106, 109, 126, 203n5
  Gentile Christians, 121
  See also Jew and Gentile believers together
Gnosticism, 156
God, 20, 37, 48, 55, 139, 141, 189
  covenant of with the Jewish nation, 35, 99–100, 156
  design of for creation, 39, 77–78
  divine joy of, 77
  glory (Shekhinah) of, 174
  government of, 28
  hostility toward, 204n3
  of Jacob, 29–30
  justice of, 163–64
  love of for believers, 66–67
  as protector and defender, 113, 132–33
  relationship of to mankind, 55
  and the restoration of Israel, 170–72
  revelation of, 16
  righteousness of, 160
  view of time, 88
  Word of, 128–29, 133
  See also Great Tribulation, actions of God during
Gospel of the Kingdom, 25
grace, 94–95, 105
Great Commission, 16, 134
Great Tribulation, 152, 158, 177–78, 181–82
  actions of God during, 179–80, 185
  and Israel, 182–84
  and the Levitical feasts, 186–87, 209n20
  necessity of, 184–85
  and the new heaven and new earth, 187–89, 208n11
  rehabilitation of earth after, 165–66
  suffering of all nations during, 183
  summary of, 178–80
Guyon, Madame Jeanne, 95

Hebrew Scriptures (Old Covenant Scriptures [Tanakh]), 19, 25, 172
holiness, 92–93
  fulfillment of the Law (Torah), 97–99
  and the law of love, 95–97
  passion for, 93–95
Holocaust, the, 137
Holy Spirit, 18, 23, 29, 33, 34, 83, 84, 99, 120, 189, 202n1, 209n19
  commitment of to holiness, 94
  and the empowering of the church, 94

Isaiah, 92
Islam, 36, 139
Israel, 19, 24, 25–26, 51, 198n3, 207n16
  Christians standing with, 36–37, 119–20
  convergence with, 33–34
  military inductions in, 130
  poverty in, 123
  prayer battalions for, 34
  redemption of, 52
  repentance of, 51
  salvation of, 34–36
  spiritual heritage of, 17
  See also Israel, as Christ's bride; Israel, restoration of; Israeli Defense Forces; Six Day War; War of Independence
Israel, as Christ's bride, 57–58
  and the bride as kiddushin ("sanctified one"), 61, 62, 181
  marriage contract of, 58–60
  and the New Covenant, 60–62
  and the tale of the ten virgins, 62–63
  unfaithfulness of, 60
  and the wedding celebration, 61–62
  See also Song of Solomon
Israel, restoration of, 170–72
  and the cleansing of Israel, 173
  regathering of the Jewish people, 172–74
Israeli Defense Forces, 136
  and the "Khazak v'amats!" motto, 135

Jerusalem, 188
  See also Jerusalem, battle over; Millennial Jerusalem
Jerusalem, battle over, 116–18, 184
  and the armor of God, 129

and the biblical (Hebrew) concept of war (*milkhama*), 124–25, 126, 127
and biblical protocol, 122–24
Messianic war room strategy, 118–20
shedding of blood as atonement for sin, 127–29
and spiritual plunder, 126–27
See also Millennial Jerusalem
Jesus Christ (Messiah; Yeshua), 18, 19, 22, 24, 26, 33, 50, 121, 155, 189–90, 197n7, 208n9, 209n19
as Bridegroom-King, 89, 133, 140, 150, 164, 166, 168, 188
as Commander of the Armies of Heaven, 111–12, 117, 118
as Conquering King, 32
and the fulfillment of the Law (Torah), 99
intimacy with, 74, 76
Kingdom rule of, 156–57
as Kinsman-Redeemer, 51
as Lord of the Sabbath, 89–90
Olivet Discourse of, 197n1
promise of to His disciples, 151–52
relationship of to His Church (the bridal relationship), 57–58
return of (the Second Coming), 27, 30–31, 35–36, 89, 117, 158–59, 183, 200n7
Sermon on the Mount of, 100–101
as Suffering Servant, 32
supremacy of, 105
teaching of, 25
ultimate sacrifice of, 59
Jew and Gentile believers together, 40–41, 119–20, 122–24, 147
redemption for, 53–55
See also Ruth, book of
Jews, 16, 24, 39, 105, 106, 208–9n17
and Christians, 33–34, 36–37, 197n8
identification with, 16
Jewish Christians, 119–20, 121, 203n10
Messianic Jews, 17, 46, 115, 119, 121, 123–24, 203n8, 206n15
in the Soviet Union, 114–16, 118
traditions of, 19–20

treatment of, 38
See also Jew and Gentile believers together
John, 93–94, 152, 188
John the Baptizer, 92
justice, 111–12, 162–63
and military force, 131–32
See also Jerusalem, battle over

Kaddish ("The Mourner's *Kaddish*"), 170, 207n1
ketubah, 99–100
Kingdom of God, 21–22, 23, 24–27, 30, 187, 190
and the Davidic Covenant, 153–54
and the Davidic throne, 154–55, 174, 176
Israel-related dimension of, 30
righteousness and peace in, 159–62
Kingdom of heaven, 32
Kingdom Revelation, recapturing of, 28–30

Law, the (Torah; Law of Moses), 79
embracing the Law as "Judaizing," 108–9
fulfillment of, 97–99, 200n4, 201n6
and a *ketubah*, 99–100
and legalism, 102–4, 201n10
obedience to, 106
parameters for reevaluating God's Law in our lives, 104–6
and the revelation of the Lawgiver, 102–3
and the Sermon on the Mount, 100–101
and a Torah-observant lifestyle, 106–8, 202n13
lawlessness, 109–10
Lekha Dodi, 75, 200n1
Levitical feasts, 186–87
Day of Atonement (*Yom Kippur*), 186–87
Feast of Trumpets, 186
Feast of Tabernacles, 186–87
love, and the way of the warrior, 32–33

Meir, Golda, 205n9

Messiah. *See* Jesus Christ (Messiah; Yeshua)

Messianic age, 26, 156, 161

Messianic faith communities, 143

Messianic Millennium, 150–51

and heaven on earth, 151–53

and the Millennial Temple, 174–75

and progressive restoration, 164–65, 166

and rehabilitation after the Great Tribulation, 165–66

role of the resurrected saints in, 166–68

Messianic Warrior Bride, 16, 19, 24, 34, 47, 55, 110, 140, 146, 180, 183, 190

Millennial Jerusalem, 175–77

Millennialism, 157–58

Millennium, the, 88, 89–90

Messianic, 89

miracles, 33

misogyny, 145–46

Moab, 43–44, 46

moral relativism, 138

Moses, 100

Mount of Olives, 184

Mount Zion, 174–75, 208n6

New Covenant, 15, 16, 25, 26, 60–62, 76, 78, 96–98, 104–5, 121, 134, 178, 201n7

eschatology of, 176

as a legal and spiritual covenant, 201n8

New Covenant believers, 94

and Yahweh's revelation of Himself, 98

New Covenant Scriptures, 76, 91, 154, 198n4

and the restoration during the Messianic age, 156

Old Covenant, 17, 24, 49, 97–98, 104–5, 201n7

Old Covenant Law, 121

See also Hebrew Scriptures (Old Covenant Scriptures [Tanakh])

Paradise, restoration of, 27–28

Paul, 35, 103, 109, 121

and the Law (Torah), 106–8

on the relationship of Christ to the Church, 57–58

Peter, 106

postmillennialism, 157–58, 207n10

premillennialism, 158

prophets, 56

Rapture, the, 181–82, 208n14

replacement theology, 30, 202–3n4

Revelation, book of, 88

revelation, of our role in the prophetic age to come, 30–31

Ruth, book of

as an account of historical events, 42

as allegory, 42

Boaz as kinsman-redeemer in, 49–50, 53

and divine reciprocity, 50–52, 53

and Israel's desolation, 42–44

Naomi and Boaz in, 52–54

Naomi and Elimelech in, 42–44

Naomi and Ruth in, 50–52

Naomi's gleaning, 47–48

Naomi's return, 46–47

and the new "man" (humanity), 41–42

Obed and the lineage of David, 54

Orpah in, 44, 45

Ruth's commitment to Naomi, 44–46

Sabbath (*Shabbat*), the, 74, 75–76, 201n11

association of with faith, 80

creation's enjoyment of, 79

designation of Sunday as the seventh day, 90–91

developing a Sabbath lifestyle, 84

and the fourth commandment, 80–82

as a gift to all, 81

and the Hebrew calendar, 88

in the Holy Land, 85–86

and idolatry, 86–87

and the importance of remembering, 81–82

Jesus as Lord of, 89–90

and the Kingdom of God, 87
  legalism regarding, 76
  observance of, 76
  and the rest of God, 76–78
  as a sign of the covenant, 81
Satan, 23, 117–18, 132, 134–35, 162
secular humanism, 136–37, 204n7
  and appeasement, 138–40
self-preservation, as an idol, 87
shalom, 91, 190
  protective and settled *shalom*, 83
Shema, 56
Six Day War, 138
Song of Solomon, 63–64, 200nn11–12
  and the dark night of the soul, 70–72
  as God's song to individuals, 64–65
  as the "holy of holies" of biblical writings, 64
  and the image of doves, 200n13
  and the kiss of God, 65–67
  and the love/desire of the Lord for His people, 72–74
  mutual love of bridegroom and bride, 67–68
  and the separation of bridegroom and bride, 68–69
  submission of the bride, 70
  and voice of the bride (voice of worship), 73–74
Soviet Union
  "anti-missionaries" in, 115–16, 202n2
  disintegration of, 114
  missionary work in, 114–16, 202n2
  missionary work in Belarus, 126–27, 202–3n4
spiritual warfare, 114
  and the armor of God, 129
  and Israel's warfare in the natural world, 131
  See also Jerusalem, battle over
Spurgeon, Charles H., 96

Temple Mount, 117, 175, 202n1, 208n6
ten Boom, Carrie, 96

Ten Commandments, 59, 79
Torah. *See* Law, the (Torah; Law of Moses)

Union of Soviet Socialist Republics. *See* Soviet Union

war
  conception of in heaven, 132
  God's feelings concerning, 131–32
  necessity of, 132–33
  rules of engagement (per the Torah), 133–36
war, and women, 140–41
  female fighters, 143–44
  and the healing of ancient hatreds, 144–46
War of Independence, 137
Wesley, John, 95
women, 205nn11–12, 206n16
  and Christ's calling, 142–43
  and a Messianic Jewish challenge, 147–48
  Messianic Jewish men and women, 148–49
  See also misogyny; feminism/women's liberation movement; war, and women

Yahweh, 19, 131
  as Creator/Sovereign of the Universe, 88
  written revelation of, 98
Yeshua. *See* Jesus Christ (Messiah; Yeshua)
Your People Shall Be My People (Finto), 181–82

Zion, 136
  as a signpost of contention, 137–38, 139–40
Zionism, 173

Sandra Teplinsky is cofounding director, together with her husband, Kerry, of Light of Zion Ministries. Ordained by Harvest International Ministries, Sandy is an American-Israeli, Jewish believer in Jesus with a passion for revival. Her teaching and pastoral ministry to the Church imparts a distinctly prophetic, Jewish reality to the Word of God, drawing believers into Messiah's love in the power of the Holy Spirit.

From an Orthodox Jewish background, Sandy now mobilizes intercessory prayer for Israel. She ministers internationally on God's prophetic heart and plans for Israel, and on the Church's Old Covenant heritage. She also speaks at Christian conferences, on Christian TV and radio, and has written numerous magazine articles. Sandy has served intensively in Jewish evangelistic outreach in Eastern Europe.

Sandy is a former litigation attorney, with a J.D. from Indiana University School of Law and a B.A. from the University of Illinois in political science. She has also attended Talbot Seminary in Los Angeles. Her previous books include *Why Care about Israel? How the Jewish Nation Is Key to Unleashing God's Blessings in the 21st Century* (Chosen Books, 2004), *Out of the Darkness: The Untold Story of Jewish Revival in the Former Soviet Union*, and *The Blessing of Israel.*

When in the United States, Sandy and her husband live with their daughter in Southern California. Their ministry house is located in Israel and is dedicated to establishing prayer and worship, as well as humanitarian outreach, in the Negev. You may contact Sandy at:

Light of Zion
P. O. Box 27575
Anaheim Hills, CA 92809
www.lightofzion.org

More from Sandra Teplinsky

God has a plan for you. It starts with Israel. From the moment God created the Jewish nation, His plan for her was immense-nothing short of blessing the nations of the world. Yet, as this Messianic Jewish author explains, this calling has yet to be fulfilled. Sandra Teplinsky guides you through the mystery of God's relationship with Israel and the implications for Gentile believers today. Be part of this great unleashing of blessing in the twenty-first century as you share in God's passion for His ancient covenant people.

"Sandy Teplinsky asks all the right questions and gives all the right answers with passion and precision and prophetic insight."

—from the foreword by Dr. Michael L. Brown, president, FIRE School of Ministry, Charlotte and New York

"A brilliant and anointed book that is theologically sound and yet prophetically timely."

—Che Ahn, senior pastor, Harvest Rock Church, Pasadena; author, *Into the Fire*

***Why Care about Israel?: How the Jewish Nation Is Key to Unleashing God's Blessings in the 21st Century*
by Sandra Teplinsky**